The Eye and Other Tales

THE EYE

AND OTHER TALES

ANDREW FISCHER

ISBN: 979-8-9890839-0-9(Paperback)
ISBN: 979-8-9890839-2-3 (eBook)
ISBN: 979-8-9890839-3-0 (Audiobook)

Library of Congress Control Number: *to come*

Book cover and book design by Glen Edelstein, Hudson Valley Book Design

Printed by IngramSpark, in the United States of America.

First printing edition 2024.

Contents

"Whoever listens to a witness, becomes a witness,"

—*Elie Weisel, April 2002.*

Preface

In January, 1990, my mother, your Nana, getting too old to travel alone, asked me to accompany her on a trip to visit her Uncle Adolphe in Paris. This turned out to be the last we would see him, as he died the following year, 1991, at the age of 92. It was a wonderful trip. There was breakfast with Nana and Uncle Adolphe, at his favorite café. There was one special afternoon at Uncle Adolphe and Aunt Maggie's apartment. Their son and daughter, Jean Claude and Anna were there with Nana and me, as was Nana's cousin, Solange, and we had boisterous conversations over tea and pastries. That trip was the last time we saw Uncle Adolphe.

On that trip, Nana and I spent a lot of time with her cousin, Solange, much of it sitting around Solange's kitchen table together. We talked, we sang and Nana and Solange reminisced about their days as girls growing up in Lodz every morning over breakfast and again at lunch and dinner. We had many good times around that table. I remember Nana and Solange singing songs in Polish, folk songs, children's songs, lullabies, smiling and singing as one would interrupt the other. They talked about their children, their families, their life as girls growing up in Lodz, and on that trip I resumed taking notes.

I already had some notes from conversations late in life with my father, and then, after he died, with his cousin, Abe Fischer. At first, I was hoping to document something about our family, the Fischers and the Glantzes on your grandfather's side, and the Sylberstajns on your Nana's side. After many more trips to Paris, where I enjoyed the pleasure of sitting with Solange at her kitchen table and listening to her, the story began to grow.

Much of what I know about the Sylberstajn family's life in Lodz came from those chats in Solange's kitchen and elsewhere on that visit and my later visits to Paris to see her. Solange not only told me the family history and the stories that are documented here. We also discussed politics, Zionism and a host of other things. Solange always asked about my wife Linda and our children and about my sister Vivian and her family. Solange was never hesitant to offer me advice about how to treat my wife or children or to give her opinions about your grandfather, Hillary Clinton (whom she adored much more than she adored my father) or a host of other topics. She was not just loving, but also wise and thoughtful and to her last days was perceptive and had thoughtful, insightful and wise advice to give to me. I miss her very much, as she was a second mother to me after Nana died and was a guiding voice and constant inspiration.

This work originally was intended to be the story of your grandparents, my parents, so you would know their stories and where they came from. Over time, it has also become the story of Solange, whose sons predeceased her, and so she has no sons to remember her. It has also become the stories of Uncle Adolphe and his son, Jean Claude, and his daughter, whom I first knew as Lilian but has become Anna. It now ends with the story of Solange's two sons, Maurice and Charles. They have no one to remember them – but you. So I have tried to tell their stories for you, as well, so that that you will know and remember them all, as your family in Europe, before your Nana and your grandfather came to this country, your family that came to this country before them, and your family that stayed in Europe, in France, as well.

CHAPTER 1
Coming of Age in Galicia

My father, Jan Bernard Fischer, grew up in and around Lvov, a beautiful old city in eastern Poland, dating back a thousand years. Both his mother's family, the Glantzes, and his father's family, the Fischers, lived in Boiberke, a small town some 20-25 kilometers south of Lvov. Boiberke, or Boiberek in Yiddish, was a small provincial town, but a regional center, with a village square, a post office and a courthouse, several banks, a Catholic church, school and grounds, a synagogue that still stands today, although now just an empty building, and a local open-air market that also continues today.

Boiberke center 2015

Boiberke was burned down by the Cossacks in 1914. When the Cossacks burned Boiberke again, in 1918, Sruel and Miriam Glantz, my great-grandparents, moved to what my father, Jan Bernard, called their "country estate" in Budkow. Budkow was a small rural village, a few miles from Boiberke, but closer to the train station in Chlebowice than Boiberke was. What my father and his Uncle Herman used to call the "country estate" was the small home of the parents of Sruel Glantz, Berko "Dov" Glantz, after whom my father was named[1], and his wife Malka. It was hardly a "country estate": it was a small hut in a shtetl village much like the shtetl Anetevka in the musical "Fiddler on The Roof".

Sruel and Miriam Glantz

Nonetheless, Budkow was refuge for Sruel and Miriam, as everyone would flee with each burning of Boiberke by the Cossacks. Salo Fischer took his wife and children to Austria and the first burning was when Morris Glantz left to join his brother Abe in America. Much was in flux at the time as World War I was followed by fighting throughout Eastern Poland, Galicia and the Ukraine, as part of the war between the White Russians and the Red stemming from the Russian Revolution.

---

1 Berko was his Polish name. It meant "Bear", thus the Yiddish/Hebrew name was "Dov", or "Bear". My father, Jan Bernard, was named after his grandfather, and was often called Bernard, or Bernie, rather than Jan, as Berko became Bernard in English.

Boiberke Synagogue ruins, 2015

I visited both Boiberke and Budkow on my 2015 trip to eastern Europe with my friend, Robert Strauss. We hired a driver in Lvov who took us to Boiberke. It was market day and we saw farmers selling produce, and other vendors selling kitchen wares, clothing, crafts and other assorted things, not unlike the shouk or other traditional outdoor farmers markets. We also found the synagogue. After thoroughly exploring the small town, we asked the driver to take us to Budkow, but he did not know where it was and it took us a while to find it. After some exploration, we discovered that Budkow still exists.

Budkow was a small village which, when my father was growing up, and his grandparents lived there, was near the train stop Chlebowice. When Strauss and I visited, it was still like the shtetl in Fiddler on the Roof. It had one street, a dirt road maybe a quarter mile but no longer than a half mile long, with a few dozen houses on each side, each with a vegetable garden and maybe some chickens or a horse to pull a plough, along the single dirt road. We walked through it and took some photos. We did not find what my father used to call "the Glantz country estate." The photos in our hallway with the carpet hanging as the backdrop were likely taken outside that house for what was obviously a family photo session.

Budkow

In one of the photos that hangs in our living room, the Sruel and Miriam Glantz family portrait, my grandmother, my father Jan's mother, Bluma (or Blanka)[2], her four brothers and her one sister, Baila (or Bertha), are all pictured around their parents, my father's grandparents Sruel (Israel) Glantz and Miriam Glantz. This and the other pictures taken at this session were more likely also taken in Budkow, where they lived, than in Boiberke, where Sruel's parents, Berko "Dov" Glantz and his wife Malka lived. This and the other pictures were taken before World War I, probably in early 1910.[3]

Sruel was one of eight children of Berko and Malka Glantz, four boys and four girls. His three brothers were Chaim, Jacob and Izydor and his sisters were Minna, Chana, Zipporah and Sarah. Sruel's brother, Izydor

2 Vivian's middle name, Blanche, is English for Blanka, after both our two grandmothers.
3 This estimate is based on Herman's apparent age and the fact that it is before Morris and Abe came to America.

4

"Iszu" Glantz, probably an older brother, had been to America around the turn of the century and had returned. He was a business venturer, successful with a saw mill and several other large wood processing plants. Iszu was a risk taker who gambled with rich Polish noblemen. He married well, marrying the daughter of a Polish landowner. Through that marriage he acquired or managed timber rights to forest land in nearby Carpathian forests with a company called Oikos. Uncle Isydor's connections got Sruel's son, Nathan Glantz, a management job with Oikos. From Oikos, Nathan went to work for Morris Kopleman, who exported timber, mainly railroad ties, from the Polish Carpathians to western Europe.

Sruel and Miriam Glantz, center, clockwise from top, Baila, Nathan (inserted later), Bluma, Salo Fischer, Herman, Morris, Abe,

Nathan is in the picture of Sruel and Miriam and all their children. Nathan is in the back row, between his two sisters. If you look carefully, you can see that he was inserted into the photo of Sruel, Miriam and their children. He was not there when the photograph was taken, but his head was added to the picture, in the back row, between his two sisters.

Nathan later used the name Mathew, or Mateus. Nathan was a prisoner in Russia during the fighting at the end of World War I. Before the war he had married Bertha Shuman and they moved away, likely to Vienna. Nathan and Bertha had two daughters, Anna (Hannah) and Miriam, or Mia, who were roughly your grandfather's age. My father remembers that when these cousins came to visit their grandparents in Boiberke or Budkow, they slept in his bed, and one of them peed in his bed while she was sleeping in it. That must be what he remembered most about them, as that was the only thing he told me about them.

Nathan's baby brother, the youngest child of Sruel and Miriam, was named Hirsch. As a young man, Hirsch also worked at Oikos. Standing 6'3' or 6'4", he was young, big and strong. He started out cutting trees, but he soon was doing more sophisticated work. Eventually he was moved from working in the forest and promoted to a better job, although not as sophisticated a management job as his older brother, Nathan. It was his job to pick which trees to cut and then to designate which logs would be cut into lumber, which would be designated for pulp to be made into paper, and so forth. Years later, when he would take his daughters, Elaine and Marsha, for a walk in the park or the woods, he would tell them how old a tree was or what kind of tree it was. As a youth in Poland, Herman also kept and trained pigeons, homing pigeons, which were still used to send messages in these rural parts of Galicia that still lacked telegraph or telephone lines.

Hirsch worked at Oikos until he left for America in 1938, just in time, before it was too late. He became Herman in America. Vivian and I knew him well as our Uncle Herman. He followed his older brothers, Abe and Moishe, who became Morris after he got to New York. They are the two young boys in the family picture, and Herman is the little boy in a dress-like outfit. Abe and Morris had come to America earlier, Morris maybe to avoid conscription in the Austrian army during World War I or maybe not until 1922, and Abe before that. The records are not clear.

Abe, who was the oldest brother, quit school and left for America sometime between 1900, about ten years before my father was born, and 1910. From this we know two things: first, the family photograph, in fact all the photos taken in that session, were taken before my father was born, on December 22, 1910, because Abe, who is in the photo, had left for America by then. We also know that the first time my father met his Uncle Abe was in 1950, when he arrived in New York, because Abe left for America before my father was born. The picture was probably taken earlier that year, as Herman, who, in the picture in what looks like a dress, looks two or three years old, and was born in 1908. So this and the other photos from that shoot must have been taken in 1910.

After arriving in New York, Abe met and married his wife, Anna. They settled in the Bronx, where they had three children, Selma, Norman and Murray. Selma married Willie Heller and they had two daughters, Marlene and Rhonda. Marlene married Steve Riback. Marlene and Steve had two daughters, Laurie and Amy (after whom Shira, as a little girl, named two dolls). Laurie married and divorced Mitchell Cooper. She lives in North Carolina with son and daughter, adopted from the former Soviet Union, Alek and Anastacia. Amy married Atilla Ballogh. The two of them had a daughter, Skyler. Amy lives in Florida near her parents, who live in Lake Worth, where they moved from Wappingers Falls, where they lived while Steve was working for IBM.

Rhonda married Alan Hollander and they had two boys, Adam and David. Rhonda was a trusts and estates lawyer at Palmer & Dodge and then for a smaller firm. Rhonda and Alan lived in Massachusetts, first in Newton, then in Needham. They have retired to Austin, to be near their son, Adam, and their two grandchildren, a granddaughter named Anali, born 2016, and a grandson, Jackson, born in 2019. Adam is an entrepreneur, who moved to Austin in the course of working for Harte Hanks Communications, now a global marketing services company headquartered in Boston. Originally **Harte-Hanks Newspapers**, a newspaper chain that started in Texas as a newspaper chain, it now still has a large Texas presence in Austin.

Adam was developing training games for the marketing department but has moved on. He and his father, Alan founded their own company, Fantasy Sales Team, selling a training game used for corporate education and training. Adam moved to Seattle for a while, when Microsoft bought the fantasy sales game, but has returned to Austin, where his next venture

---

*Weblinks to proper nouns boldfaced, like Hart-Hanks Newspapers, can be found in the endnotes, p.323

was designing training games for doctors training for medical certification exams.

Adam's brother David lives in Hoboken. He shares custody of his daughter, Harper, born in 2019, with his ex-wife, who lives across the street from David. He commutes to New York City, where he works for Google, running programs tied to sales teams engagement. Before that he worked for advertising agencies in New York and in Atlanta, where he attended college at Emory University.

Abe and Anna's middle child, Norman, drove a cab for many years. He and his wife, Jackie had four children, Sharon, Reesa, Barry and Penny, all of whom eventually settled in Manalapan, in central New Jersey.

Murray, the youngest of Abe and Anna's three children, married Arlene, who worked for American Airlines for many years. They had two children, Clifford and Ilene. Clifford moved to Washington state, where he worked in the eastern portion of the state, as a meteorologist for a company that did contract work for NOAA. Long after divorcing his first wife, Clifford found true love and married Tikva.

Clifford had a son, Logan, by his first wife. After a short stay in Washington, D.C., where he met Miriam, Logan has returned to Washington state, and married Amanda Semanoff. Ilene, who lived with us in Cambridge for a short time, had a tough time for a number of years, until she moved to Washington, with her then young son Avery, to be closer to her brother, Clifford. She and Avery still live in the Seattle area.

Morris Glantz followed his older brother Abe to America. They both left Boiberke around the same, just before or at the start of World War I. They left as young boys, perhaps to avoid being drafted into the Austrian army. Morris settled in the Sheepshead Bay section of Brooklyn, and married an American Jewish woman, Ruth Weiss.

My father was not old enough to have known either Abe or Morris before they left for America. However, he did meet Morris in Poland, as Morris returned to visit twice after leaving for America. Morris was quite successful in the garment business in New York and eager to show off his success. He returned to Boiberke in 1928, when my father, Jan, was still a teenager. Jan was very impressed with how successful his Uncle Morris had been in America when he saw him on that visit. My father saw his

Uncle Morris again in 1933 when his uncle returned a second time with his wife, Ruth, and their very young redheaded daughter, Beatrice, who was called "Bea" or "Beady." Little did my father guess that years later, he would one day knock on Morris' and Ruth's door, as an immigrant with his own new wife and baby.

Morris was not the first Glantz to come back and show how successful he was in America. His uncle, Isydor, had returned some years earlier with "plenty of money" according to my father. Aunt Clara once told me that Isydor was a bootlegger. I don't know whether Isydor returned to Poland to stay, or just to visit. I wish I knew what happened to him, but I don't.

Abe and Morris are in the Glantz family portrait that hangs in our living room. They are the two boys on the left side of their parents, Sruel and Miriam. Directly behind Sruel and Miriam is their daughter, Bertha. Bertha didn't come to America, like her younger brothers, but she was also successful, marrying a wealthy doctor named Shuman who most likely was from Vienna, but may have been from somewhere else in Poland if not from Vienna.

Morris, Ruth, and baby Beady, 1934

When her brother Morris came back to Poland to show the family his American wife, Ruth, and daughter, Bea, my grandmother, Bluma, gave Ruth several needlepoints she had made, which Ruth brought back to Brooklyn and framed. Years later, these were passed on to me after Ruth died. Bea tracked me down through Herman's daughter, Elaine. You can see the two of the needlepoints, of Polish peasants, hanging in the library of our home, above the TV. The other two hang behind the door in my study.

When I first met Bea, she was a very attractive grown woman. She was a nurse. She had two daughters from her first marriage, Michelle ("Shelley"), who is maybe a year older than me, and Vicki, who is my sister Vivian's age. We visited them often in Brooklyn, and Shelley and Vicki's father, Eli Arenberg, would take the four of us, Shelley, Vickie, Vivian and me, to Coney Island and to shows at Radio City Music Hall when we were kids. After she and Eli were divorced, Bea moved to Florida and remarried. With her new husband, Stan Frielich, she had another daughter, Randi, and two sons, Scott and Shawn. Bea's three children with Stan Frielich, who all grew up in Florida, are also my second cousins, but I have never met them.

I had not heard from Shelley since we were kids, but Shelley found me on Facebook, in 2010. She lives in Florida, married to Greg Thomas. Her mother Bea, and grandmother Ruth had moved to the same area, as did Selma (Abe's daughter and Rhonda's mother), with her husband, Willie, to be followed by their daughter, Marlene and her husband Steve, and their daughters, Amy and Laurie (who since moved to North Carolina). Thus a good portion of the New York Glantz family ended up moving to the warmer weather of the Florida coast north of Miami.

Morris and Ruth also had a second child, a son, Stanley. They had a two-family house off of Avenue U in the Sheepshead Bay section of Brooklyn, not far from Coney Island. They lived on the second floor. When Jan Bernard and Litka arrived in America, with me as a little baby, that was the first place we stayed. Later, that was where Vivian and I would go, when we were growing up, for week long visits, sometimes in the summer, sometimes during school vacations. It was in Morris' living room that I first saw baseball, watching Yankees games with Uncle Morris.

Bea and her husband, Eli, lived on the first floor, with their two daughters, Shelley and Vickie. When Stanley finished law school and got married, to his first wife, Cookie, they lived in the basement apartment. Stanley and Cookie had a son, Bradley, and a daughter, Tami. Stanley and Cookie and their two kids lived in the basement of a two-family that had become a three-family. Bradley grew up and, in the sixties, became a hippie and a deadhead. I don't know much else about what became of him, except that he still lives in Woodstock, New York. Tami is now Tami Breimann, a mother and grandmother living on Long Island

After Stanley and Cookie divorced, Stanley married Ellen. Stanley and Ellen had seven children: Stephen, Stanelle, Martine, Janina, Sonny, Shayna and Kenny. They all lived in a house in the same Sheepshead Bay neighborhood in Brooklyn where Stanley grew up. Stanley was a successful lawyer. Through his involvement in the Brooklyn Democratic party, he was elected a local judge, in what is the New York equivalent of the probate court. After retiring, Stanley joined his long-lived mother, sister and other relatives in the migration to Florida.

Back to the family picture from Budkow that hangs in our living room, Herman, was the youngest of Sruel and Miriam's six children. He was not that much older than my father, maybe five or six years older, but maybe only two or three, if he was born in 1907 or 1908, as I have been told. He was born at least 15 years, maybe more, after his oldest sister, Blanca, my grandmother, who was born in 1893, who was, thus only seventeen or eighteen when my father was born. My father and Herman grew up together almost like brothers. My father used to tell Vivian and me how Herman carried him on his back through the snow home from school.

As you know from the photo of my grandfather in his military uniform, my father's father, Salo (Solomon) Fischer served in the Austrian army during World War I. After the war, Salo and his wife, Blanka, moved to the big city, Lemberg, as Lvov was called when it was in the Austria Hungarian Empire. After the war, it once again became known as the Polish city of Lvov, in the re-established nation of Poland. Lvov, just 18 miles from Boiberke, was the capital and major city of Galicia, which never was an independent nation, but was the home of many, many Jews, known as Galicianers, and the center of Yiddish culture.

Salo Fischer

Lvov was not just a business and commercial hub, it was a beautiful historic medieval city, with a five-hundred-year old university and a cultural center where artists, intellectuals and writers such as Sholom Aleichem gravitated. It had a large Jewish hospital, a Jewish cemetery and several large and famous synagogues. The synagogues were all burned down by the Nazis, except for one, which remained because the Nazis used it as a stable. It is now functioning again as a synagogue. The Jewish hospital is now a state-run hospital, and the land behind it, where the main Jewish cemetery was, is now a farmers market. The gravestones from the cemetery were taken by the Nazis and used as street pavers. Some of these gravestones were found and recovered when streets were repaved and can be seen at the one remaining synagogue.

In the period between the two wars, Lvov was a thriving city and the center of Jewish life in Galicia. The Jewish population was large, one third of the population, some 75,000 of the slightly over 200,000 total population in 1939. Lvov attracted writers, artists, intellectuals and all sorts of people seeking their fortune, many of whom were Jewish,

It was here, in Lvov, that Salo and Blanca Fischer tried to build a life together after the war ended. Salo Fischer was trained as an accountant, and worked for a while at the Galizische Sparkasse Bank, but did not like sitting at a desk all day, and he was not paid so well. At the urging of his wife, Blanca, he began selling insurance on the side. Sometime around 1921 or 1922, he went out on his own selling insurance. Salo began as an agent for an insurance company but he and Blanca were entrepreneurs, always trying something new venture, and he and Blanca had a number of business ventures in the early twenties, some more successful than others. Sometimes, they sent Jan and his brother and sister to stay with their grandparents.

The fighting in eastern Poland and the Ukraine and Russia did not stop with the armistice that ended World War I. The Russian Revolution that led to the fall of the Tzar continued, as did fighting between White Russians and Cossacks and the Polish Army. After the fighting ended, the newly established independent nation of Poland controlled Lemberg, which became Lvov. Everything was changing and new. New economic distribution systems developed and Salo, always encouraged by his wife, Blanka, saw an opportunity.

With a partner named Adler, Salo began distributing food for a local farmers co-op. They would give the food to salaried workers, on credit, and collect the money owed them when the workers were paid, at the end of the month. The business lasted until Adler left town with all the money in the bank that they had collected, like the farm shares we have today. Salo's "partner", Adler, turned out to be a conman who disappeared with the money.

Salo and Blanka had other business ventures, some more successful than the food coop. I know that one of these ventures was a pet store, because my father used to talk about how, as a boy he liked playing with the monkeys, birds and other animals. My father's cousin, Abe Fischer remembers the shop, as well, the monkeys and birds. My father also liked that there were always kids in the shop, also attracted by the animals. My father's father Salo did not run the shop or spend much time there. He had other business – or businesses – to tend to.

When they were busy with their ventures or when the businesses were not doing so well, they would send their son, Jan Bernard, to his maternal grandparents, Sruel and Miriam Glantz. They had a big house, with three or four bedrooms, plenty of room for Jan and Jan loved spending his summers in his grandparents' house, in Boiberke. There were chickens in the back yard and with his grandmother, Miriam always preparing baked goods, the Glantz home always smelled good. The home was around the corner from the synagogue. Later Jan's brother, Max, would go with Jan to their grandparents. Eventually, their much younger sister, Bertha, would also join them, but that was much later.

Boiberke was a beautiful town, in a valley, surrounded by green forest and fed by the cleanest spring water. It was a pleasant place. There was an outdoor market. On market day, Thursday, Jan Bernard's grandmother, Miriam, had a stall, in which she sold teas and baked goods, and his grandfather, Sruel, would sell chickens. When we were in Boiberke, Strauss and I visited an outdoor famers market, on the other side of the town square that the synagogue faced. It was probably the same market where Miriam Glantz had her little café and Sruel sold his eggs and chickens.

Jan's grandparents, Sruel and Miriam, had plenty of room in their house in Boiberke for their three grandchildren, Jan Bernard, Max and Bertha, their little sister, and a big yard with chickens in the back. It was just a few hundred yards down the street from the back of the synagogue on one side and only a few doors from Laizer Fischer's house and mill and stable on the other. Consequently, Jan was happy to spend a lot of his childhood with his Glantz grandparents, more than just weekends and summer vacations.

My father spent a lot of his time in Boiberke with his Uncle Herman. Jan talked more about Herman than about his own brother and sister, his younger brother Max, or his baby sister, Bertha, who was born 1923 or 1925. Maybe that was because it was hard for Jan to think about his brother and sister. Maybe it was easier to for Jan to talk about his childhood with Herman, who was alive with us in America. Max and Bertha were gone. Grandfather hadn't seen them since he was taken by the Russians to Siberia in 1939. Maybe it was just too hard for him to talk about them.

Abe Fischer, also a few years older than my father, remembered being at Max's bris with my father, Abe also remembered Max as a young man, describing Max as smart, even smarter than his smart older brother, Jan Bernard. However, according to Abe, Max never applied himself like his older brother. Max also grew up ideologically very different than his older brother. He was a leftist, and maybe this distanced him from his older brother. He became a pharmacist. He never married. He never had the chance to.

My father also spent time with his other Fischer cousins, Abe's brother Chaim and sister Gertrude, the children of Salo's older brother. Salo was the youngest son of the seven children of Ephraim Fischer. Ephraim's oldest, Hersh, or Harry, came to the United States before World War I, and had three children, Sidney Fischer, who died in Florida, Saul Fischer and Leo Fischer, according to Abe Fischer. Next came two daughters, Brondle and Sura, who married Shloime Pelz. Next was Eliezer, who whose wife Sura, or Sara, was my father's second Aunt Sarah. After Eliezer came a daughter, Laiche, who also came to America.[4] After Laiche came my grandfather, Salo. The youngest was a daughter, Hannah, whose married name was Hannah Labener.[5] If you are confused, look at the Fischer family tree [*Appendix 2B*]

All seven of Ephraim's children lived in Boiberke, except for Salo, who lived, at different times, in Boiberke and Lvov. Hirsch, Laiche, and Hannah also lived in Boiberke until they left for America.

Abe Fischer's father, my father's Uncle Eliezer, "Laizer" Fischer had five children. Sruel, or Israel, was the oldest. Sruel also left for America. He had a son, Arthur who lived a full life in New York, but I never knew or met Arthur. I only learned about Arthur in the nineteen-eighties, after he was dead, when I learned about him from Abe Fischer. I don't

---

4 I learned from Abe Fischer that Laiche was married in the United States, to a man named Nash. Abe told me that they had at least one child, Dorothy, whose married name was Platzner. She had a son named Robert Platzner who was still alive in the 1980s, when Abe talked about our cousins "the Platzners".

5 I am not sure of the spelling.

know that Arthur ever married or had children. Next was Abe, then Chaim, whom I knew as Uncle Hymie, when I was a boy. Then there was a daughter, Beila, or Bertha, and the youngest, Gertrude. I also knew Gertrude, whom I also knew as Aunt Trudie who lived in the Bronx with her husband Max, and her brother, my Uncle Hymie.

Laizer was financially quite comfortable, with a mill that ground flour from a variety of grains that included oats, barley, rye, and buckwheat, known in Yiddish as kasha. Indeed, the mill ground everything but wheat, according to Jan. There were work horses, to power the mill, and there was a barn near the mill, to house the horses. Jan remembered the leather saddles and fancy leather boots in the barn, just a few hundred yards from where he lived with his Glantz grandparents and uncle, Herman. Jan also remembered that his cousin, Abe Fischer, would take him riding.

Abe ran the mill from an early age until he left for America. Then Hymie took over the business. According to Abe, his younger brother Hymie was a much better businessman than he was. Abe called his younger brother, Hymie, "real smart, a conniver". The mill continued to be a thriving business and, so the story goes, Hymie had accumulated a fair amount of money that he had hidden when the war broke out.

My father's maternal grandparents, Israel [Sruel] and Miriam Glantz, with whom he spent much of his childhood, were much more religious that his parents, Salo and Blanka Fischer. But while Sruel may have been more religious than his daughter and son-in-law, Blanka and Salo, he was not a scholar like Jan Bernard's paternal grandfather, Ephraim.

Ephraim was born in 1845 or 1848. His mother, Beila, died giving birth to Ephraim, according to Abe Fischer. Both my father, Jan, and Abe relate that she was fifty years old when she gave birth to Ephraim, so it is not surprising that she would have died in childbirth given her age. If she did not die in childbirth, she died soon thereafter, within the year after Ephraim's birth. According to Abe, Ephraim Fischer had an older brother, Herzyl, and the two of them had a much older brother Eliezer "Laizer" Yankel, who was born in 1820 from an earlier husband. Beila had at least two grand-daughters named after her. Both my father, Jan Bernard's younger sister and Abe and Hymie's first sister were named Beila, after their great-grandmother, but they were both called Bertha in Polish.

Ephraim the melamed

Ephraim, who lived well into his eighties, died in 1932. He was a melamed. According to Wikipedia "In Russia and Poland, the word '*melamed*,' is synonymous with respected and *rav*." My father talked about Ephraim, his grandfather the melamed, as a learned scholar who taught Tanach, not just to bar mitzvah boys, but to the teachers in the local *cheders*. My father went to *cheder* as well as to public school. He also studied Hebrew and learned Tanach with his grandfather, Ephraim. Ephraim travelled frequently throughout Galicia as a melamed. When a synagogue, a yeshiva or a wealthy Jew would buy a torah or pay to have a new torah written, they would hire Ephraim the melamed to read and check the torah scroll for mistakes.

Sometimes the torah scroll would be brought to Ephraim in Boiberke, where he stayed with his daughter, Sura (or Sarah) Pelz, who was married to a *shochet*[6]. They had eight children, including Hersch, who was a rabbi, but they all perished in the Shoah, the Holocaust. Other times, Ephraim would stay with his son, Laizer, whose wife was also named Sura[7]. Frequently Ephraim would take his grandson with him when he

---

6 A **schochet** is butcher who performs ritual slaughters. See https://en.wikipedia.org/wiki/Shechita
7 Their son, Chaim Fischer, is sometimes called Chaim Pelz. I am not sure why. Sometimes Jews were married under a chuppah by a rabbi, and not married civilly, and thus their legal Polish name was their mother's last name. This might have been why. Or maybe it was Eliezer's wife, and not his sister, who was the Pelz in the family tree.

traveled to neighboring towns. This was always a special treat for my father.

Although my father learned Hebrew and Tanach with his grandfather, Ephraim, he was primarily a secular scholar. He attended a Jewish *cheder*, but his primary studies were in Polish, in a secular primary school. He was an excellent student, who attended university and then law school at Jan Kasimer University[8] in Lvov. After that, he studied in Switzerland, perhaps in Italy and at the Sorbonne in Paris for a year.

Jan and Ola at the Notre Dame

My father spoke many languages as a consequence of where and how he grew up. He spoke Polish (and some Ukrainian) in the streets, Yiddish at home, Hebrew at the *cheder* and knew some German as the language

8 The university was founded in 1661 by the Polish king Jan Kasimer II, who granted a university charter to a "Collegium" founded by the Jesuits in 1608, giving it "the honour of an academy and the title of a university". It was known as the University of Lvov, but was later given the name Jan Casimir University, in honor of its founder. It is presently known as the Ivan Franko National University of Lviv, named after a Ukrainian military hero who also was known for his role in leading pogroms.

of the Austrian government when he was a child. After graduating high school, he went to work for a Dr. Boleslaw Czuruk, doing translations. This was even before he learned French and Italian in his studies abroad.

After four years at Jan Kazimierz University in Lvov, from 1929-1933, he completed a Magister Iuris, a law degree, in 1933. He also earned a Diploma from the Academy of Foreign Trade, a separate university in Lvov that may have been affiliated with Jan Kazimierz University in 1932. Pursuing his interest in international law, Jan Bernard continued his studies abroad, in Italy, Switzerland and at the Sorbonne in Paris after completing his studies at Jan Kazimierz University. I have a picture of him with his first wife, Ola Stark Fischer, with the Notre Dame in the background that I used to put away whenever Nana would come to visit.

Jan Bernard never got to practice law, as by the time he completed his studies, antisemitic laws were being passed that prevented Jews from entering certain professions, such as law and medicine. When he returned from his year studying international law at the Sorbonne, Jan taught languages in a Lvov high school, and resumed doing translations for his patron, Dr. Czuruk. Boleslaw Czuruk, a professor of Slavic languages at the University of Lvov, had a translation business on the side, translating birth certificates, marriage documents and other legal papers. He hired Jan Bernard to translate these legal documents.

At one point, Jan Bernard wanted to become a translator for the League of Nations[9] in Switzerland. This never happened, so Jan Bernard's professor, Dr. Czuruk sent him to his brother. My father remembered this Czurok brother as a successful lawyer, who was a retired military officer with a distinguished military career, who led army units in World War I and the spillover fighting that continued after that in eastern Poland, Russia and the Ukraine. Boleslaw's brother, the retired general who became Atty. Czurok was so impressed with Jan Bernard that he wanted to sponsor Jan to serve in the Polish Foreign Service. But to do that, Jan would have had to convert to Catholicism, which Jan was unwilling to do.

By the late thirties, things were getting worse for the Jews. Antisemites killed several Jewish students at the University of Lvov, changing the

---

9 The League of Nations, founded on January 10, 1920 by the Paris Peace Conference that ended World War I, was the forerunner to the United Nations, and was the first worldwide intergovernmental organization whose principal mission was to maintain world peace. It ceased operation on April 20, 1946 but many of its components were relocated into the new United Nations.

status quo. Poland, like other countries, followed Hitler's lead and began prohibiting Jews from practicing law, medicine and other professions. Now it was not a matter of entry into the elite status of the Polish Foreign Service. Jan Bernard just wanted to sit for the bar exam, but by this time, even taking the Bar exam was forbidden if you were a Jew. Either Jan's mentor, Dr. Czuruk, or his brother, Jan's boss, Atty. Czuruk, still protecting and advocating for his talented Jewish law clerk, offered to adopt him and have him baptized. This would have allowed Jan to take the Bar exam and work as a lawyer in the gentleman's office. Again, my father refused.[10]

Jan Bernard was not the only Jew or the only former student that Boleslaw Czuruk helped. Jozef Intof was one of the others. Intof escaped and made it to Palestine in 1946, only because Dr. Czuruk helped him escape from Lvov when the Germans took the city in 1941. Intof submitted the story of how Dr. Czuruk saved him to Yad Vashem, where Boleslaw Czuruk is now listed as a Righteous Among the Nations. When you find his name and story in the Yad Vashem archives – you can do so online – you will first see Josef Intov's story, but read to the end. The last paragraph starts "Among the Jews helped by Boleslaw Czuruk were . . . Bernard Fischer (another former student, from the university) and his family Gabryel Stark, Maria Stark, and Ola Stark." It was much later, just after Teddy was born, did I learn that Ola Stark was my father's wife.

Olenka "Ola" Stark[11] was beautiful, smart, and educated. She came from a wealthy family. Abe Fischer said the Starks were the richest family in Lvov. Ola's parents, Ludwig Stark and Maria Stark, née Grutz, owned a large department store and other businesses. Many men would have been happy to marry Ola Stark. But while Ola was a good catch, so was Jan Bernard Fischer. He was handsome, well mannered, well-educated and well-travelled. He spoke many languages, had completed law school and was sponsored as a candidate to go into the foreign service by his

---

10 One of your grandfather's favorite stories, and mine, too, was about "animum revertendum", a phrase this Czuruk brother, the attorney, used to refer to his clients, the low lifes and criminals, many of them Czuruk's former soldiers, who Jan would see sitting in the law office. Literally the phrase means "the beast returns". In Roman law, if a cow or other farm animal had wandered from his master and two farmers were arguing over whose cow it was, the Romans would let the animal loose and see to which barn it returned. The farmer who owned the barn was declared the owner of the animal, because "animum revertendum", the beast always returns -- to his home. So when Jan Bernard asked "why do you have all these unsavory clients?", Atty. Czuruk would answer "animum revertendum" – the beast returns. Indeed, I have told the same story explaining some of my clients.
11 Sometimes in English she is called "Caroline".

patrons, the Czuruks. He was a good candidate to help manage the Stark businesses. Jan Bernard Fischer's marriage to Ola Stark was a good match for the Stark family, as well.

However, my father never talked about his first wife, Ola or his son. He talked freely about many other things. He told stories about his time in the Siberian labor camps and as a soldier in the Polish Army, serving with the British in an intelligence unit in Egypt. He would talk about staying up nights to monitor and translate radio transmissions from Brazaville, in the French Congo, of the advances of the Free French in Africa against the Germans. Most of all, he liked to tell the story about the ten zlotys and the eye.

Father talked about his life as a child. He told me about his brother, Max, two years younger, and his baby sister, Bertha, fifteen years younger, born after his bar mitzvah. He talked often about being close to Herman who was like an older brother, and about his parents and grandparents, but there were some things that were too painful to talk about. He never said anything about being married or about his son. Just like Nana didn't talk about a lot of the things she went through. She didn't talk much about her husband. She didn't talk much about her time in the labor camps, either. There were lots of things she never talked about.

I didn't know until after I became a father, and I had my own son, Teddy, that my father had been married in Poland before the Shoah, or that I had a half-brother. I found out by accident, when my father's first cousin, Selma, and her husband, Willie Heller, visited us in Brookline. Selma, if you followed my genealogy above, was the daughter of my Father's Uncle Abe, the first Glantz to come to America. You may remember Selma's daughter, my second cousin Rhonda, who lived in Newton at the time. Selma and Willie were in the process of moving from Riverdale in the Bronx to Pembroke Pines in Boca Raton, Florida.

Selma and Willie were in Boston to visit Rhonda and her husband, and their two grandsons, David and Adam, before driving to their new home in Pembroke Pines. While in Boston, they stopped to see me and the new baby, Teddy. Selma had also brought something for me, a box of photos, old photos. In cleaning out her Riverdale apartment while packing for the move, Selma had found some old photos in some drawers. Some of these photos were photos that her father must have brought with him from Poland,

Among the photos that must have come from my father was one with him standing in front of the Notre Dame Cathedral with a stylish and attractive woman, his first wife, Ola. Father and Selma were always very close as first cousins. Later, when Nana and Jan Bernard came to America, Selma was one of two American born stylish New York women that taught Nana, then a young "greener", how to be an American. Aunt Ruth, Uncle Morris' wife, was the other. They gave Nana dresses and clothes, took her shopping and taught how to dress, how to style her hair, how to use make up and many other such necessary things.

Jan and Selma knew each other even before the war. They would not meet in person until my father came to America with Nana and me, as a baby, but they corresponded regularly and that is where the second group of pictures Selma showed me came from. I hadn't yet seen the one of grandfather and his first wife in front of the Notre Dame when Selma pulled out one of grandfather and a young woman, his age, and a little child, a boy maybe five years old. I was seeing these photos for the first time and, as with the other pictures, I innocently asked "Who's that?", pointing to the woman with father, in front of the Notre Dame.

"That was your father's first wife" Willie answered, matter of factly, not realizing that he was revealing a secret my father had kept my whole life. He also mentioned that my father had a son, my older half-brother.

I wanted to know more. Sometime not too long later, I tried to confront my father with this picture, part of the collection Selma bequeathed to me when she moved to Florida, but he acted like he didn't recognize the woman or the boy in the picture. He was very flustered. Nana recognized the photo and what I was doing and tried to shoo me away, to protect her husband.

By this time, shortly before my father's death, his Alzheimers had taken most of his active mind and, while I always felt like he recognized who was in the picture, I feel like I should not have shown him the picture. If he did recognize it, it was more likely to upset him than accomplish anything else. It was something he never talked about all my life growing up.

CHAPTER 2

Ten Zlotys, or the World's Biggest Sucker

When my father used to tell this story, he always said that at the time he thought he was the world's biggest sucker. On the other hand, he also said that you never knew when God would repay you for the good deeds you did. He said this when he talked about the Polish soldier with the bandage on his head, covering one eye, who asked for ten zlotys – the equivalent of ten dollars.

In September, 1939, the war that was to become World War II had broken out in Poland. Hitler had attacked Poland from the west and Stalin had attacked Poland from the east. Within days the Polish army was in disarray and retreating. As valiant as Poland's soldiers may have been, within weeks the defenses had collapsed and the country was in disarray. My father, Jan Bernard, was living in Lvov at the time[12], with his first wife and son. Lvov was a disaster with deserters and others coming back from the front. One soldier came up to Jan, pointing to the bandage around his head covering his eye, and asked for ten zloty for cab fare to the hospital.

He said that there were many wounded soldiers at the front, there weren't enough ambulances for all the wounded and the overwhelmed medics told him he should walk and he should get to the hospital on his own. He said that he had made it back to Lvov but had no more money

---

12 "At the time" was between the two world wars. Before World War I, it was part of the Austria-Hungary empire and was known as Lemberg. After World War II, it was part of the Soviet Union, the U.S.S.R. It is now Lviv, in the Ukraine. When Uncle Herman, Elaine and Marsha's dad, was asked "Where did you come from?", he used to answer "What year?" and would explain that he was "born in Austria Hungary, raised in Poland and it is now Russia." After Uncle Herman died, it became part of the Ukraine, which is where it is today.

and asked if he could borrow ten zlotys for cab fare to the hospital. Grandfather gave him the ten zlotys but never expected to be repaid. The soldier took the ten zlotys and disappeared. My father was sure he would never see him or the money again Whenever he told the story he joked that he was the world's biggest sucker. Then he would add that you never knew when God would reward you for the good deeds you do.

CHAPTER 3
Leaving Lvov – Saved by Deportation

Within days of this encounter, the Russians took Lvov. The soldier and the ten zlotys were the last thing on my father's mind. By then, there were thousands of refugees fleeing the front and overwhelming Lvov. The Russians began rounding up people and sending them east as prisoners.

When the Russian occupying authorities looked at my father's passport and saw the customs stamps from Italy, Switzerland and France, they accused him of being a spy and deported him to a labor camp. Father used to say that they knew he was not a spy, but they were rounding up anyone who was educated or a potential leader, in order to eliminate any possible dissent or opposition. Since my father had a law degree and was a teacher, he was viewed as a potential opposition organizer.

He did not realize it at the time, but like hundreds of thousands of others – not just Jews, not just Poles, but hundreds of thousands of others caught behind enemy lines, my father's life was saved by deportation. He was saved from Hitler by being deported by Stalin. My father was taken prisoner and sent to a labor camp somewhere in Siberia. Nana was also saved by deportation and sent to a labor camp in Siberia, because she was caught behind enemy lines and could not get home, but I will get to that story later.

CHAPTER 4

The Shema

I always think of my father when I say the *shema*. Every time I say the *shema*. And I think maybe there is a god that protects his chosen people. When my father was deported, he was separated from his wife and son and taken by train to somewhere in Siberia. He would never see his wife or son again. I am not sure he ever knew exactly where he was, but it was cold and the accommodations were hardly ideal.

The prisoners were a mix of people. Some were political prisoners. Some were picked up because they were in the wrong place without papers. That's why Nana and her first husband were picked up, but we'll get to that later. Others, like my father, were identified as potential opposition leaders and removed for that reason. My father was accused of being a spy. That was the reason given for his arrest, but he always suspected that the real reason he was taken was that he was a potential organizer and opposition leader.

My father's group of prisoners was assigned to cutting down trees. The work was hard and there was not enough to eat. Most of the prisoners smoked because smoking suppressed their appetite. My father had never smoked before, but he started smoking in the camp, as the nicotine would mask the hunger.

Both my father, and my mother, Litka, your Nana, started smoking when they were prisoners in Russia, as the tobacco helped diminish their appetites. My father soon learned that cigarettes were a valuable commodity that he could trade for food. Trading the cigarettes for food turned out to be a better use of the cigarettes than smoking them, but both your grandparents acquired a bad habit that was with them for the rest of their lives. My father switched from cigarettes to a pipe when he got older, but that was not much better. Nana also smoked until her last years.

My father talked about trading his cigarettes for food, but he never starved. This was because of the *shema*.

The first day in camp, my father and all the other prisoners lined up for their one meal a day, a bowl of thin soup. My father moved forward with the line, and as he moved forward in line, closer to the pot of soup, he could hear the man ladling the soup out, muttering under his breathe. As my father got closer he tried to make out what the man was saying, but the man was muttering under his breathe, so that the guards wouldn't hear him talking to the prisoners. Not until my father was next to the man could he hear what the man was saying.

"Shema yisrael adonai eloheynu . . ."

Standing in front of the man, with his bowl in hand, my father realized what the man was doing, and answered, also muttering under his breathe so the guards wouldn't hear.

"Boruch shem k'vod malchuso."

The man didn't say another word but dipped the ladle deep into the pot, reaching for the one bone, with a little meat on it, and put it into grandfather's bowl.

The next day, when they lined up for food, the man looked at my father, recognized him and, again, dipped the ladle deep into the pot and delivered the one piece of meat into father's bowl. This continued every day. I don't think that the two ever spoke, except for that first time, when my father completed the *shema*, but my father never starved to death. He had a *shomer*, a guardian taking care of him. Did he have someone looking after him because he knew the *shema*?

My father told other stories about his two years in a Siberian labor camp. He always smiled when he talked about his "welcome" to the labor camp. When he arrived, the guard at the entrance told him "you'll like the weather here." My father looked back at him, wondering what he meant. The guard continued "the weather is good here. Only ten months of winter and all the rest is summer." Father never tired of telling that story.

He talked about the work he did. He said the labor was hard. Their job was cutting down trees for lumber. What made the work hard was that had to dig down through many feet of snow to get to the base of the tree, and then widen the hole so that they could manipulate the saw. Needless to say the saws were not power tools.

My father told many stories and jokes about his time in the camp. He loved to tell the joke about the good weather in Siberia. But his story of the *shema* was different. For him, the story was about his reason for believing not just that there was a god but that G-d was a just god.

My father was very proud of the fact that he was a rational man. He was never very observant, although we did celebrate the holidays, and he always had a rational explanation for Jewish laws that he found primitive and no longer relevant. For example, he said that pork went bad quickly in the desert, so that the wise men made a rule against eating pork to keep the people healthy. Father would say that we do not need to keep these rules today. With modern medicine and science, we know about refrigeration, and we know how to keep meat, so there was no more need for the rules of kashruth.

He also did not keep the Sabbath. He was not a religious man. But he had a great respect for Jewish learning. He also used to say that the reason he had a son was so that there would be someone to say kaddish for him. Little did he – or I – realize that having me say kaddish for him was how he continued the Jewish education of his son, even after his passing. My father also used to tell the story about the man muttering the *shema* under his breathe. He would tell it often, and when he told it and when he told the story of the eye, he also used to say that God always rewards you for the good deeds you do, and that you never know when the reward will come.

CHAPTER 5
The Eye

Late in 1941 Hitler turned on his ally, Stalin, and attacked Russia. This changed the war – and changed the world. Now, instead of being aligned with Nazi Germany, the Soviet Union was at war with Germany, on the same side as the Allies, which at this point was mostly just Great Britain. The Nazis had rolled through Europe. Along with their ally, Italy, the Germans had occupied France and much of Europe. They were bombing London, and, as the United States had not yet entered the war, Britain was standing alone against the Nazi onslaught, until Hitler turned on Russia.

All of a sudden, Britain and Russia were fighting the same enemy. Stalin and Churchill became allies. As Hitler's troops crossed through what was left of Poland and the Ukraine and into Russia, Stalin could not feed or shelter his own people, let alone the hundreds of thousands of refugees, who had fled east from Poland and prisoners, like my father and Nana, who had been sent east by Stalin. Stalin turned to Churchill, the prime minister of Great Britain and asked him for help, for food, blankets, clothing and money. Poland had been England's ally prior to the Nazi invasion, and the remnants of the Polish army leadership, Generals **Wladyslaw Anders** and **Wladyslaw Sikorski**, were in London.

Churchill answered that Great Britain would provide blankets, tents, food and shelter, but he had a condition.

"If we take care of them, then they are ours," Churchill said.

The British set up refugee camps, tent camps, across southern Russia, along the border with Persia, which was then controlled by the British. The British brought food and supplies into the camps from Persia. General Anders and other exiled Polish officers came from England and began organizing a second corps of the Polish army in exile.[13]

Hitler attacking Russia also meant changes for my father. All the Polish prisoners in the Russian labor camps, including my father, were no longer prisoners. The prison guards opened up the gates to the labor camps, and told the prisoners "you are free." This only meant that the challenges were different. They had no warm clothing, no money, no food. They were not even sure where they were.

The Russians offered their former prisoners the opportunity to enlist in the Russian army and help liberate Poland, their homeland. As soldiers, they would be clothed and fed. The big inducement that the Russians offered was that the former prisoners would be given the opportunity to be the first to charge the German lines. My father explained that he thought about this offer. Then he began to wonder whether, being the first to charge the German lines, he would be shot from the front or from behind, and realized that maybe enlisting in the Russian army and being the first to lead the charge maybe was not such a good idea.

That was how my father decided to head south. He led a group of former prisoners from his labor camp. That was only one group. They were all headed south, to the Soviet frontier in Kazakhstan, looking for the British. The British had come north into Kazakhstan, from where they were occupying what is now Iran but what was then British occupied Persia.

The liberated prisoners knew that if they headed south and traveled far enough, they might reach the British refugee camps, where the Polish army was recruiting and organizing under the auspices of the British. They began walking. Because my father spoke Russian, German, English and other languages the other freed prisoners made him their leader.

They walked for a long time. Days became weeks, even months. Jan never explained how they found food or survived. Late one night, a Sunday night, they reached an outpost of Polish soldiers under the British. They

---

13 The First corps of the Polish Army in exile was formed from the Polish soldiers who were evacuated from Dunkirk, along with the French. The French soldiers became the Free French, led by DeGaulle, and the Polish soldiers with them became the Polish Army in Exile, led by Generals Sikorski and Anders, until General Anders went to Asia, to organize the Second Corps of the Polish Army in Exile.

knocked on the gate and the lone sentry doing Sunday night guard duty answered. Jan asked if he would let them in. The guard answered that it was Sunday night and everything was closed.

Jan explained that they had come a long way and that they were tired and hungry. The guard told them to come back in the morning. My father asked the guard to get his commanding officer. The guard said no. The sergeant was asleep and there was no way the guard was going to wake him. My father insisted and the guard said "the sergeant will kill me if I wake him. No way!"

Jan would not quit. His whole group was as tired and hungry as he was, and they had no place to wait until morning. Eventually my father persuaded the guard to get the sergeant, his commander, and the guard went off muttering about how angry the sergeant would be and how he didn't want to do this.

He came back in a few minutes with a grumbling, angry sergeant, upset about being awakened and yelling at the guard that he had disobeyed orders not to wake him. Then he saw my father, looked at him and everything changed. He went up to grandfather and gave him a big hug. Then he started kissing him on the cheeks.

Feeling awkward at this stranger hugging him, father said "excuse me. I don't even know you."

"Yes, you do," the sergeant answered, and he pointed to his eye. Father looked at the sergeant's eye. It took a minute before he realized that it was a glass eye. Then he realized who the sergeant was. By then the sergeant was yelling at the guard again. "Why didn't you let these men in! Go wake the cook! These men are hungry! Have him get these men some food! Why didn't you wake me?"

Whenever he told this story, Father would say, with utter faith, "There is justice in this world: God always rewards your good deeds, although you may never know how or where or when.

CHAPTER 6

The Dancer

Nana grew up in Lodz, Poland. At the time, Lodz was a thriving city of textile mills. Nana used to say that Lodz was known as the "Manchester" of Poland, referring to Manchester, England, famous as the center of the Britain's 19th-century textile industry. During Poland's industrial revolution, wool and cotton mills were built at the end of the 19th century. The mills needed workers, and people poured into Lodz from surrounding towns. The population grew from 50,000 in 1872 to over 351,000 in 1900. Close to 100,000 of those living in Lodz were Jews.

A strong Jewish community had begun to emerge in Lodz in 1848, when the Czar of Russia lifted the limitations on Jewish settlement in Polish cities. Then, in 1861 and 1862 decrees from the Czar eliminated the requirement of a "separate Jewish Quarter", that is, a ghetto, in Lodz. Jews began to settle throughout the city, although many decided to remain in the former Jewish quarter, the "Alstadt."

An orthodox synagogue, the Alte Shul or the Stara synagogue, was opened in 1860. Renovations took place in 1897, but the Nazis burned it down in 1939, soon after they occupied Lodz. A Reform synagogue opened in 1883. The wealthy, Jewish factory owner, I.K. Posnanski oversaw its construction. At the time, it was the largest structure in the heart of the city and was known as the "Great" Synagogue. The Nazis burned it down, too, in 1939, during the Nazi occupation. The Vilker Shul, opened in 1899, was also demolished by the Nazis in 1939, with the rest of the synagogues.

Nana's father, Joseph Sylberstajn, who was born either in Lodz or in Kielce, where his parents came from, worked as a manager in one of the mills. Later, Joseph was a "Director" of a large factory. He was the only Jew to hold such a high position. He was both a sharp businessman and an intellectual. Nana says that many years later, in Florida, her Uncle Harry, her father Joseph's brother, described Joseph as "so brilliant that had he come to America, he would be either a Wall Street millionaire or in jail".

Joseph Sylberstajn

Joseph adored his daughter, Litka. Nana adored him, as well. She was very proud of her father, Joseph. She described him as smart and shrewd and very successful in business, saying that he was well educated, a sophisticated intellect, well read and cultured. In addition to Uncle Harry, Solange confirmed what a brilliant man Joseph was. The highest praise she would bestow on me was that I looked like Joseph. Nana used to say the same thing.

Joseph had a son named Henyik, or Henry with this first wife. That first wife died, perhaps while giving birth. Joseph married Nana's mother after his first wife died. Nana's older half-brother, Henyik, was much older than Nana or their other siblings. Henyik was a good older brother and Nana adored him like she adored their father. Henyik taught his younger sister, Litka, to dance. He not only taught his younger sister to dance, he taught her to dance the tango, a daring and sexually provocative dance, now as well as then, and certainly not always considered "proper" in those days.

Joseph's second wife, Nana's mother, was Bluma, or Blanca, the same as my father's mother. My sister, whose full name is Vivian Blanche Fischer, was named after both our grandmothers, Nana's mother and my father Jan's mother. Bluma, or Blanca in Polish, was born in Maciowice. Her maiden name was most likely Eisenbaum , but possibly may have been Eisenfeld or Eisenberg or Eisen. . . something.

After your Nana, Litka, was born, Joseph and Bluma had two more children. Their second child was a boy, named Abramik, or Adam, as he was known in Polish. Adam was born in 1918 or 1919, a year-and-a-half younger than his big sister, Nana, and a year-and-a-half before the 1921 birth of their second daughter, who they named Miriam, or Manousha, (a diminutive for Mary, her Polish name). Manousha was the baby. When Shira and I were in France in 1996, for the high school graduation trip I had promised my daughter, Solange described Manousha as "brilliant", saying she had a head "like Shira". Both Solange and Nana were very proud that Manousha had received an award from Josef Pilsudski, then the president of Poland.[14]

Joseph was the oldest of the ten Sylberstajn siblings, five brothers and five sisters, with an alternating birth order of male, female, male, female, as Adolphe would later explain to me. There was an eleventh child, another sister, Leah, who died young. Nana, whose Hebrew name was Leah, was named after her Aunt Leah. After Joseph was Malka, who was married to a man named Shlomo, whose last name is unknown. Next was Hirsch, or Harry. He was the Uncle Harry, in Miami, that Vivian and I knew when we were little, Harry Silby. Then came the second daughter, Miriam, then Maurice, Solange's father, and then Rachel, or Rose. In Polish, this was Ruzia or the diminutive Ruszeke. Next was Adolphe, then the fourth daughter, Tola, and then Henry

---

14 Josef Pilsudski was the marshal, or general, in World War I, who led the Polish forces against the Austrians and the Russians (who became entangled in their own civil war, the Russian Revolution that led to the overthrow of the Czar and the establishment of Communist Russia). The first Polish state in centuries was established in 1918, and Pilsudski became the first chief of the state, or president, serving from 1918 to 1922. During this time, Pilsudzki continued to serve as Marshall Pilsudski, leading the Polish army in border disputes with Bolshevik Ukraine, Germany, Lithuania and Czechoslovakia that went on for several years. Both Nana and my father admired him and spoke of him as the Polish George Washington. They were not the only ones to treat him with this honor.

and Sonya, or Sarah. Henry, the youngest son, was, according to Nana and Solange, "the poet" and "the artist". He was also special according to both Nana and Solange.

L to R, Unknown man, Harry, unknown woman, Maurice and Adolphe

Joseph and his wife Blanca, Joseph's brother, Maurice, and his sisters, Malka and Miriam and Rose, or Ruzia, and the "poet", Henry, were all killed in the Shoah. In addition, most all of their children perished. Nana's brother Abramik, and baby sister Manousha, and Solange's brother Abramik were also killed. There were other cousins who also perished, two brothers named Henry and Munik, who were the sons of either Malka or Miriam, and other cousins as well.

Joseph and Blanca lived with their children in an apartment at 51 Wschodnia Street, in a Jewish section of Lodz. They lived upstairs from Joseph's parents, Meilich, or Myetek, and Bronya Szylberstajn, in the same building on the third floor. Joseph's younger brother, Maurice, or Moshe lived across the courtyard, on the second floor, with his wife, Miriam, and children, Abramik and Zlata.

Harry, Joseph's next oldest brother, was old enough that he no longer lived with his parents when Nana was a child, but Nana knew him as he lived nearby with his wife Gustave, or Gustie. Gustie was from a Jewish family in Lodz that the Szylberstajns knew. Harry and Gustie married in Lodz and were together until Gustie died, in Miami Florida, many, many years later. Harry wanted to be a doctor but, as a Jew was not permitted to enter medical school in Poland, so in the early twenties, he followed his brother, Maurice, who had already gone to Vienna to study orthodics.[15]

In Vienna, he and Gustie planned that he would study medicine, while she opened a pharmacy to support them. Unable to study medicine in Vienna, as well, for the same reason, he ended up studying chemistry and pharmacy. He joined Gustie in operating their pharmacy until they fled the *Anschluss*, the German occupation of Austria in March 1938, to the United States, where Gustie had an uncle or a cousin. They eventually settled in the Coral Gables section of Miami, where Harry lived the rest of his life.

Adolphe was born in 1899 or 1901. According to Solange, Adolphe was born in Skarzysko, a village just south of Radom. Adolphe was a musician from the beginning. He studied violin as a child in Lodz and joined his brother, Harry, in Vienna as a teenager. Adolphe was on his way to Vienna around the time Nana was born in 1916. It's possible that Nana never really knew Adolphe before they found each other twenty years after the war.

Henry, the youngest brother of the five brothers, still lived with his parents, Myetek and Bronya when Nana was a child. Nana probably knew him best of her uncles, as he lived downstairs from Nana when she was growing up, and was pretty close to the same age as Nana's half-brother with the same name. Like his brother, Joseph, Nana's Uncle Henry would take Nana to the cafes and poetry readings and out dancing.

As for Nana's five aunts, the five sisters, it is not clear which of them was living where in the years when Nana was growing up, in the 1920s and 1930s. The sisters were, in order, Malka, Miriam, Rachel or Ruzia (Rose), Tola, and Sonya or Sarah, the youngest. The youngest sisters, Tola and Sonya, were not so much older than Nana, or even Solange.

In 1963, Tola's brothers Adolphe and Harry would find their long lost

---

15 In Europe, an "orthodist" was a medical related professional who made braces and other medical devices meant to support an injured knee, or leg, or wrist, or foot. The orthodic device might be a cast for a broken bone, a shoe insert, such as arch supports, or a brace for a knee.

niece Litka, your Nana. Vivian and I spent a summer or two in Orlando in the early sixties with Tola and her son Martin, who quickly became like a big brother to me. My sense, from listening to Tola and Nana talk about each other and the family, was that Nana and Tola were very close, not just in age, when they were growing up. They were closer in age than my father, Jan Bernard and his Uncle Herman. Tola and Nana were probably more like sisters than aunt and niece, just as Jan Bernard and Herman were more like brothers than uncle and nephew.

It is hard to say how many Sylberstajns were living in the building in Lodz at any given time. For example, there was a period before moving full time to Vienna that Adolphe would stay with his parents when in Lodz and with his brother Harry when in Vienna. Maurice may have been the first to go to Vienna to learn a profession. He studied orthodics in Vienna and was still studying there to welcome his brothers, Harry and then Adolphe, when they sought their fortunes there.

Maurice returned to the family home on Wschodnia Street after completing his studies. He had his own apartment after he married Miriam Luxembourg, first cousin to Nana's mother, Blanca. The Sylber-stajns stayed close and there were always aunts, uncles and cousins in the building. Nana and her brother and sister, and their cousin Solange, who was then called Zlata and her brother Abram lived across the courtyard. They all grew up together and were close.

Nana and Zlata, who became Solange when she moved to Paris after the Shoah, were actually double cousins, through their mothers as well as their fathers, as Joseph and Maurice had married first cousins. Maurice's wife, Miriam, or Manya, as Nana always called her, was first cousins with Nana's mother, Blanca. As two cousins who had married Sylberstajn brothers, they were very close. Miriam and Blanca were always very close, sticking together through many quarrels with their Sylberstajn in-laws. Perhaps the two were close because the two sisters, Bluma and Miriam, came from a more religious family than the Sylberstajns.

Their three daughters, Litka, as Nana was called, Manousha and Zlata, were all also very close growing up, even though Nana was a few years older than her little sister, Manousha, and her cousin, Zlata, who were almost the same age. Even closer were their two brothers, Nana's younger brother and Zlata's older brother. The two cousins were both named Abram, both the same age, and had a special bond. The Sylberstajns were a close knit family, but especially the two cousins with the same name, Abram. They were especially close. Both Nana and Solange said that their two brothers had always been inseparable, from as early as either can remember.

As a child growing up, Zlata always looked up to her older cousin, Litka. Her older cousin was smart and fashionable. Most important, her cousin Litka was a dancer. As children, they grew up together and shared stories and sang songs together, but your Nana was the cool and hip older cousin. Nana was always dressed in the most stylish new clothes. She went to the cafes with her father. She went out dancing and went out not just with her older brother Henyik's friends, but her own boyfriends, too. This won admiration for Nana from her younger cousin, Solange, then Zlata, but also sometimes got Nana in trouble.

Nana's mother, Blanca, didn't always know about Nana's boyfriends, like Solange did, and often Solange's mother, Chacha Manya, as Nana would call her, knew about them, too. When Nana's mother heard that Nana was riding on the back of a motorcycle with her boyfriend, Nana ran for help to her Aunt Miriam, Chacha Manya, who interceded with her cousin, Blanca, on Nana's behalf. What is not clear is whether Nana got into trouble for riding too recklessly on the back of a motorcycle or for going out with a young man who was not Jewish.

Nana taught Solange to dance the tango in her play "Dancing School", where she let Solange come "for free". Nana must have been a good teacher and Solange a good student, as years later, in 1990, at Solange's kitchen table, Nana smiled when she talked about how Solange danced the tango with their Uncle Henyik, the youngest of the five Sylberstajn brothers. Both Nana and Solange thought the world of their Uncle Henyik, referring to him as "the poet" or "the artist".

Nana was a dancer and partier. She loved going to the cafes with her father or older brother, Henyik, where they introduced her to writers, poets and intellectuals. Nana's father Joseph, like his siblings, was not religious like their father, Nana's and Solange's grandfather, Meilech Sylberstajn, who, according to both Solange and Nana, did not work but spent his time praying. His wife, Bronya, Nana's grandmother, was a Poznanski. Jean Claude told me that we have cousins named Poznanski in Paris that he knew as a child and he also told me that the richest man in Lodz, who owned the biggest mill in Lodz was named Poznanski. Jean Claude was curious whether maybe we were related to him.

Henya, Henry the Poet

Young Nana the Dancer

When I visited Lodz in 2015, I visited the mill and the Poznanski palace, which is now the Museum of the City of Lodz. The beautiful palace sits at the corner of Ogrodowa Street and Zachodnia Street, and houses a collection of local and Polish art, and European masters, as well as a history section. One can imagine the elegant parties that took place there at the one-time home of Izrael Poznanski, who in the late nineteenth century was one of the richest textile magnates and perhaps the major philanthropist in the history of Lodz.

In addition to his home, now the Lodz Museum, and his factory, a third major site in Lodz is the huge domed Poznanski family mausoleum in the Lodz Jewish Cemetery, which is the largest Jewish graveyard in Europe. Founded in 1892, the cemetery was too large for the Nazis to destroy. It contains 68,000 surviving memorials and an area called Polem Gettowy, or the

Ghetto Field, the final resting place of 43,000 who died in the Lodz Ghetto.

At first I thought Jean Claude's question was a fair one, until I realized how many Poznanskis there were in Lodz. The "sky" or "ski" at the end of a Polish name meant "from", so the name "Poznanski" meant "from Poznan", another city a little under a hundred miles west of Lodz. So the name Israel Poznanski meant "Israel from Poznan", and there were many Poles, many of them Jewish, who immigrated to Lodz in the second half of the nineteenth century and early twentieth century, like both Izrael Poznanski and Nona's grandmother's family.

Nonetheless, the Poznanski from whom we are descended, Nana's paternal grandmother, Bronya Poznanski Sylberstajn was quite an entrepreneur herself, running a small hosiery business from their first floor flat at 49 Wschodnia Street. It must have been a busy apartment, for in addition to various grown sons and daughters coming and going, and staying there from time to time, there were seamstresses. Some seamstresses worked there daily, sewing hosiery. Others came to drop off the hose they had sewn. Customers also came to purchase the fine men's and women's socks and stockings.

However, the seamstresses and customers were never there on Shabbat. It was not just that Nana's grandfather, Meilich, was such a pious and observant Jew. Indeed he was. Lilian and Jean Claude would laugh about how their father, Adolphe, described their grandfather, Meilich. He would sit at home all day, praying and studying, while Grandmother Bronya, the Poznanski, ran a thriving cottage business. No wonder Jean Claude thought that his Grandmother, Bronya Poznanski, may have been related to the wealthy Israel Poznanski. After all, Jean Claude and Lilian had some Poznanski cousins in Paris. They would have been our cousins, too. But as good a businesswoman Grandmother Poznanski may have been, she was also a religious and observant Jew.

This often caused conflict in the Sylberstajn home, because the younger generation, Meilich and Bronya's five sons and five daughters, were not as religious as their parents, nor, for the most part, were they interested in being observant. Solange described her childhood family as Jewish but not religious: her father, Maurice was not at all religious, but her mother, Miriam, kept a Kosher home and Solange remembered that

Friday afternoons were special. Every Friday afternoon at 5:00, Solange's friends and her brother's friends would come for a "Shabbat party", where they would eat cakes and sing and dance. On holidays, Rosh Hashana and Yom Kippor, they would go to synagogue.

Solange's mother, Miriam, was more traditional than her Sylberstajn husband, Maurice. Maurice, like his siblings, was not religious. According to Solange, her father was "a bit of a Trotskyist" when he was young. Yet he had a profession, as an orthodist, mostly making inserts for shoes and boots. He made a good enough living. It was not "fashionable" yet for women to work outside the home, but Solange's mother worked in her mother-in-law's hosiery business. While the standard of living in Poland in the twenties and thirties was not so great, the families of the Sylberstajn brothers, Joseph and Maurice, lived comfortably. Like Nana, Solange spoke fondly of her life as a child growing up in Lodz.

Nana's father, Joseph, the oldest of the five brothers and five sisters, was not religious at all. When he went out Saturday morning, he did not tell his wife or his mother where he was going. He let them think that he was going to shul. But as his daughter, your Nana, grew older, she knew where her father was going, because, when she grew older enough to keep his secret, he would take here with him.

Joseph went to the cafes to sit with the poets and writers. He and his brothers were modern, Bohemian and intellectuals. Nana always talked about her Uncle Henry, the poet. Solange also would reminisce about their Uncle Henry, saying the same things as Nana about their fathers' youngest brother being a poet, a writer, a creative intellectual but mostly a poet. Henry Sylberstajn was about the same age as Jules Tuwim, also a Lodz native, and one of Poland's most popular poets between the wars.

Jules Tuwim was born in Lodz in 1894 to a secular, assimilated Jewish family. He grew up in Lodz, perhaps frequenting the same cafes as Joseph and Henry Sylberstajn. He was not just a poet, but a major figure in Polish literature. He wrote cabaret sketches, children's stories, translated foreign poets like Rimbaud and Heine, and authored humorous pieces, satires and *szmonces*, comic pieces rooted in and alluding to Jewish tradition. He was attacked as a Jew, accused in a 1930 magazine article for "Jewing up

Polish literature". At the same time, he was attacked within the Jewish community as an anti-semite.

When Strauss and I visited Lodz, we spent time on Piotrokowska Street, now a pedestrian mall for many blocks in the center of the city, with cafes and restaurants, much like Lodz must have been in the thirties. We came upon a statue of Tuwim, seated on bench in a mall where today, students and young writers and artists still gather in the outdoor cafes. Reading the plaque about Tuwim made me wonder where I knew the name. I think there was a book on the shelves in our den at home with his name, perhaps his biography or a collection of his poems. I'm not sure if Nana used to talk about him, also, but seeing him seated on the bench on Piotrokowska Street made me wonder if Joseph or Henry Sylberstajn knew Jules Tuwim, and made me think about Nana's uncle, Henry Sylberstajn, and what he would have become.

Statue of Tuwim, 2015

Nana's mother's family was more scattered than the Sylberstajns. Her mother, Blanca, was born in Maciejowice, not Radom, like her mother's cousin, Miriam, Solange's mother. Blanca's parents were Hersh Baer Eisenbaum and Hannah Leah Eisenbaum.[16] Like Nana's father, her mother also was one of ten siblings, five brothers and five sisters. Nana remembered visiting one of her mother's sisters, an aunt who had moved to Kudnow. What Nana remembered was that the aunt's husband threw Nana out of the house in Kudnow when Nana forgot to wash her hands before eating. Nana remembers that one of her aunts married a rabbi. I am not sure if it was this one in Kudnow.

Feige was another of Nana's mother's sisters. Nana remembers her Aunt Feige as "beautiful, with long black wavy hair, like my mother." She was married to a goldsmith or a jeweler. They separated and she went to South America, perhaps to Argentina or Brazil, in the 1930s. Feige and her husband had two children, an older son and a younger daughter. Nana remembered that the girl was disabled and couldn't walk. From Nana's description, it sounded like she had polio.

Nana also once talked about a cousin who was a big Zionist. She thought that he was the son of one of Nana's uncles, one of her mother's brothers, an Eisenbaum. Nana said she really liked this cousin, even though he was always trying to get her to join the Zionist youth club he belonged to. She said that this cousin left for Palestine. She wasn't sure when or if he made it.

So maybe we have Eisenbaum cousins in Israel, descended from Nana's uncle and cousin. Or maybe we have cousins in Argentina or Brazil, descended from Nana's Aunt Feige. But we don't know her married name, so we don't know what their family name might be.

---

16 Although it is possible the name was Eisen . . . something else. According to Solange, Nana's mother's maiden name was Paznich, or Pasnick, but more likely Solange was remembering Nana's grandmother, Bronya Poznanski.

CHAPTER 7

Two Cards That Said "Seal Your Lips"

The Sylberstajns were bright, motivated and ambitious. So it is not surprising that Vienna, a grand city with its operas, music, universities and culture would attract the Sylbertajn brothers from Lodz, with its mills and factories, as it attracted many Jews, who in return, contributed to Vienna's culture. Solange's father, Maurice, went to Vienna first when he went to study to be an orthodist. Uncle Harry moved to Vienna for good in the early twenties, with his bride, Gustie, but likely had already been studying there before then.

Adolphe traveled back and forth from the Lodz family home on Wschodnia Street in Lodz to Vienna perhaps as early as before World War I. That's what his children, Jean Claude and Anna say. Adolphe was born at the turn of the century, in 1899 or 1901, so that would make him a still young teenager when he started playing his violin in Vienna, but it is very possible. He became interested in the violin from watching his older brother, Maurice, play. Responding to this interest, Maurice gave Adolphe his first violin. At some point, his other older brother, Harry, invited Adolphe to stay in Vienna and study music. This might have been right at the end of the first world war. Adolphe was still a teenager at the time. When he arrived in Vienna, he changed his name, which by best accounts was Avram or Abraham, to Adolphe.

In Vienna, the young Adolphe began to play in larger cafes, playing violin and leading small orchestral ensembles of five, six or seven musicians. This was the beginning of what would be a long full life of playing Viennese music, especially Viennese waltzes. Adolphe lived in the same building as his older brother, Harry. Adolphe lived on the third floor, Harry on the first, with his wife, Gustie. Sometime, probably in the early twenties, Adolphe married a Catholic woman in Vienna. He tried to keep this hidden from his mother, Bronya. When she came to visit, Adolphe and his brother, Harry, conspired to keep their mother on the first floor, in Harry's apartment, for if she went upstairs to Adolphe's flat, she would discover his Austrian Catholic wife.

But according to Nana, Bronya, who was Nana's grandmother as well as Adolphe's mother, learned about her son Adolphe's Catholic wife. This happened when Nana's mother, Blanca was having problems with her eyesight. Nana's father, Joseph, took his wife, Blanca, to Vienna where his brother Adolphe found an eye doctor to treat her. However, Blanca would not stay at Adolphe's apartment with his Christian wife. When she returned home to Wschodnia Street in Lodz, and talked about her trip, Blanca told the family about Adolphe's Catholic wife. First she told her mother about Adolphe's *shiksa* wife. Then she told her mother-in-law, Bronya, Adolphe's mother, about Adolphe's wife. Adolphe responded by sending Blanca a card. On the front of the card was a face with the lips buttoned closed.

After that, when Bronya, went to visit Adolphe, she would not go up to his apartment. They would meet in a park. Nana explained to me that her grandmother did this out of courtesy to Adolphe's *shiksa* wife. Nana said that Grandmother Bronya did not want to be rude to Adolphe's wife or reject her daughter-in-law. To the contrary, she wanted to avoid a confrontation. She was afraid that if she visited the apartment, she would be offered food, and she would have to refuse it because she would not know if it was kosher. This would have been rude, so instead of taking the likely chance that she would have to refuse the food she was offered, Bronya instead avoided visiting at all.

When Nana told this story, she made a point of comparing the way her grandmother Bronya handled the situation to the way her Aunt Miriam, Chacha Manya, Solange's mother treated Adolphe years later in Paris. However Miriam had good reason to be unhappy with Adolphe. Her husband Maurice had a mistress, or maybe more than one. Maurice first had an affair with the family maid, a Polish woman. Later Maurice began traveling to Vienna to meet with a mistress. He would stay with his brother, Adolphe, a wrong that Chacha Manya, would remember, years later in Paris, when Adolphe would come to her for help.

Adolphe sent a second similar card sometime later to his sister-in-law, Manya. He did this after a visit from Manya, who brought her daughter, Zlata, to Vienna for Adolphe to help find a doctor. This must have been in the 1930s, as Zlata/Solange was not born until 1922 and Adolphe would have had to have been older, too. Solange was suffering from some sort of malady. Perhaps it was a back problem that caused Zlata, as she was then known, to hunch her back.

Once again, upon the return to Lodz, Adolphe's mother heard a report about her son's Catholic wife. Once again, Adolphe sent a card to the offending party. This time the card had a face with the lips zipped shut, rather than buttoned. In both cases the message was clear.

CHAPTER 8

Nana's Story – Also Saved By Deportation

Nana was married before the war, something she never talked about when Vivian and I were growing up. Like Jan Bernard, she didn't talk about being married, or about other things that maybe were too hard to think about. She never talked about a lot of things. Perhaps to avoid telling us she was married before the war when we were growing up, Nana never really explained how she got the name Kantor on her passport and papers, brushing us off when we asked with the explanation that she took the name of a famous Polish soccer player.

At some point, Nana, like other survivors, began to talk about certain things. Maybe it was because enough time had passed that she was able to talk about these things. Maybe it was because she was getting old enough to worry that if she didn't talk about certain things, they would be lost. By the time she was more willing and able to talk more about these things, there were things she did not remember so well or no longer remembered at all. It was many years and Nana was already a grandmother before she first revealed that she was married before the war. In fact she was married on August 23, 1939, exactly a week before Hitler invaded Poland on September 1, 1939. She was twenty-three at the time. She had married a good looking but hot-tempered guy. His name was Myetek Kantor.

According to my notes, Nana told me one time in the 1980s that Myetek was the grandson of a rabbi. I am not sure if this is accurate, for she also said, another time, also in the 1980s, that Myetek's grandfather was a judge. This is likely more accurate, as it was corroborated by Solange.

Maybe it was Myetek's other grandfather who was the judge. In any event, the story continues that Myetek Kantor's grandfather, the judge, had converted, at least outwardly, in order to become a judge. Unless it was Myetek's father who was the judge. Nana may not have remembered forty or fifty years later such details of the family into which she had married only a week before the Russians took her prisoner.

In any event, Myetek's generation of the Kantor family was quite assimilated, especially after Myetek's father died, and Myetek was a quite secular and assimilated Jew. Nana explained that the Kantor family was so secular that Myetek's mother did not speak any "Jewish", which is how Nana and everyone from that generation referred to Yiddish. According to Nana, the family was much more secular than even the Szylberstajns. I suspect that the Kantors were probably a bit of mix, somewhat secular but with strong strains of observance and tradition, much like the Szylberstajns – or the Glantzes and the Fischers, for that matter. That's what Jewish life was like in Poland between the wars, a constant push between the secular modern world and a long and still strong Jewish tradition, religion and culture.

Litka and Myetek's wedding was very small. The wedding was in a private house in Lodz, perhaps the judge's house. The wedding was that small. But it was a traditional Jewish wedding, with a rabbi officiating. Nana even remembers going to the mikveh before the wedding. Nana remembers that Myetek's brother and widowed mother were there but Nana never said who was there from the Szylberstajn family. Litka and Myetek never had a civil marriage, as the war started before they had the chance to.

After the wedding, Litka and Myetek went to visit family, to introduce Litka to Myetek's family and Myetek to Litka's family. It seems like a variation of *sheva b'rachot*, in a broad sense. First, the newlyweds went to Radom, where Nana's mother had family. Then they continued to Rovno, so that Myetek could introduce his new bride to his relatives there. Litka and Myetek were still visiting with Myetek's relatives in Rovno on September 1, 1939, when the war broke out.

Rovno was part of Poland then, but now is deep in the Ukraine, far to the east of Lodz, even further east than Lvov. It is now called Rivni, like Lvov is now called Lviv. It is some 600 kilometers, or 400 miles east of Lodz. Rovno was deep in what is now the Ukraine and within days the Russian forces had advanced almost to Warsaw and Nana and her husband, Myetek were many miles behind the Russian lines. There was no way they were going to get back to Lodz. With a war now raging, they did not know what to do.

The Russians solved that problem for them, taking them both prisoner, as they did not have proper papers to be in Rovno. Once they were taken by the Russians, they were separated, both put on trains headed east, to labor camps in Siberia. Nana saw her husband once, in those following weeks of transport and transition. She was in a line of female prisoners being marched one way, passing a line of men being marched in the other direction and she and Myetek passed each other, but they had no chance to speak.

As Nana was moved about, she would ask other prisoners about her new husband, just as all the prisoners would ask about family and friends as they crossed paths with others. Occasionally she heard stories, but she held little hope. She knew that Myetek was hot headed. He had a quick temper and his temper would likely get him into trouble. She was sure, quite regretfully, that he would not survive. She never learned for sure.

She was alone and did not know when, or if, she would ever get back to Poland or see her family again. She did not know exactly where she was except that she was well into the eastern portion of Russia, if not exactly in Siberia. Nana never smoked before but, like Jan, she started smoking as a prisoner, because the nicotine in the cigarettes suppressed the hunger. She kept the name Kantor, as she thought it was less Jewish than Szylberstajn. She acted as if she was not Jewish, as if she was not anything, because it was easier to survive that way. She did everything she could to be as invisible as possible. She said you had to lie, to steal, to do whatever was necessary to survive.

Smoking was just one of the problems that Nana acquired while a prisoner in Russia. From as early as I can remember, Nana always had stomach problems, problems that got worse later in life. Nana said that she first developed these problems when taken to Russia. Whether in transit in cattle car type trains, or in the prisons and labor camps, often there were no private toilets, or toilets at all. Despite being a bit wild as a teenager and young woman, Nana was a very modest woman. Reluctant to go to the bathroom in front of others, Nana would hold it in. When she developed stomach problems later in life, she attributed the origins of her digestive problems to the things she had to do while a prisoner in Russia.

There were other habits that Nana acquired while a prisoner. Many of them, which had to do with eating, arose from being hungry all the time. You might remember some of them. Nana would not throw away an empty jar or container of food without taking the last bits of food off the jar. She did the same with serving plates before putting them in the sink. Growing up, Vivian and I first wondered about why she did such things when she taught us better table manners. Only later did we learn to excuse behaviors like this in both our parents.

Nana also spent two years in a work camp, the same as my father. Unlike my father, Nana never talked much at all about being a prisoner or what life was like in the labor camps. Perhaps the hardest part for her was being alone. She had no family, not even a friend. She had no idea what had happened to her parents, her brothers and sister, or her newlywed husband. She was truly alone, doing whatever she needed to do to survive. Many around her died, but Nana survived. Like your grandfather, Jan Bernard, and many, many others, she was set free, after two years as a prisoner, when Hitler attacked Stalin's Russia in 1941.

After Hitler's attack, Russia switched sides, joining the allies, and your Nana, like my father, like hundreds of thousands of these other prisoners, was no longer a prisoner of war. They were "set free". The gates to the prisons and labor camps were opened up and these hundreds of thousands of prisoners, mostly Polish, and many of them Jewish, were free to go. But where were they going to go? They were in the middle of nowhere, somewhere in Siberia, as best they knew.

Nana had nowhere to go. She had no friends or family. She was on her own. She did not speak Russian or other languages, like my father. She had to count on the fact that Russian and Polish were similar enough to communicate when she encountered locals. She had no food, she had no money.

Nana knew she had to head south, and she managed to do so, although she never talked much about how. She hitched rides when she could, hopped trains when she could, but mostly she walked. Mostly she was by herself. At some point Nana could go no further. She was tired. She was hungry. Her clothes were ragged. She was ragged. She was somewhere in open country. Maybe it was farmland or pasture. Maybe she was off the road. She was in a field or an orchard. She did not know where she was, but she could go no further. She collapsed and lay down under a tree.

CHAPTER 9
No We Have Never Met Before

When Nana woke up, she did not know where she was. She was still lying down under the tree, and not in good shape. She looked up to see an Englishman in uniform attending to her, and a native Kazakh, a farmer or a shepherd. The native Kazakh had found Nana passed out under the tree. Nana was a light skinned, European, a white woman. The Kazakh assumed she was English and he went looking for an British soldier, or some other Englishman, to report that one of their women passed out under a tree and needed help.

As fortune would have it, the soldier he found was a doctor, a military doctor. However, the doctor did not speak Kazakh, and so did not understand the shepherd, who was jabbering in Kazakh and pointing to the tree. The English doctor thought the shepherd was accusing him, or other soldiers, of stealing fruit from the tree and tried to back away. The Kazakh shepherd was persistent, however, and kept pointing to the tree. Eventually, gesturing with arms waving, the shepherd got the English soldier to look under the tree, and see the woman and managed to communicate to the soldier that this woman was European, that she was "one of yours".

If Nana were a woman of faith, she might have felt, when she opened her eyes and saw a white doctor in a British uniform attending to her, that the Lord was watching over her and had send this hero to rescue her. She was grateful to both the doctor and the Kazakh shepherd for rescuing her. In her eyes, they had rescued her. She never saw her survival as the grace of a god watching over and protecting her. To the contrary, if anything, she was angry about how she suffered solely because she was Jewish, although she may not have ever recognized her anger, or its source. If her bitterness about being Jewish ever changed, it was only years later, when she was blessed with six grandchildren. She loved these grandchildren as a blessing and this was when her feelings changed.

Nana was very grateful to this handsome doctor in uniform who rescued her and brought her back from near death. Much later Nana had her chance to thank the doctor, but that would come after many more travels. Nana was taken to the nearby British refugee camp where she slowly recovered her strength and health. As she became stronger and able, she enlisted in the Corps II of the Polish army in exile that the British were organizing in Samarkand under General Wladyslaw Anders.

General Anders would go on to command the 80,000 Polish refugees enlisted from the eastern, or Russian front who formed the second Polish Corps. The First Corps, under the command of General Sikorski, who was also serving as the Polish prime minister in exile, also started as a force of 80,000 troops consisting of soldiers who escaped the initial attack on Poland and who fought, quite bravely, under General Sikorski in Switzerland and France before being evacuated to England, when France fell. It regrouped in England, as the Polish Army in Exile, fighting under the British command. Its pilots played a large role in the air battles over Britain. By late 1941, the First Corps was reduced to 20,000 troops, when General Anders was send to Samarkand to form the much needed Polish Second Corps, made up of well bodied Polish refugees who had been scattered in Russia and the Balkans and from Persia to the Middle East.

Nana trained in this Second Corps, and, at some point, she shipped out to Persia. It is not clear whether her training was in the camp in Kazakhstan or in Persia, both, or somewhere in between. In any event, it was a long way from her home and family in Lodz. The British had a strong presence in Persia, which was victim to the politics of oil, just as it was after it became Iran, as it is called today. Back then it was the British Empire, taking oil from Persia through British Petroleum, now BP. At the end of the twentieth century, it became the United States and Exxon-Mobil taking oil from Iraq and Iran. Oil was important to Britain's war effort.

As Nana, and other volunteers in the Second Polish Corps, completed training, the British had begun massing troops, literally, from all over the world in Egypt. Field Marshall Erwin Rommel had British and Australian troops under siege at Tobruk. A brilliant strategist, Rommel was known as the Desert Fox. If he took Tobruk, Egypt would fall next. The newly formed Second Corps of the Polish Army would soon be facing combat against the German tank brigades. The Polish volunteers were headed for battle, alongside not just British, but Australian, Indian, Free French, Czech, Greek, and French African forces. Rommel was threatening to attack Egypt and he had to be stopped.

Nana was not a combat soldier. She was a dancer. But it takes many people besides combat soldiers to keep an army fighting, healthy and motivated. There were huge staging areas in Egypt behind the enemy lines, where soldiers and units were prepared to go to the front, and where soldiers returning from the front that needed to recover and to be attended to before returning to the front. Soldiers on well-needed leave often needed a break from combat, and a young and attractive Nana helped to provide this.

Nana danced in a folk music troupe that performed Polish folk dances, like mazurkas, polkas and polonaises. She also helped arrange and choreograph the dance numbers and performances that were part of the shows to entertainment the troops. It may not have been fighting in combat, but it was what she did well, and it was her way of contributing to the war effort to defeat the Nazis.

Nana had a friend who was a nurse, also Polish. The nurse, who was dating a doctor, arranged for a second doctor to be a date for her friend Litka. When the two couples met, Nana's friend introduced the two doctors. Nana's date said that he was pleased to meet her.

Nana looked at him and realized that he was the doctor who the Kazakh shepherd had brought to her when she had collapsed under his fruit tree. She answered him, saying "We've met before."

The doctor answered that he did not think they had met. In fact, he insisted that "surely I would remember meeting a woman as attractive as you."

Nana smiled, graciously accepting the compliment, as she said "I didn't look this then." Over dinner that evening, she had the chance to tell the doctor the story of where they had met and to thank the young doctor for saving her life.

CHAPTER 10

A Middle Eastern Romance

Not long after her second meeting with the British doctor, Nana had another arranged meeting with another handsome young soldier. This meeting was at a beach resort in el Quassasin province, at a small resort along the waters of the Suez Canal, called Ismailia. Known in Egypt as "The City of Beauty and Enchantment", Ismailia sits in the middle of the Suez Canal, halfway between Port Said to the north and Suez to the south, some 90 miles east of Cairo. Ismailia was built in 1863, during the construction of the Suez Canal, by Khedive Ismail the Magnificent, after whom the city is named.

The British established a military base at Ismailia in 1882 and an airbase there in World War I. British forces defeated Ottoman and German forces at the Battle of Romani in 1916, establishing their control of the Suez Canal for the rest of World War I. Also notable in the town's history, the Muslim Brotherhood was established in Ismailia in 1928. However, Ismailia is probably most well known as the site where General Ariel Sharon crossed the Suez, and changing the course of the Yom Kippur War.

With this bold move, Sharon was able to move his Israeli forces behind the advancing Egyptian lines, placing them in a position to cut off the advancing Egyptian troops from their supply lines. Worried that the Israelis would soon be able to do so, the Egyptian forces, advancing boldly until then, now were on the defensive. They had to send troops to defend Ismailia, worried that Sharon's forces would take it. Not waiting for the order to attack, Sharon ordered the Israeli paratroopers forward to

Ismailia. Heavy fighting ensued, but the Egyptian advance was stopped. The course of the Yom Kippur war had changed, turning on a young general's decision to act before receiving orders.

The course of two other lives also changed at Ismailia. Ismailia was where a romance began for Litka Kantor and for Jan Bernard Fischer, a romance that lasted the rest of their lives. Each alone in the world, far from the home and family they knew, they found support – and a strong and lasting love – in each other. Your Nana was truly in love with Jan Fischer. He was handsome, smart, and even after all he went through, still had an amazing self-confidence. He equally loved and adored Nana. She was young, 27 years old, attractive and had a grace and charm. Her face lit up when she smiled and she had the ability to engage people when she spoke. He was in love with her.

Ismailia gave the two of them a respite from war. It was where the world turned around for them, too, with a romance that restored love and companionship to both their lives and initiated a lifelong partnership between them. The only problem was that, as far as they knew at the time, they both were already married. Litka was married to Myetek Kantor. Jan Bernard was married to Olenka "Ola" Stark, the mother of his young first-born son, Gabryel. They each suspected and feared that they would never see their spouses again, even if their respective spouses managed to survive. Yet, even as they knew there was little hope that either Myetek Kantor or Ola Stark was alive, as long as Litka and Jan did not know, for each of them, there was an uncertainty . . . and a hope, that had cast a somber shadow on a budding romance.

Their time together in Egypt was short and was limited. Jan was in military intelligence, a job he enjoyed. His duties included monitoring the radio transmissions, from Brazzaville radio. Brazzaville was the capital of the French Congo, just across the Congo River from Leopoldville, now Kinshasha. Leopoldville was then the capital of the Belgian Congo, now Zaire. The radio broadcasts reported the advances of the Free French, under the leadership of Charles de Gaulle, as they retook French Africa from the Germans, and moved north, from the Congo, through sub-Saharan Africa, advancing to French Saharan Africa.

Jan Bernard enjoyed listening to French more than German. His duties included teaching German to other intelligence officers, mostly British. He did not enjoy that as much as Radio Brazzaville. He also did daily translations and reports of daily newspapers and interrogations of German prisoners. Jan Bernard always preferred French, and Italian, to German. He once told me how much he hated teaching German in the Army. However, he was always interested in the German news and in interrogating recently captured German. He always hoped some prisoner or some news report might provide some information about his home or his family.

Jan Fischer, Intelligence Officer

Nana, however, was jealous of Brazzaville. She complained mightily that Jan spent all his evenings with Brazzaville while she was left alone. Jan was a dedicated soldier then, just as later he would be a dedicated teacher and educator. His work always came first, even then. The Polish Army in exile played a critical role in North Africa, in a cat-and-mouse game that British intelligence was playing with Rommel's codebreakers. The British relied on a group of Polish mathematicians, Marian Rejewski, Jerzy Różycki and Henryk Zygalski, to break the Nazi's powerful crypto-logical system created with the vaunted Enigma cipher machine.[17] These

17 Gershom Gorenberg, <u>War of Shadows: Codebreakers, spies, and the secret struggle to drive the Nazis from the Middle East</u>, 2021

mathematicians were in the same intelligence unit as my father, Jan Bernard. While my father never spoke about this particular codebreaking, he was in the intelligence unit and may well have known these fellow Polish intellectuals, as he was certainly involved in the spy versus spy maneuvering between German and Allied intelligence, as the British made effective use of their Polish assets.

As the French advanced from central Africa to the north, fortunes changed in North Africa as well, when Churchill placed Field Marshal Bernard Montgomery in charge of the British First Army for the invasion of French North Africa, in August 1942. Field Marshal Montgomery was a confident and self-assured leader who instilled a new confidence in the beaten Allied forces. There is a story that upon taking command, Montgomery remarked that "After having an easy war, things have now got much more difficult."

When his colleague supposedly told him to cheer up, that it won't be so bad, Montgomery clarified that "I'm not talking about me, I'm talking about Rommel!"

Jan Fischer was among the many soldiers who were inspired by their new leader's cockiness. He was proud to fight under Bernard Montgomery. He fought under Montgomery's command in North Africa, and followed him when Montgomery led the Allies from North Africa across the Mediterranean, from Tripoli to Sicily and then onto the invasion of Italy.

In 1943, Litka and Jan were separated. Litka was discharged. She could not return to Lodz, or anywhere in Poland, but as a veteran of the British Army, albeit the Polish Division, she was able to go England. There she spent the rest of the war waiting for Jan to join her. Jan still had more fighting to do.

CHAPTER 11

From Kazakhstan to Monte Cassino – a War Hero

Jan's journey from Kazakhstan to England was longer journey than Litka's was. His journey was also a little more complicated, and it took him a few years longer. After Field Marshal Montgomery took command in 1943, the Allied Forces turned the tide in North Africa. They defeated the Nazi Panzer divisions in the Libyan port of Tobruk, near the Egyptian border, pushing the Nazis out of Tobruk and back into Libya. After seizing Tripoli, the Allies began preparing to invade Sicily, and to hop from Sicily to the tip of Southern Italy.

This is what took my father, Jan Bernard, to what was then British Mandate Palestine. British Mandate Palestine was created in the wake of World War I as part of a compromise between Woodrow Wilson's ideal of self-determination and the European powers' desire to keep the spoils of war, the captured and occupied lands. For the British, this included much of the Middle East, including Palestine, Trans-Jordan and more, extending to Persia and the Arabian peninsula. The **Palestine Mandate** was established under the Covenant of the League of Nations, entered into on 28 June 1919 as part of the Treaty of Versailles which ended the First World War.

Under the mandate, the British had the obligation to "develop the mandate territory for the benefit of the native people", as a "sacred trust of civilization." Pursuant to this obligation, the British issued the Balfour Declaration, committing to "the establishment in Palestine of a national home for the Jewish people". Unfortunately, the Balfour Declaration was inconsistent with both the Sykes-Picot Agreement, a secret convention between Britain and France and the Ḥusayn-McMahon correspondence, an exchange of letters between the British and the then emir of Mecca, which in turn contradicted one another.

The British established a military presence, under the mandate, that grew during the time between the world wars. During that time, the British shipped oil that was piped across Syria to Haifa. For that reason they began expanding the port in the 1930s. Once the Second World War started, the British turned Haifa into a major military port, to make use of the oil lines coming into Haifa and the major rail links from Haifa across the Middle East. For the war effort Jan was sent there from Egypt, probably in 1943. Along with other troops, from Poland, and other countries, Jan trained for mountain warfare in the mountains north and northeast of Haifa, now the Galilee region and southern Lebanon, preparing for the invasion of Italy.

Other Jewish soldiers from eastern Europe, but largely from Poland, were "disappearing" from the Polish Army in Exile. Whether it was "deserting" or seizing the opportunity to fight for the Zionist cause, they were joining the Irgun and other Jewish guerilla forces already organized and fighting the British.

At some point, my father, Jan Bernard, told me he was solicited to join the Irgun, one of the underground Zionist groups then becoming active. I have some memory of my father talking about meeting Menachem Begin, who was then recruiting Jewish soldiers from the Polish army to fight in the Jewish underground. I am not sure of the accuracy of my memory or whether my father claimed to have met Begin or whether my father just said Begin was just among those recruiting Jewish soldiers for the Irgun.

While in Palestine, Jan managed to get to Tel Aviv and Jerusalem. In Tel Aviv, he visited with his aunt, Sarah Schleider. She was the sister of Jan's grandfather Sruel Glantz. Born a Glantz, she married a man named Schleider and they moved to Israel, probably in the thirties, but maybe earlier. Jan also made it to Jerusalem, looking for Jacob Hennifield, a family friend from Lvov who had moved to Israel before the war and lived in Rechavia. Finally, Jan was looking for Bernard "Ben" Kratter, who left Lvov for Palestine in the twenties.

My father told me that Ben Kratter may have been the youngest of the Kratter siblings. Their mother was a Glantz, another of the sisters of Jan's grandfather Sruel. My father recalled that the Kratters lived on Batorego Street in Lvov, across from the Court House. My father remembered that there were four or five Kratter siblings, two of whom were girls. I don't know if my father found Ben Kratter in Jerusalem in 1943, but I do know that Ben Kratter was still alive and living in Israel in the 1980s, when my Aunt Clara Glantz, the wife of my father's Uncle Herman, still had his address. I am sorry I did not take it from her when she told me this.

My Aunt Clara told me that her husband, Herman Glantz, was Ben Kratter's first cousin. She told me this late in her life, in the 1980s, after Herman had died. She said that she had met Ben Kratter sometime long before, I don't know when or where. She said that Ben Kratter was a schoolteacher in Israel and at some point, he invited her and Herman to join him in Israel. Ben Kratter's mother or grandmother was Chana Kratter. Chana Kratter was born a Glantz. She was the sister of Israel "Sruel" Glantz, your grandfather's grandfather and Herman's father. This meant that Chana Glantz Kratter was Herman's aunt and my father's great aunt. [See Family Tree, Appendix 2]

Chana married Saul Kratter.[18] This made her youngest son, Ben Kratter, Herman's first cousin and my father's first cousin once removed. I have looked for but have never found Ben Kratter's address in Israel, and so it remains a mystery for someone to research whether there are Kratters living in Israel who would be our cousins, albeit distant. That's another story, one that may still be discovered.

My father found the Schleiders and visited them in Jerusalem. Whether or not he also found Ben Kratter, we do not know. My father did not stay in Palestine much longer, although he would return after the

---

18 Chana had at least four more children from two other fathers, Malka, Harry and Sally Roher, and Murray Glanz. The Rohers and Murray Glanz all lived in America after the war. Harry Roher or Murray Glanz (or both of them) were business partners in the clothing business with Morris Glantz in Brooklyn. Marsha and Elaine knew the Rohers and I likely met them in the fifties but was too young to remember.

fighting ended, in 1945. After training for mountain warfare in the hills of Lebanon, the Second Polish Corps joined the Allied troops preparing to invade Italy. The Allies first landed in Sicily in July, 1943. It only took a few days before Sicily fell.

The Allies were assembling large numbers of troops for the assault on Italy. The troops that had taken Sicily would be joined by other troops crossing the Mediterranean from Egypt and Libya on one side and from the former French Saharan colonies, which were retaken in the North African campaign, on the other side. Allied troops from Sicily landed in Calabria, at the tip of the toe of Italy, and other Allied forces landed in Salerno, a little way up the coast. The imminent invasion of Italy had prompted a coup that overthrew Mussolini, and, in the first days of September, Mussolini resigned and the new Italian government surrendered to the Allies, now under General Eisenhower's command. However, the Germans were determined to halt the Allied advance.

The Allies began moving north, up the boot of Italy. One force, led by the Americans, advanced up the west coast of Italy. At the same time, a second large force, under the British, was moving up the eastern coast, the Adriatic side. My father shipped out with the Second Polish Corps, which was part of a large group of reinforcements that landed halfway up the Adriatic Coast. Once on Italian soil, the Second Polish Corps joined the growing army under the British, heading towards Rome to the east of the Apennine Mountains that run like a spine through the center of the Italian peninsula.

The Germans held strong, flooding Italy with many more troops. They built three lines of fortifications between Naples and Rome, designed to stop the Allied advance before it reached Rome. The strongest of the multiple lines of defense was the "Gustav Line", just below the ancient St. Benedictine Monastery. The monastery is the burial place of Saint Benedict, the founder of the Benedictine Order. It stands atop the highest peak in the area, Monte Cassino, 1,700 feet above the town of Cassino below and overlooking the whole area. The Germans had turned the holy site into a fortress that dominated the entire area for miles around. This fortress was the linchpin of German Field Marshall Kesselring's formidable "Gustav Line". This was where the Germans made their stand.

The first of the four battles that comprised what was called the Battle of Monte Cassino was in January, 1944. After two and a half weeks, the American forces, worn out and having sustained heavy casualties, withdrew. Both sides regrouped and prepared for the next round, the Germans also having sustained heavy casualties. Before the second assault, on February 11, the Americans bombed the monastery, which the allies thought was being used as an observation tower. The destruction of the monastery did no good. Again, the Allies could not advance, beyond taking the rail station at the bottom of the mountain.

The third battle began on March 15, 1944. After a few days, New Zealanders and Gurkha Rifle units led the assault, coming within 250 yards of the monastery. Meanwhile, hand-to-hand fighting in the town was measured from house to house. After a German counterattack cut the Gurkhas off, the Allies regrouped and prepared for a fourth battle. General Anders was informed that his Second Polish Corps had been given the almost impossible task of capturing Monte Cassino and its destroyed abbey.

In mid-April the Second Polish Corps took over the advanced positions. On May 12, the Poles charged the monastery's ruins. During reckless and ferocious hand-to-hand combat with the paratroopers, the Poles incurred heavy losses and had to withdraw. The Polish soldiers attacked again on the evening of May 16, and, again, fought man-to-man. Polish soldiers captured, lost and recaptured strong points again until they began running out of supplies and ammunition. The Poles eventually resorted to throwing stones at the Germans. The Poles lost so many soldiers that they were sending any able-bodied men from the rear areas into battle. Clerks, cooks and drivers were armed and sent up the mountain. It was all in vain. The Germans still held the monastery at the end of May 17.

The following day, as the Poles prepared for another assault, a white flag appeared above the ruins. After the surrender, Lt. Kazimierz Gurbiel of the 1st Squadron, 12th Podolski Lancers led a 12-man patrol up into the ruins. He was to raise the Polish flag above the rubble, but no Polish flag could be found, so the pennant of the Podolski Lancers was the first flag to be raised in victory. A day later, General Anders climbed the mountain and had the Polish troops hoist a British flag above the monastery ruins. Anders recalled corpses of Poles and Germans entwined in deadly embraces as they died together in vicious combat.

"22 days under constant fire, in terrible conditions, seven days of fierce struggle to break German defenses. . . . It was not just the Battle of Cassino, it was a battle for Poland," General Anders recalled years later in his book titled *Without the Last Chapter.* In fact, it was a battle for all Europe. The D-Day invasion of Normandy would not have been possible had the Nazis not diverted so many troops and other resources to stopping the Allied advance through Italy. But the Poles paid a steep price breaking the German line of defense at Monte Cassino.

During the battles for Monte Cassino, the Polish II Corps had almost 4,000 casualties, nearly half of the Polish infantry involved. Atop Mount Calvary (Hill 593), the last German position to fall, there now stands a monument dedicated to the memory of the 1,100 Polish soldiers lying in the Polish cemetery, only a portion of the 3,800 Polish soldiers that gave their lives at Monte Cassino.

Jan Bernard Fischer was one of the soldiers who survived the combat. The mountain training he had in Lebanon paid off, as he was awarded a medal for what he did at Monte Cassino. Actually, he was awarded several medals, the Cross for Valour, for acts of bravery in the field, the Cross of Merits, and the Cross of Monte Cassino. My father was very proud of these medals, but other than to tell that he was there and was awarded the medals, I never heard father talk about the battles there, or his role in the fighting. My father had a scar on his forehead, on his left temple. I remember the scar quite well, but I don't remember him ever talking about how he acquired it. Vivian says he told her that he got it at Monte Cassino.

In total, some 200,000 soldiers from both sides lost their lives in the five months and four battles it took before the allies took the rubble that had been the monastery of Monte Cassino. It is hard to imagine what the soldiers who survived saw and experienced in those five months. Jan talked a lot about his life in Poland and his time in Siberia and in the British army, but there were some things he never talked about. What he saw at Monte Cassino was one of them.

CHAPTER 12
Becoming English

While the battle front moved north, from Africa to Sicily and then Italy, Nana went to England. She would spend nearly seven years there, several before her beau and future husband, Jan Bernard, would join her there. She was able to go to England in 1943 because she was a veteran of the British Army, albeit as part of the Polish Corps fighting under the British flag. She was still in uniform when she arrived in London. She probably remained in uniform for some time after arriving in London. She did secretarial work in London and it is likely that she first learned secretarial skills while in uniform.

Nana worked at becoming English, rather than Polish, and certainly not Jewish. Somehow she had become an adequately proficient enough English speaker to be working as a secretary. This was no easy task. She would tell with a smile how she resisted learning English in school in Lodz. She would recall that as a schoolgirl, she would say "Why will I ever need to speak English?" Instead, she studied German as her foreign language in school. Little did she know. Could she have ever imagined that she would end up an American, living her late years in San Antonio, Texas and Albuquerque, New Mexico.

As an English speaking soldier in a British uniform, Litka was able to shed her identity as a Jew, and it seemed she was eager to do so. From her point of view, being Jewish had never been any good for her. Being Jewish in Poland, indeed in all of eastern Europe, had its disadvantages even before the rise of Hitler and the laws banning Jews from certain professions. In Lodz she had seen her uncles, Harry and Adolphe, leave Poland because they could not pursue their respective careers there. Harry left Poland to attend medical school in Vienna, but then switched to pharmacy because as a Jew he could not become a doctor. Adolphe, also, left Poland for Vienna, because his options as a Jewish musician were more limited in Poland.

While she may not have known yet what had happened to her parents and family, news was leaking out about the death camps. As a soldier and veteran, she was welcomed in England. As a Jewish refugee, she would have had problems getting into the country. There was no benefit in being Jewish. It only caused her grief, the loss of loved ones and immense suffering. At this point in her life, alone in England in 1943, Litka anglicized her name to Lidia.

Lidia made friends in London. Indeed, she made friends everywhere she lived. It was in England, living on her own for the first time, that Lidia learned to learned to cook and keep a house, although she would later joke that she was so inexperienced that the first time she made tea, she left the water boiling and burned the teapot. She settled into a flat, and, for the first time in years, was settled and no longer on the run living by her wits. Jan remained in uniform until 1947, when he joined Litka, now Lidia, in England. He continued to call her Litka, as he did the rest of his life.

CHAPTER 13

The Aftermath – Learning What Happened Lvov and Boiberke

Neither Jan nor Lidia knew what had happened to their spouses. Consequently, they were reluctant to marry. They could not go back to their homes in Lodz and Lvov, but made what inquiries were possible. Jan Bernard actually obtained an affidavit, from a Polish woman in Lvov, Dr. Celestyna Jonasowa, that "it is known to her that Ludwik STARK, Maria STARK nee GRUTZ and their daughter Olenka were murdered by the Germans in 1942 in Lwow."

How did Jan Bernard get such a document? I do not know. Lidia had no such documents. She had no family to help her search. For Jan Bernard, it was easier. He was in touch with his uncles in the States, Herman, Morris and Abe Glantz. He was also in touch with his cousins Abe Fischer, living in Montreal, and Abe's sister, Trudie, who was living in the Bronx, where she had settled and married Max Ziebert long before the war. From them, Jan knew that their brother, Chaim, whom I always knew as Hymie, was alive and had gone back to Budkow.

Hymie had taken over running the Fischer family mill after Abe left for America. Hymie was still running the mill when the war broke out and the Russians overran first Boiberke and then Lvov. My father had told me that Hymie was "caught" by the Russians, like him, but that was not exactly the case. I later learned from Abe Fischer some things my father never told me. I learned from Abe not just that Hymie was a leftist, but that my father's brother, Max, was as well.

```
                    C e r t i f i c a t e
                    ------------------------------


        The undersigned, aware of the responsibility by law for making statements
not based on true facts, certifies hereby that it is known to her that Ludwik
Stark, Maria Stark née Grätz and their daughter Oleńka were killed by Germans
in Lwow in the year 1942.

                              Zabrze, December 30, 1947.
                              (Signed)  Dr. Celestyna Jonas.


Registry No: 4284/47.
        I certify hereby that the above certificate was signed in my presence
in her own hand by Dr. Celestyna Jonas known to me personally and residing in
Zabrze, ul. Bohaterów Warszawskich, no. 13.
        Notary fee according to para 21 of scale received.
        Zabrze, on the thirtieth day of December year nineteen hundred and
fourty seven (30/12/1947).


                         (Signed) Mieczyslaw Galewski, Notary public.

        Round Seal: Mieczyslaw Galewski, Notary in Zabrze.
```

Affidavit that Jan's wife and parents were killed by Nazis

Hymie was not just a leftist. He was an active communist. At one point before the Shoah he was sent to prison for owning a bookstore that sold communist books. So it made sense that he was one of the locals that were put in charge of the town under the Russian occupation. According to Abe, his brother Hymie was a "big shot" in Boiberke for the two years of the first Russian occupation. That lasted until Hitler turned on Stalin and attacked Russia, in 1941. So Hymie was saved by the Russians, but not by deportation. Hymie was able to escape with the Russians, when they retreated. He then joined the Russian army, where he was a sergeant, according to Abe, and he received Stalin's Medal.

This was Abe's version of how Hymie was able to escape the Nazis. Abe's story is that Hymie never wanted to leave Boiberke, but the Russians would not let him stay there as long as he was in the Russian Army. Hymie's son, Ismor, has a slightly different story: Hymie was in the Polish army, and this was why the Russians sent him to Siberia, notwithstanding his political leanings. In any event, it was a good thing the Russians did not let Hymie stay in Boiberke. If they had, he would have died with his first wife, Pearl, and their daughter. Hymie was the only other Fischer besides your grandfather, Jan Bernard, to be saved by deportation.

Hymie returned to Boiberke in 1946, after the war ended, looking for his wife, child and family. He was the sole Fischer to return after the Shoah, the sole Fischer to go back to Lvov and to Boiberke and bear witness. Hymie was how Jan found out what happened. In 1946, Hymie had no idea that his cousin, Jan, was even alive, let alone where he was. Nor did Jan know that his cousin Hymie had survived and returned to Boiberke. After Jan got to England, he learned from either Trudie or from Abe what Hymie had discovered: all the Fischers and Glantzes who remained in Boiberke and Budkow were dead and gone

Hymie did one other thing when he returned to Boiberke. Before he had left, in 1941, Hymie had buried some valuables and money before he fled the Germans. When Hymie returned in 1946, he dug up the money he had buried. This money was what he used to get out of what had become the Ukraine, SSR, part of the Soviet Union. Initially, Hymie made it to Montreal with his older brother, Abe's help. Abe says that when Hymie arrived, Abe came into his kitchen and was surprised to see Herman Glantz, who had traveled up from Philadelphia to see Hymie, sitting at the kitchen table. For Herman, who had left Poland in 1938, it was his chance to hear what had happened in Boiberke directly from the one witness, Hymie. Hymie stayed with Abe for three years, then got an American visa and went to the Bronx, where he lived with his sister Trudie.

Hymie was still living with Trudie and Max when, as a small child, I first met him. I remember Hymie and Trudie well, and Trudie's husband,

Max. I remember Max and Hymie taking me to play when I was very little to parks in the Bronx and to the Bronx Zoo. When I was a little older Max gave me my first baseball bat, a beautiful black bat with a thin handle, a 34" bat that was a little too big for me then, but which I came to love.

I had that bat for a long time, even bringing it to Brookline, where I first taught Teddy to bat, and it was too big for him, then, too. Teddy may have used the bat later, when he played youth baseball. I no longer have the bat, much to my dismay. I don't know what happened to it, but that bat, that beautiful black bat, always made me think of Hymie and Trudie and Max.

Jan had a falling out with Hymie. Hymie did not come to my bar mitzvah, and Jan was angry at him that he did not come. I never saw Hymie again. Years later, after I met and grew close to Abe Fischer, Hymie's brother, Abe told me that Hymie had remarried and had a son who was a professor in Madison, Wisconsin. Eventually, I was able to find this son, Ismor, and contacted him. Ismor told me that he had a younger brother, Saul. So Hymie actually had two sons with his second wife, Tillie, his American wife. Ismor was born in 1956 and Saul in 1959. At the time of my bar mitzvah, in February, 1963, they were both young boys. In those days, traveling from the Bronx to the Philadelphia area was big trip and Hymie, living in the Bronx, did not have a car. Traveling to South Jersey in the winter with a pregnant wife or a little baby was not so easy. Indeed, I don't remember any of the other New York relatives at my bar mitzvah, either.

Like Hymie, Jan had a wife and a child in Poland that he had lost. Jan knew that you never replace that loss and Jan understood how precious it is to be able to have another son. It seems strange, given his own experience, that Jan did not understand why Hymie was so protective of his sons, his new family in America. For two cousins who grew up together, who suffered similarly, each losing a wife and child, each somehow surviving Siberian labor camps, one would think there would be a bond. The depth of the harm to them went beyond what was inflicted upon them and onto the next generations.

I never saw Hymie again. Nor have I ever met his two sons. My father never told me about them. I did not learn about these two cousins until I visited Abe Fischer after my father died. Aside from the stories he told, Abe would give me a number of photos and other family items, including the Boiberke Memorial book, from where I took the picture of Ephraim, the melamed. It is from one of the photos Abe gave me that I first learned that Hymie had two sons.

Hymie, Saul, Tillie and Arthur Fischer, photo taken by Ismor Fischer

At some point Abe told me that Hymie's older son was living in Wisconsin, but I did not follow up on it until many years later, when I was already far into writing this family story and realized it was part of this story. I found an Ismor Fischer, on the faculty of the University of Wisconsin, in Madison Wisconsin. I found a phone number but it was not a working number. I turned to my private investigator, Jay Groob, who provided me with an email address and a working phone number. Score one more for Jay and for me, for now I was in contact a long lost cousin, but not until 2023.

I have started communicating with Ismor by email. He has retired from his position on the faculty at the University of Wisconsin, where he taught various advanced mathematics and biostatistics courses and did consulting and authored or co-authored a number of peer review research articles in biostatics, particularly relating to mental health issues. Upon retiring he moved to Monterey, where he was an adjunct professor for several years at the Naval Postgraduate School there. Ismor is a widower, with no children. His wife, Carla died in 2006.

Ismor has told me about his brother, Saul, born in 1959, who lives with his wife, Estelle, and their son Lucien, born 2006, in Riverdale in the Bronx. I hope to track him down, as well, but that's one more still open quest.

CHAPTER 14
Abe Fischer

I didn't know Abe Fischer until after my father died. When Jan died, Nana had plenty to deal with and so I asked her what I could do to help her. The one thing she asked me to do was to call Abe Fischer in Montreal and tell him that father had died. I had known about cousin Abe Fischer in Montreal, but I had never met him or even spoken to him. Nonetheless, that was the one thing Nana asked me to do, so I called him.

Abe answered the phone and when he realized who I was, he chided me for never having called before, but he did so in a warm and welcoming way. He asked why I had never come to Montreal to see him, and I promised him I would. Not long thereafter, I did. In May, 1987, I drove to Montreal, by myself, and met Abe and his wife, Eva. This began a relationship that would become very close until Abe's death in 1997.

That first visit, Abe and I sat at the kitchen table in Abe and Eva's small apartment in a public senior housing building and we talked for a long time. Abe showed me his copy of the Boiberke Memorial Book.[19] It was from there that the picture of his grandfather, also Jan Bernard's grandfather, the picture of Ephraim the Melamed, in the first chapter of this book came. The memorial book also had a photo of a soccer team in Boiberke. Abe is in the front row of the picture, on the left, with his right hand on his knee.

---

19 "Memorial" books were put together some years after the Shoah by "landsmen", or people from the same town, when survivors who found each other were able to assemble lists of those who perished. As with the gift Abe passed on to me, these memorial books often contained other material of historical or cultural relevance.

Boiberke Soccer Team

In addition to playing soccer, Abe was also a boxer. He was not that big, but he was stocky. He had a solid built and was strong, even as an older man. I could see from his manner and movements that he was sturdy and tough, someone who did not back down. In Boiberke he was the one, sometimes with his brother, Hymie, who would protect other Jewish kids from the Polish or Ukrainian gangs.

Abe left Poland in 1933. He got to the port city of Gdansk, but had to pass a physical before he was allowed to board the ship. That should not have been a problem for him, but the doctor declared that Abe was not healthy enough to sail, and would not sign the paperwork. Abe came back the next day and again the doctor said that he was not healthy enough to sail. Twice Abe failed the physical before he figured out what was wrong. The third time, Abe brought some cash for the doctor. This time he passed.

When Abe got to New York, where his younger sister Trudie, who had sponsored him, lived with her husband Max, immigration officials required him to take another physical. He failed, and was not permitted to enter the United States. I am not certain but it may have been because he tested positive for tuberculosis. He was put on a train for Montreal, where he lived a healthy life for the next sixty-four years, passing away at the age of 89.

Trudie and Abe, 1936

Not long after settling into Montreal, Abe met Eva Cramer. Abe and Eva married and Abe went to work for Eva's father, who had a business called Cramer's Import Company. In 1936, Abe and Eva had a son, Gerry. His Hebrew name was Eliezer, after his grandfather, Abe's father, Eliezer "Laizer" Fischer. Gerry was Abe and Eva's only child. As a teenager, he fell ill with a debilitating kidney disease. I am not sure what the disease was, only that no cure for the disease was discovered until some years after Gerry's death. Gerry suffered for several years before passing away at the age of 19. His mother, Eva, never recovered from losing her only child. After losing his only son, Abe spent the next thirty years caring for an invalid wife, who never recovered from losing her only child.

Eva and Abe with their son Gerry

Abe took great pleasure in telling me of his family, which was also my family, our family, too. Abe told me about his grandfather, Ephraim's seven children, four boys and three girls. Eliezer, or Laizer, Abe's father, was the oldest. He operated the mill, down the road from Salo, my grandfather Fischer, who may have been the youngest of Ephraim's children. Abe always called my grandfather "Shloimie". Ephraim's other five children, Abe explained, were Hersh, Sura (Sarah Pelz), Brondle, Laiche and Hanshe.[20]

Hersch Fischer, Ephraim's oldest son, was also my father's uncle, my grandfather Salo's oldest brother. Hersch's Jewish name was Herzyl. He later went by the name Harry when he came to the United States, before World War I. Hersch had three sons, Abe told me, Sidney, Saul and Leo. Sidney had lived in Florida, where he died. Saul and Leo lived in New York. Abe said that both Saul and Leo Fischer had children, who were grown and living in New York or California. Abe also gave me a photo from Poland labeled "Fischer Family 1928", with a rug in the background much like the backdrop in the Glantz family portraits, but the only person I can identify in it is Trudie, seated to the right.

20 When my father, Jan, related the family history to me, he at one point described Sura "Sarah" Pelz as Laizer's wife, Sara, Abe and Trudie's mother. I think after so many years, Jan had confused Sura "Sarah" Pelz with Sura/Sarah, Laizer's wife. Abe knew better who his mother was. Thus I am confident that Sura Pelz was Sura Fischer, who married Schloime Pelz, or Peltz, and not Abe's mother.

**Eliezer Fischer Family 1928, Back row; Izzie, Yitzak Rapp, Abe, Hymie,
Front row: Bayla, Sura Pelz Fischer, with grandson Lizer Rapp, Trudie**

Abe told me about his and Jan's aunts, Aunt Laiche and Aunt Hanshe,
or Hannah. They were the younger sisters to Abe's father, Eliezer and Jan's
father, Salo. Aunt Laiche, had come to New York and married a man named
Nash. Aunt Hannah, who married a man named Labener, also may have
come to the states. Aunt Laiche had a daughter whom Abe identified as
Hannah Nash (not to be confused with Aunt Hanshe, who became Hannah
Labener). Hannah Nash had a daughter, Dorothy, whose married name was
Platzner. Dorothy Platzner had a son, Robert Platzner. He or his children
may be living somewhere in the United States, perhaps on the west coast.

Abe also told me about his siblings. I knew about Hymie and Trudie,
whom he called Gertie, but not about Izzie or Beila. Abe's youngest sister,
like Jan's sister, was named Beila, after their grandmother, Beila, Ephraim's
wife. According to Abe, she died in 1900, but according to my father,
she may have died earlier, in 1890 or 1895. She may have died giving
birth to her last child.

Together with the Boiberke Memorial book, Abe gave me some
pictures of the Platzners and other relatives I did not know I had. As

with Ismor Fischer, I regret that I did not track them down then, as I had intended to do while Abe was still alive to help me. That is a job that will be harder for one of us to do now.

Dorothy Nash Platzner, son Robert and Joe Platzner

That visit was also the first time I met Abe's wife, Eva. I also met Arthur Greenberg on that first trip. Arthur was Gerry Fischer's best friend growing up. After Gerry died, Arthur and his very sweet and gentle wife, Ruth, "adopted" Abe and Eva as the Greenberg family's surrogate grandparents. Arthur and Ruth had three children, Debbie, Dannie and Paul. Abe and Eva spent Passover seders and other Jewish holidays with the Greenbergs, as well as attending weddings, bar mitzvahs and other Greenberg family events. As Abe and Eva aged, Arthur took it upon himself to take on the responsibilities of the son they no longer had. Arthur's wife, Ruth, was a willing and capable partner in taking on this obligation. They certainly derived some mutual benefit from this relationship, but they deserve to be remembered for the kindness they showed to Abe and Eva over many years.

The next time I visited Abe was for Eva's funeral, I stayed in Debbie Greenberg's former bedroom. I stayed with the Greenbergs again, perhaps several times, and was the beneficiary of their friendship and kindness for the remaining years of Abe's life. Both Arthur and Ruth were as kind to me as they were to Abe. Linda and I became friendly with their daughter Debbie, but a close relationship with her was difficult because she lived in Toronto.

When Arthur's youngest son, Paul, came to Boston to work for The Consulting Group, and moved to Brookline, Linda and I reached out to him and his wife Marla. For a while, we saw Arthur and Ruth when they came to visit Paul and Marla, and later, their grandchildren, Talia, Morris and Micah. Paul and Marla lived in a condo on James Street in Coolidge Corner and then moved to a very nice house on Dean Road, going up Fisher Hill. We often saw them on Shabbat as they attended Kehillath Israel, where the Washington Square Minyan, our minyan, also meets, but we never developed a close relationship.

Abe and I developed a warm relationship that lasted for the rest of his life, until he died in 1995. He was a great storyteller. However, there were some things he said that I have wondered about. In relating family history, Abe claimed that we were related to Moritz (Zvi) von Hirsch, also known as Maurice de Hirsch or Baron de Hirsch.

Born in Munich in 1831, Baron de Hirsch was one of the richest Jews in Europe. He married Clara Bischoffsheim in 1855, and became part of the banking house in which her father was a partner, Bischoffsheim & Goldschmidt, of Brussels, London and Paris. Baron de Hirsch amassed a large fortune, by purchasing and working railway concessions in Austria, Turkey and the Balkans, and by speculating in commodities like sugar and copper. Baron de Hirsch then became a philanthropist, establishing charitable foundations.

Through these foundations. Baron de Hirsch gave millions to charity, mostly to Jewish charities. His greatest efforts were on behalf of the Jews in Russia and the pale of settlement. He gave millions to resettle Jews from eastern Europe in Palestine, but he also gave to charities in the

United States, Canada and South America. Among his many charitable endeavors for the Jewish community, Baron de Hirsch also established a network of primary and technical schools in Galicia and Bukowina in the last years of the nineteenth century.

According to Abe, Ephraim Fischer's father was Baron de Hirsch's brother. As Abe figured it, that made all of us Fischers relatives to Baron de Hirsch, and may entitle us Fischers to an inheritance from the Baron de Hirsch fortune. Abe seemed to believe this sincerely and he always wanted me to look into it. In one sense, this was no crazier than Jean Claude asking me if Nana and his grandmother were related to Izrael Poznanski.

CHAPTER 15

The Romance of Abe and Lottie, or How We Acquired Our Fine China

After Eva died, Abe was liberated in a way. He was no longer house-bound, no longer caring for an invalid wife, as he had been doing for many years, a loyal and faithful husband. Now he was free to travel. First, he visited me in Boston. I asked him what he wanted to see and offered to take him anywhere he wanted. The one place he wanted to go was to the race track, Suffolk Downs. Suffolk Downs was not open. It wasn't the right season. So we went to Wonderland Park, in Revere, the dog track where the greyhound dogs used to race.

It was the first time I had ever been to Wonderland. I remember that Nana and your grandfather used to talk about going to the dog track in England. They would say "watch when the dogs are brought out to the starting gate and see which dog relieves himself. That's the dog you should bet on." My parents were never real gamblers and that was the extent of their expertise. Abe was different. He knew what he was doing and clearly enjoyed the thrill of betting on the races. However, he cautioned "Take $50 or $100 and put it aside. That will be your evening's entertainment. If you win, great. If you lose, when you've lost the $100, it's time to go home." Abe continued that he learned that this way you could enjoy your evening out.

We had a good time and on the next trip to Boston, we went to Suffolk Downs, the real thing, the horse races. Abe bought a program and carefully looked at the horses' names and their racing history. We bet on a few races and maybe won one or two, and had a good time.

Abe came to realize that he was now free to travel for the first time in close to fifty years. We began to talk about him traveling and, at one point, I asked Abe where he wanted to go. He was now over eighty, so I offered to go with him. We had become close and were both interested in traveling together. Abe answered that there were two places where he wanted to go. The first was Boiberke. The second was Israel.

The idea of going back to my roots with Abe, to Boiberke, my father's family home in Poland had long intrigued me. The chance to do so with the only family member still alive who had lived there before the Shoah had become a very real possibility. I began to do some research regarding travel to the Ukraine, where Lvov, which had become Lviv, and Boiberke were now located. I inquired about travel, speaking to some people who had traveled to the area before, either in support of the Soviet Jewry movement or on their own family history "roots" trips.

In 1989, the Soviet Union had not yet fallen apart, but it was on the verge of doing so. The Ukraine was not yet independent, and as I would learn, was not a safe place for two westerners to travel, not in the city, but especially outside the big cities, venturing to a small town like Boiberke. I was given the advice that in order to travel safely outside of Lvov, I should hire a driver and a guide. I correctly understood this to be a euphemism meaning "two armed men".

I spoke with Abe and we decided that he would travel to Israel. Linda and I were already planning a trip that summer and Abe arranged to fly directly from Montreal once we were there and we agreed to meet once Abe was there. Abe arrived and contacted us after he checked in to his hotel, a big tourist hotel in Jerusalem, perhaps the Dan. Linda and I and the three kids met Abe for lunch.

Over lunch, Abe told us about meeting an older woman in the hotel. After arriving and checking in, he had been sitting in the lobby, mid-afternoon. Hungry for a snack, he ordered a piece of fruit and he was brought a huge serving of watermelon, much more than he could eat by himself. So he tried offering some of the watermelon to other people in the lobby. A small, well dressed, older woman accepted his offer. That was how Abe met Lottie. Lottie Slimmon was visiting Israel, not for the first time. She was there for a family wedding or bat mitzvah. Over the watermelon, the two of them struck up a conversation.

We had arranged to meet and spend time with Abe over the week or so of his trip. We somehow managed to do so, even traveling with three children. On his last night in Israel, Abe and I had dinner together. Over dinner Abe said he had a question for me: would it be improper for him, as a single man, to stay overnight with a woman. I was a bit taken aback as Abe was in his eighties, but he was quite serious. He explained that Lottie had invited him to visit her at her home in Glen Ridge, New Jersey. He wanted to accept, but he did not want to do anything improper. I encouraged him to go and he did.

The next thing I heard from Abe was that he and Lottie were getting married. He moved out of his small public housing for seniors apartment in Montreal and moved to Glen Ridge. Lottie took him shopping for new clothes and he began dressing in a suit and tie. His hair was neatly trimmed and he face more cleanly shaven. He was a new man, flashing a new smile.

Abe and Lottie

Lottie had no children but she had two nieces and a nephew. The nephew and one of the nieces lived in the Boston area. One niece lived in Acton or Wayland and the nephew was a student, living in Brookline near us. So Lottie and Abe each had good reasons to come to Boston and they came fairly often. It was always a pleasure to have them, as they were so clearly so happy together and happily in love. At our Shabbat table they would hold hands and look at each other like two teenagers excited by their first love.

During this time, we managed to visit them at Lottie's home in New Jersey at some point. It was a nice older home in the very nice New York suburb of Glen Ridge. We knew that Lottie had a china shop, selling high-end bone china and silverware. It was one of those shops that would be listed for gifts for expensive weddings that were given notice in the Sunday New York Times. I think that Lottie may have driven us past the shop so we could see it.

Before we left, Lottie took us out to her garage. There were boxes of chinaware, dishes and other inventory from her shop. Lottie began rummaging through them looking for something for us. After some time hunting through the boxes she found what she was looking for. She told me which boxes to take and I loaded the car. The boxes contained the green fine china milchig set of dishes that we use on Shabbat and special occasions. Lottie also gave us the silver milchig cutlery that we use regularly to this day.

At Lottie's insistence we began to use the silverware regularly. Lottie explained that silver would tarnish if it sat in the drawer. She insisted that silver needed to be used. We accepted her expertise and our regular use of the silverware she gifted us has proven her to be right. It has not tarnished and we continue to use the silverware regularly. More important, we think of Lottie every time we use her silverware. For me that's every morning when I get up and make a cup of tea. And every time we eat with the green bone china, I think of Abe and Lottie, holding hands and smiling and crooning at each other at our dining room table.

CHAPTER 16

Epilogue to the Romance of Abe and Lottie

In addition to her home in New Jersey, Lottie owned a condo in Florida. Lottie and Abe spent their winters there. That is where they were when Abe called to tell me that Lottie had died. Shortly thereafter, Abe called me again, seeking my legal help. Lottie's nieces and nephew were claiming that they had inherited the condo unit and wanted to evict him. I was not sure of his legal rights as Lottie's surviving spouse, as I did not know Florida law. Whatever the law or legal rights, it was cruel and selfish to throw an 86-year-old man out of his home, especially one grieving the loss of his wife.

Abe did not want to fight with Lotttie's heirs, her two nieces and nephew and so he vacated the condo. Abe took his possessions, including some things that Lottie had given him. One of the gifts from Lottie was a watch that he had showed me before. It was engraved with the name of one of Lottie's earlier husbands. Abe was her fourth husband. She had outlived each of her first three husbands.

Abe moved in with his brother-in-law, Max Zeibert, his sister Trudie's husband, who had an apartment in Miami or Miami Beach. Abe and I remained in touch. We talked from time to time and were close until he died. Much to my regret, I never got to go to Lvov and Boiberke with Abe. I took that trip in 2015, with Robert Strauss, who has been my good friend since I was nine or ten years old. I am sorry Abe and I were not able to take that trip together, not just because of what he could have showed me and told me, but because both of us enjoyed each other so much in the time we had together.

When Abe passed away in 1997, the last Fischer who had lived in Boiberke, in the old country, was gone.

CHAPTER 17

Coming to America

Jan and Lidia were married in London on October 23, 1948. By
then they were planning to come to America, but I delayed their plans.
When they learned Lidia was pregnant, they decided to wait until after
I was born rather than have Lidia take a weeklong ocean voyage while
pregnant. I was born February 12, 1950, in Queen Charlotte's Hospital
in Wimbledon.[21] Four months later, in June, 1950, the three of us set
sail on the M. V. Georgic, a sister Cunard Line cruise ship to the Queen
Elizabeth.

It was a difficult decision to leave England. Jan and Lidia had lived
in London for several years after Jan joined Lidia there and they had
built a life in England. They had friends, and a full life. They thought
about staying and settling in England, but it would have been difficult.
Once he was discharged from the Army, Jan feared he would no longer
be afforded the status of a soldier in uniform but would be considered
either a displaced person or a refugee. He did not want to go back to
Poland, nor did he or Lidia feel fully comfortable as a Jews, given what
they had been through since September, 1939.

Yet Jan was not only openly but actively Jewish and was clearly
connected to Jewish Palestine, despite not accepting the offer to leave the
British and fight for Zionism. This was just one of the many decisions
Jan faced, both during the fighting and after the war ended. It is hard

---

21 Now known as Queen Charlotte's and Chelsea Hospital, the hospital is one of the oldest maternity
hospitals in Europe, founded in London in 1739.

to gauge how strongly he felt tied to the Zionist cause, as he had other passions that were stronger. In 1943, after fighting in Italy, at Monte Cassino, still hoping to find out about his wife and son, he chose to stay with British military intelligence, where he thought he would be most likely to learn of their whereabouts. After Jan and Litka fell in love, and the likelihood that Ola Stark had survived diminished, ascertaining what happened to her became not just important but a pre-requisite to Jan's ability to re-marry, something he managed to do, although it is no longer clear exactly how.

When the fighting had ended and the British de-militarization had begun, Jan began to think about his future. Litka had already been discharged and had become a civilian in London but British command had sent Jan back to Egypt with the Polish Second Corps. Still with military intelligence, he was also writing for the camp newspaper and teaching English and perhaps other skills.

Jan was still stationed in Egypt for several years after the war ended, and this allowed him to maintain his connection to what was still Palestine but soon to become the independent Jewish state of Israel. Jan kept his bank account in the Barclay Bank's Jerusalem branch. He was still looking for Ben Kratter, or for other possible relatives.

Among the papers Jan kept was a weathered clipping of a classified ad from a Yiddish newspaper placed by Natan Rubin, or Natan ben Leib Rubin, of Shkunah (neighborhood) Hapoalim, in Herzylia, the only survivor of his family from Pshemishel Poland. The ad sought information regarding his two cousins Abraham and Hershele Glantz from Boiberke. The missing cousins, both named Glantz, were cousins of Natan Rubin who had the same last name as Jan's grandmother, who was Miriam Rubin when she married Sruel Glantz, my father Jan's grandfather. Was my father thinking that Natan Rubin's missing Glantz cousins or even that Natan Rubin, from Herzylia, was a lost relative?

In 1946, still in uniform in the Middle East, my father tried to arrange leave to attend a Passover seder in Jerusalem. He did this through his friend and colleague, Rabbi D. Fajngold, the Chief Jewish Chaplain with the headquarters of the Polish Second Army. By this time, Jan and Rabbi Fajngold had known each other for some years, from before the

Italian campaign. They were together in Egypt again, and remained in touch even after Jan Bernard was deactivated and left North Africa to join Litka in London.

Ad seeking lost relative

Passover leave to Jerusalem could not be arranged. Instead, Jan Bernard attended Rabbi Fajngold's seder in Cairo in 1946. He did, however, manage to send an Israeli hagada to Herman and Clara in the Spring of 1946, one more indication that, upon his return to the Middle East, he was again visiting what was still British mandate Palestine.

In the spring of 1946, Jan Bernard still had pressing questions. Did he know, yet, what had become of his wife Ola, and their son? Was he free to marry his new love, Lidia? Where would they settle? Was Jan considering Palestine, soon to become Israel? As much as he may have considered doing so, it is unlikely that Lidia would have agreed to leave England for the turmoil of Mandate Palestine. She had had enough of war and peaceful London was much more attractive to her than what could be expected in Palestine. Zionism was not her cause.

So the choices were to stay in England, where Lidia had settled in, or to join the only surviving family that either of them knew of, Jan Bernard's three uncles in America, Herman, Abe and Morris Glantz. Going to America would not be easy, but neither would it be easy to start a life in England, with no family, no community, no one. Lidia grew up in a large and close family, and now the only family she could have was the family of her fiancé, Jan Bernard Fischer. In the end she was happy to be adopted by his family and happy, as well, to adopt it.

For Jan Bernard, whether in England or the United States, he would be starting over. The idea of coming to America, where he had family, seemed preferable for that reason. He had been in touch with his three uncles in the United States, since leaving the labor camp and joining the army, particularly Herman, with whom he had grown up in Boiberke. Herman, fortunately, had arrived in the states in 1938, just before the invasion of Poland. He was now settled in Philadelphia, married to Clara Polis and soon to be the father of two daughters, Elaine and Marsha. Jan Bernard had been corresponding regularly with Herman and his wife, Clara, mostly with Clara, who was more comfortable writing.

In a February 28, 1946 letter to Clara, Jan Bernard wrote that while he looked forward to shedding his uniform and "putting on civil clothes", he appreciated the respect the uniform afforded him and "will not be very pleased to be after demobilization a 'displaced person' or a 'refugee'". Like Lidia, Jan Bernard felt that their new life would not be in either the Jewish or Polish communities in exile. While there were both Jewish and Polish communities established by post-war immigrants, Jan Bernard and Lidia spent their time among their English neighbors and acquired English friends.

Neither Jan Bernard nor Litka had a conspicuous Jewish or Polish accent. Although my father had a noticeable accent when he spoke English, one that my ninth-grade classmates would mimic, it came from the mélange of languages he spoke, rather than from his first childhood languages, Yiddish and Polish. In fact, in addition to Yiddish and Polish, his childhood languages included German, the official government language, Hebrew from *cheder* and his grandfather, Ephraim, and enough Ukrainian to get by in the streets. He studied Greek and Latin in school and also knew French and Italian from his pre-war university studies. He acquired enough Russian in his years in Siberia to lead a group of liberated Polish prisoners to the British frontier. Yet, while he spoke perhaps a dozen languages, there is no indication that he ever formally studied English before the war. Nonetheless, he clearly acquired adequate proficiency during the war to serve in British military intelligence.

In this post war period, Herman and Clara continued to send Jan funds from time to time, wiring deposits into Jan Bernard's Barclay Bank account in Jerusalem. In the same February 28, 1946 letter to Herman and Clara, Jan Bernard wrote of his concerns "about the future possibilities of the ex-soldiers". The letter first dealt with affidavits and other documentation necessary "to bring me over to the United States". Before ending, Jan Bernard, then in his mid-thirties, revealed what he had been through, writing:

> I feel still young and I am not afraid to work, even to work hard. I am sure that I will find a job and will earn my living. One who has lived through these years in Europe, these years of war and unhappiness, will never be afraid of working hard if he knows that he will have a quiet life without all these sufferings that exist in Europe.

Seeking work as a lawyer was particularly difficult. Had Jan been a tradesman, an electrician, a plumber or a chef, he could have found work anywhere. But the practice of law is a local profession: the law that one learns in one country is of no use in another. His two degrees from Jan Casimir University in Polish law were not accepted in England and would not be in the United States. Jan Bernard enrolled in the law school, the "Faculty of Laws" of University College London, but he was starting over again, having to learn the constitutional laws of the British Empire.

Jan Bernard continued his study of English law at University College London until the end of 1949. In November 1948, he submitted a dissertation in Conflict of Laws. This involved how to resolve legal questions when the laws of European countries differed. He planned to take his qualifying examination for the LLM

At the same time, Jan Bernard was also looking for work in England, both in the short term and long term employment that involved a career path. In the short term, he submitted an application on June 2, 1948 for a position teaching English and other skills to the Committee for the Education of Poles in Great Britain, an agency working with Polish refugees, many of whom settled in England. In the long term, he sought an academic post as a university professor. In fact, he was ready to accept an academic position at the University of Edinburgh.

If he moved to the United States, Jan Bernard would have to start again, learning American law. It seemed he would have to start over wherever they ended settling. But the notion of being near family was appealing. Jan Bernard had been in touch with his uncles in America, particularly Herman, about coming to the United States since he first came to Palestine from the Soviet labor camp. Yet coming to the United States was not a certainty, and Jan Bernard was at the same time pursuing not just a law degree in Great Britain, but other job possibilities in Great Britain, primarily teaching positions.

I remember father telling me how close he came to accepting an academic post at the University of Edinburgh, joking with me about how close I came to being Scottish. In the end, it was the opportunity to be with family, the only family he had, that sealed his decision.

Litka had faced her own difficulties getting settled in London. Growing up, she spoke Polish and Yiddish, or "Jewish" as it was called then, and little else, when the war started. Although technically a British soldier, she was with the Polish army under the British flag, so she was with Polish speaking troops. Yet, somehow by the time she got to London, or some time thereafter, she managed to acquire a fair proficiency in English.

Language was just the first handicap. Although she completed gymnasium in Lodz, Litka had never worked in Poland, and had no vocational training or job skills as a newly arrived immigrant in London. Even as a soldier, there is no indication that she acquired any job skills. During the war, in the service, she danced and organized dance performances. What she did have as a soldier, however, was the benefit of being in the service. This allowed her to come to England as a veteran and not as a refugee.

In England, Litka became Lily or Lidia, ultimately settling on Lidia. It did not take her long before she found secretarial work. It appears that job was either within the military or through connections from her military service, as she had no prior secretarial experience. This first secretarial job was the beginning of a long and successful secretarial career. She was smart, learned quickly and knew how to figure out what she needed to do and how to do it. She did not have the formal education of the man who would become her husband of thirty-eight years, but she had street smarts, and both a good business sense and a lot of common sense.

Most of all, Lidia had great social skills. She knew how to deal with people, how to meet people and how to make friends. Soon she had many friends in England. But she had had no contact with anyone from her family, indeed from anyone in Lodz or Poland. She had no idea what had happened to her husband, although she had a good basis for assuming he was dead, or her parents, siblings or any relatives at all. This would soon be confirmed.

After she was settled in London, in 1947, Lidia wrote to the city government in Lodz, asking for the names of anyone still alive on Wschodnia Street, the street where she lived with her parents, grandparents and so many other Szylberstajns. The only name she got was the name "Lola Servich". Lidia actually knew Lola Servich, a Catholic Polish woman who was a neighbor in Wschodnia Street. From London, Litka contacted Lola, who was still living in Lodz. She wrote asking if Lola knew what happened to her parents and family, or if she knew what happened to any of the Szylberstajns.

Lola's response was "Don't come back. There's nothing to come back to." Lola continued "Don't ask anything else", saying that if she did not know what happened to her parents, that was better. From this, Litka presumed that there was no family that survived, no one that returned to Wschodnia Street, no one that had returned to Lodz. This was also her basis for concluding that her husband, Myetek, was also dead.

Lola's response also confirmed her belief that she was now an orphan, with no family, with no one except her fiancé, the handsome and brilliant Jan Bernard Fischer, whom she loved and adored. Without him, she was truly alone in the world. This may be why she was so happy to adopt and be adopted by Jan's family, and to sail to America only a few years after just having established herself in England.

When Jan Bernard arrived in London in 1947, two years after the hostilities ended in 1945, Lidia was quite settled, with a flat, a job and new friends. This made it easier for Jan Bernard, who, like Lidia, also had had no contact with his home or family in Poland. He also did not know whether his wife was alive, whether his son was alive, whether his parents, brother and sister or grandparents were alive, or what had happened to his home and their homes in Boiberke and Lvov. He did have one thing that Lidia did not. Jan had his family in America, with whom he had been in touch already from the Middle East for the last several years, especially Herman, with whom he had grown up.

Jan Bernard's family promised to be waiting at the dock, as letters from Abe and Anna and Herman and Clara, assured. Clara's words, in an April 6, 1950 letter were that, while the Glantzes can't promise who, "some or maybe all will be there with bells on to welcome you to our shores. . . . Morris will have to be there to meet you because he signed for you and I believe you know Herman well enough to know that he'll be around. Don't worry about that." Abe and Anna and their sons would also be there to greet their nephew, his wife and newborn baby at the dock.

Lidia only had Jan's family to greet her. She did not even have her family name. She had become Lidia Kantor, when she married, in 1939, just a week before the war started. That was the name on her papers throughout the Shoah and afterwards. Like Jan, for many years she did not talk about her first marriage before the war. The story she told to explain the name Kantor was that she had no papers and when the British asked for her identifying information, she gave the name Kantor after a popular Polish soccer player. She explained that Kantor did not sound as Jewish as Szylberstajn. I did not know her true maiden name was Szylberstajn until much later, after I was grown and her uncles, Harry and Adolph had found her.

CHAPTER 18

The Only Time Uncle Herman Ever Got Angry at My Father

Jan's older uncles, Abe Glantz and Morris Glantz had been in America since before the First World War. Jan hardly knew them, even though Morris had returned to Boiberke twice, with his wife and daughter, Bea. Jan did know his Uncle Herman well. They had grown up together in Boiberke and Budkow, and Herman was more like a brother to him than an uncle. Herman did not leave for America until 1938.

Herman arrived in New York City in August, 1938, with the help of his brother, Morris, and Morris' two business partners in the garment business in Brooklyn, his cousins Murray Glanz and Harry Roher. Murray and Harry were the sons of Chana Glantz, Sruel's sister, the same Chana Glantz who was the mother of Ben Kratter and three or four other Kratter children with her first husband, Saul Kratter. In addition to the four or five Kratters, at least one of whom, Ben Kratter, went on to Israel, Chana had at least four other children. Harry and his two sisters Malka and Sally were named Roher.[22] Most likely Chana had a second husband named Roher, whom she married after her marriage to Saul Kratter. We don't know that for sure. The fourth of her other children was Murray Glanz. We do not know who was the father of Murray Glanz or why his name was spelled Glanz, a spelling that appears from time to time with other family members, and not Glantz.[23]

Murray Glanz, his brother, Harry Roher, and their cousin Morris

---

22 When Sally Roher married, she became Sally Widrich.

23 Herman Glantz' daughter, Elaine, says that the family name was Glanz in the old country and the "*t*" in his name was added, for some reason, by the immigration official at Ellis Island, but this does not explain how his brothers, Abe and Morris, acquired the "*t*" in their names, as they both came to the United States many years earlier and not together.

Glantz were successful partners in the clothing business in Brooklyn. They had a factory that made women's clothing, and they did very well.

Although Morris was clearly doing well enough to sponsor his youngest brother Herman, he only needed to do so because the United States immigration laws required that every immigrant had a sponsor. Herman was doing quite well when the rapid rise of the Nazis and imminent war prompted him to leave Poland. Herman was leaving a good job with the Oikos Company, managing the wood cutting and designating the wood for particular uses – wood pulp, lumber, various wood products. He traveled first class, not in steerage, at the bottom of the ship, as so many eastern European Jewish immigrants had to do. Herman even traveled with a hairnet, to protect his well coifed hair, and with custom pillowcases embroidered with his initials.

When the ship landed in New York, Herman did not have the same tired and ragged manner or appearance of the typical Jewish immigrant who had a rough trip crowded in steerage, the cheapest and most meager accommodations. This turned out to be a good thing, as Herman was positive for tuberculosis, something he did not yet know, but would soon discover.

Herman moved in with Morris and Ruth Glantz, who were "sponsoring" him for immigration purposes. Herman went to work in Morris' clothing factory. The factory was hot and crowded and Herman had trouble breathing. When he saw a doctor, the doctor diagnosed Herman with tuberculosis. Fortunately, Herman apparently was never examined when he got on the boat in Gdansk or when he got off the boat at Ellis Island. Herman was large, over six feet tall, and well built. He was a healthy looking 31-year-old who was well dressed and traveling first class. If the doctor at immigration had examined him the way Abe Fischer had been examined, Herman would not have been allowed into the country.

Herman stayed for a while with Morris and Ruth but soon left for Philadelphia, where he was able to find work that was not factory work. His cousins, Zalman "Sol" Goldman and Ben "Bernie" Goldman from Rovno, were already in Philadelphia. Ben Goldman found Herman his first job as a waiter, a catering job at the White Manor Country Club. His cousin Ben Goldman was a caterer there. This would begin Herman's long career as a waiter. He later worked for many years at Hesbe's, an elegant German restaurant in downtown Philadelphia. Herman was well thought of there. When the owner met Clara, Herman's wife, he remarked to her that Herman was the only employee who never ate the food. Perhaps it was because Herman was the only employee at the German restaurant who kept kosher.

Herman met Clara Polis soon after arriving in Philadelphia. There was a neighborhood variety store where Herman would stop for his morning cup of coffee. The store was owned by Clara's brother, Jack Polis, and Clara, then still a teenager, helped her brother, Jack behind the counter, serving coffee, pastries and sandwiches. Herman stopped there often for a cup of coffee. Clara brought Herman his coffee and the next thing they were dating.

Herman was still getting medical treatment for tuberculosis from the doctor that Morris and Ruth had found for him in New York. When Herman traveled to New York for his doctor appointments, he stayed overnight with Ruth and Morris. He did not want to tell his new girlfriend that he had tuberculosis. Clara, not getting a good explanation for these regular trips to New York, naturally suspected the worst: that he was having an affair with Ruth. This goes to show that you should never keep secrets from your lovers.

Over the years, between the first catering job for his cousin Ben Goldman, until his years at Hesbe's and at other restaurants in the years after Hesbe's, Herman spent his life as a waiter. It was a profession in which you could earn a fair living, especially if you were working in an elegant restaurant like Hesbe's or some of the country club restaurants where Herman worked. I remember Uncle Herman leaving for work mid-morning in a tuxedo, as that was his working uniform. It was not the same as the job he had at Oikos, but Herman worked hard to support a family and raise two daughters.

In addition to the full-time job at Hesbe's, Herman did catering jobs, weddings and affairs at the White Manor and other country clubs, on the side. These were often arranged by or for his cousin, Ben Goldman. Herman worked at other restaurants besides Hesbe's, but at Hesbe's he had fewer problems. Because he spoke Yiddish he had no problem with the German names for the dishes on the menu. Herman was much happier at Hesbe's than he was at an Italian restaurant. In the Italian restaurant, Herman had a harder time with the menu, having to learn a new vocabulary of Italian foods like prosciutto and parmigiana and rigatoni.

Herman always worked hard. He was able to save by supplementing his full-time waitering job with the catering jobs, often for his cousin Ben, and he and Clara lived very frugally. Soon they were able to purchase a modest row house on Eastwick Avenue, just down the block from Harry Polis, Clara's brother and Herman's brother-in-law.

The modest home on Eastwick Avenue was where Jan and Litka stayed when they first came to Philadelphia, with their five-month-old son. My "crib" was the top drawer in the dining room cabinet, which Herman and Clara had emptied out. Clara, who had two daughters but no son, quickly came to calling me her "little man" and as I grew, I became as fond of my Aunt Clara as she was of me. I would always be her "little man", the infant that used to sleep in a drawer in the dining room cabinet, even as an adult.

Herman and Clara, 1941

Jan and Litka stayed with Herman and Clara for some months. Herman and Clara's house was a small row house, one room wide. The front door opened directly into the living room, with no entryway or coat closet. Behind the living room were the stairs to the second floor, the dining room and then the kitchen. Upstairs there was a bedroom on one side of the stairs, where Marsha and Elaine slept, a bedroom on the other side of the stairs where Herman and Clara slept, and a narrow bathroom in between. That was it.

Bernard and Litka were clearly welcome guests. For years we all spoke about how Marsha, then maybe five years old sang "If I knew you were coming, I'd've baked a cake, baked a cake" when we arrived. Nonetheless, for our first months in America, the small row house was crowded. I was oblivious, sleeping in the top drawer of the dining room cabinet. I do not know where my parents, Jan and Litka, slept. Perhaps in the living room, or perhaps Herman and Clara sent the girls, then eight- and five-years-old, to sleep in the living room. In any event, the house was crowded. Yet neither Herman nor Clara ever complained. They were glad to open their house and Jan and Litka never forgot.

But after only a few months, Jan was ready to be in his own place. Once he found fulltime employment, he was ready to get his own apartment, despite how close he was to Herman.

The Eastwick Avenue location, way down in southwest Philadelphia, was not convenient. Jan's first fulltime job was doing translations for Dr. Francis Botelho, but Dr. Botelho's translation business had its office in downtown Philadelphia. In the fall, Jan would be returning to school at the University of Pennsylvania, which was in West Philadelphia. Neither location was easily accessible from the Eastwick neighborhood.

Jan found an apartment at 3407 Powelton Avenue, in Powelton Village, near the campuses of Penn and Drexel University. Powelton Village was then a Bohemian neighborhood, where writers, artists and intellectuals lived and gathered, Philadelphia's equivalent of Greenwich Village, or, in Jan's case, the Left Bank in Paris. He would soon buy a house, only two blocks away, at 3207 Powelton Avenue, where we would live until 1957, when we became the last white family on the block to move out of a rapidly changing neighborhood. Proud to have his own place to live, Jan was excited to share his good news with Herman that he had found an apartment. Little did he expect Herman's reaction.

Herman was not at all pleased to hear Jan would be moving out. "What, is my home not good enough for you?" was Herman's response.

Jan would later say that this was the only time that Herman ever got angry at him. They remained as close as they were growing up in Boiberke. Growing up, especially in those early years, we spent a lot of time at Herman and Clara's. I remember many meals around Clara's kitchen table. It seemed like there were always people sitting around her kitchen table and eating, or drinking seltzer water that was delivered to the door by the case, in returnable glass bottles in wooden cases. This was the 1950s version of Soda Stream, and just as green as any recyclable today.

My earliest memories of going to shul were walking from Herman's house with Herman and my father. We would turn left out of the house, onto Eastwick Avenue, then left on Eighty Second Street, past Mima Pesel's house to the synagogue. Mima Pesel was Clara's relative, and her kitchen also always had people sitting at the table eating and drinking and just hanging out. There was lots of family, often speaking in Yiddish and it always felt good to be there.

Not only was I Clara's "little man", Herman also enjoyed having me around. I remember his big smile and his teasing. When Nana gave birth to Vivian, I stayed at Herman and Clara's for maybe a week. Marsha was in her tomboy phase and wore cowboy clothes and her toy guns and holsters. That was where I first learned about cowboys and Indians. Later, Marsha and Elaine would also take us for walks to the playground, and sometimes for a longer walk to the then new Philadelphia airport, where we could sit and watch the planes take off and land.

Herman was also quite fond of Vivian. Vivian and I both remember being sprawled across the dining room floor coloring, when Uncle Herman would come down for breakfast late in the morning, after a long night at work, to find us in his path. He would pretend to step on us, saying he liked the new rugs and then pretending to be surprised when we tried to move away.

My first Passover seders were at Herman and Clara's, with Herman leading the seder. I remember them fondly, a noisy and boisterous table surrounded by family and friends. What I remember the best was when Uncle Herman would open the door for Elijah. Herman and Clara's house was on Eastwick Avenue, right across from the streetcar stop. Consequently, there were often people out on the street, even late in the evening. Herman would open the door and look around. Much to Clara's dismay, Herman would invite whoever might be passing by to come in, offer them a seat at the table, and ask Clara to give the guest a plate of food.

When Clara complained, he would turn to her and say, "You never know who Elijah might be."

CHAPTER 19

Bernie "Ben" Goldman and the Goldman Brothers

When I was a boy, we often took family trips to New York City, for family affairs, weddings or bar mitzvahs, or sometimes just to visit. Sometimes we drove up with Uncle Bernie and Aunt Helen. They would drive out to Jersey and pick us up because we were on the way. We'd get into Uncle Bernie's big fancy car, always a Cadillac Coupe de Ville, if I remember correctly, and Uncle Bernie would let me sit next to him, in the middle of the wide front bench seat so that I could be the "Navigator". I would read road signs and hold the map and give him directions. This always made me feel grown up. It was not until years later that I learned that Bernie did not do this just to make me feel good: he did it because he could not read. Getting me to read the map for him was his way of compensating for the fact that he couldn't read. He knew how to overcome his limitations.

Ben "Bernie" Goldman was a rough and tumble character, a smuggler, a gambler, and a shrewd and successful businessman. Bernie Goldman was like a character from a Damon Runyon story, a bit of a caricature and a bit larger than life. His son, Steve, used to say, "My dad could take two pennies, rub them together and end up with three cents."

Bernie was never afraid to take chances. That is probably why he was such a gambler. He and his oldest son, Jackie, ran regular card games at the Goldman house, penny a point or a dollar a point, in an upstairs room at their three-story Locust Street home. Bernie's trips to visit us in Cherry Hill often included a stop to the Garden State Park Race Track. His son, Steve, remembers weekend double-header day trips: first to Delaware Park Race Track in the afternoon and then Brandywine Raceway, where the trotters ran in the evening. When the casinos first opened in Atlantic City, Ben became a favored "high roller" at Caesar's.

Bernie's mother was a Glantz, Minna Glantz. Minna was my father's grandfather Sruel's sister. This made my father, Jan Bernard, Bernie Goldman's first cousin once removed. Minna Glantz married Yehuda Goldman, from Rozdul, and they had eight children -- eight Goldmans who were also eight Glantzes. Minna and Yehuda lived in Yehuda's hometown of Rozdul between the wars. At that time, Rozdul was also part of Galicia, then in southeastern Poland, not so far from Lvov or Boiberke.

In 1980, my father told me that Rozdul was a small town about 70 miles from Lvov. I have looked for it on maps. There are several towns within a 70-mile radius of Lvov that might be the Rozdul where Minna and Yehuda Goldman raised their eight children. One Rozdul, still in Poland today but close to Lvov, was a small town, with a population of about 4500 before World War I, half of whom were Jewish. It was a rural village then and probably still is, although there are certainly few Jews there, if any. But this Rozdul is northwest of Lvov, between Lvov and Lublin, not near the Carpathians and the borders with Hungary, Romania and Slovakia, like Rozdil Lviv **Oblast.**

This Rozdil, Rozdil Lviv Oblast, is much closer to Boiberke. It is southeast of Boiberke, closer to the Carpathian borders, which is the more likely location. However, this Rozdil is a larger city, a regional center, not consistent with the more primitive farm where my father, Jan, would visit his cousins. Searching for the Goldman/Glantz farm, these two Rozdils are not the only two possible Rozdils, but the most likely. Because of its location, the most plausible explanation is that the Goldman farm may have been outside of the larger town of Rozdil Lviv Oblast, but part of the "oblast", which is analogous to the term "county" in **Russia and some former Soviet Union states, like the Ukraine.** My father, Jan, visited Rozdul often and he enjoyed going there. He knew Ben and the other Goldman/Glantzes growing up. Jan always liked going to Rozdul because there were other kids there, Ben, and his four brothers and two sisters. Jan was especially close to Ben, also known as Bernie, even then.

While Ben, the sixth of the eight children (two sisters and six brothers), was Jan's mother's first cousin, he was much younger than Jan's mother, Blanca. Like Jan Bernard's uncle, Herman, Ben was roughly Jan's age, although from one generation earlier. Growing up on the Goldman farm in Rozdul, however, Ben had a harder time than his Glantz cousins in Boiberke. The Goldman farm was a tougher and more primitive place than either the Glantz homes in Boiberke and Budkow or the Fischer homes, in Boiberke and in the big city, Lvov. There is a family story that when one of Bernie's older sisters was pregnant, she gave birth in the field where she was toiling. Having a baby in the field was not so unusual. What made her story more unusual was that after the baby was born, they brought a cart out to the field to take the baby and the mother stayed in the field, to finish her day's work.

As a young man, Ben was buying and selling goods, which, again, was not so unusual. What was unusual is that he was moving them across the border, in and out of Poland, using his knowledge of the woods, backroads and backways to smuggle the goods and avoid customs. Soon Ben was guiding people, as well as just transporting goods across the border between Polish Galicia and Czechoslovakia. At some point, in the 1930s, the story is that Ben was smuggling Jews, as well. It is not clear when he started smuggling Jews out of Poland, but what was clear was that he was getting paid for this in American dollars.

By the late thirties, Bernie was "importing" and "exporting" goods, perhaps more legitimately. He was traveling fairly extensively in the course of this business. These travels took him to Germany, where, in Cologne, he met Helen Hoffman. Helen was the second of the three daughters of Felix Hoffman, a well to do Jew who owned and operated an elegant hotel in Cologne, overlooking the waters of the Rhine River. Helen, a *yekke*, or German Jew, who had grown up in a castle on the Rhine, was smitten by the self-confident rogue from Galicia. Ben was equally smitten by the blond, young and attractive Helen. They married not long after they met. Not long after that, the Gestapo seized Felix Hoffman's river side hotel and threw him out.

Seeing the writing on the wall, Felix paid to send his daughter, Helen, and her new husband, Ben Goldman, off to America in 1938. Ben and Helen almost did not make it out. Their son, Jackie, told me that they were on the last ship to make it out of Germany successfully before Hitler took over and put a stop to ships taking Jews out of the country. That ship likely was the **TS Bremen**, a/k/a the **SS Bremen**. Jackie said "my dad knew someone, and paid him to get on the boat." The night before the ship sailed, Bernie and Helen hid in a cemetery, afraid that the Nazis would come to the hotel and take them away.

Felix, however, stayed. His first wife, the mother of his three daughters, had died, and he had remarried, shortly before the war started, to a Catholic German woman, Maria. She hid Felix in a church for six years. Other than Helen, they all stayed in Germany and made it through the Shoah without the Nazis finding them.

Like their father, Felix, Elsa and Theresa, Helen's older and younger sisters respectively, were also both married to Christians. They survived the war by hiding as well. One of the hiding places was the same cemetery where Ben and Helen hid the night before they sailed. Like Helen, they were both small women to start. In hiding, they both lost weight, one of them shriveling to sixty-five pounds before the war ended. One sister hid regularly in the graveyard. She crouched behind the gravestones to hide when soldiers came into the cemetery. Theresa had a daughter who emigrated to Peru and married a Peruvian diplomat. Although they survived the war, neither Felix nor his two daughters ever recovered what they had before the Shoah.

Ben and Helen arrived in New York in 1938. They were sponsored by Bernie's older brother, Sol. Despite his help, it was difficult for them in New York. Helen was used to a life of leisure. Like your Nana, she did not even know how to boil water. She was pregnant with her first child, Jackie, when they arrived and she soon found herself a mother with a newborn baby living in a small tenement in New York while her young husband was hustling to find work. This was a big change from the life she was used to living in her father's resort hotel in a castle on the Rhine, where she and her sisters could sit at the waterside in lounge chairs and mingle with the guests.

Bernie had a hard time finding work in New York and so he left for Philadelphia, where he joined his older brother Sol. How Sol got to Philadelphia is not clear, but he was already established there when Bernie arrived, in 1940. It was in Philadelphia that Bernie began his long American career in food services, and more short lived career as a television star. Bernie Goldman, in the early fifties, had the first cooking show on television in Philadelphia, perhaps in the country, long before cable cooking channels and Julia Child. But his career as a television chef did not last long. Bernie was fired for using a coke bottle as a rolling pin. The problem was not that he used a soda bottle, which he picked up when he could not find the rolling pin. The problem was that Coca Cola was not the show's sponsor. Pepsi was.

Bernie spent the rest of his life in food services, making a good living and helping his brother Bunya, his cousin Herman, my father, Jan, and me find work. Bernie Goldman became the Philadelphia godfather of the family. He took care of not just the Goldmans, but of the Philadelphia Glantzes, as well.

Bernie's brother, Sol, married, and, with his wife, Hannah Goldman, had a daughter, Marilyn. Marilyn married Arthur Cole and they had two children, Melissa Cole and Stewart Cole. I never met Sol or even knew who he was until I started writing this family history, but Sol Goldman was the first Goldman to come to America. Sol was the first Glantz to come to Philadelphia, as well.

With his wife Helen and baby Jackie, Bernie first lived on Locust Street, before buying the home that I knew well growing up. It was around the corner, on 38th Street, between Locust and Walnut Streets, a three-story Philly row house with bedrooms on the second and third floors. To help make ends meet in those first days, Bernie and Helen rented bedrooms on the top two floors to Penn students. Helen had to change the linens, make the beds and do the laundry, a big step down from the life she knew in Cologne.

Ben quickly began supplying food to the off-campus fraternity houses in his Locust Street neighborhood. Soon he was providing catering services, and not just fresh food, to the kitchens in a number of the University of Pennsylvania fraternity houses in the Locust Street neighborhood, then at the edge of the Penn campus. He would hire the cooks and kitchen staff who prepared breakfast and dinner six days a week. I knew that house on Locust Street well growing up. In my first two years at Penn, between classes I would visit Helen, who would feed me lunch, a white meat chicken sandwich on white bread with mayonnaise, but their house was torn down the summer before my junior year to build the Superblock high-rise dorms which were built in 1969.

In the fifties, Bernie began working for Davis Caterers, a large kosher caterer, perhaps the largest in the Philadelphia area, while continuing to do his own catering on the side. Davis had its own banquet hall at Broad and Girard Streets and also used the banquet rooms at the Drake Hotel, where I remember going for Goldman family weddings. The Davis brothers, who owned the business, were well known beyond just the Philadelphia area. They had ties to interesting celebrities ranging from South Philly singers like Fabian, the fifties idol, to the legendary Philadelphia Police Captain, Clarence Ferguson, head of a special police squad, and to Atlantic City's Paul "Skinny" D'Amato. When Davis Caterers went bankrupt, amidst some scandal, in the sixties, Bernie went to work for the Home for the Jewish Aged, managing the food services there, while continuing to do some catering work on the side.

Herman Glantz followed his cousin Bernie to Philadelphia, because Bernie got him a job as a waiter at the White Manor Country Club, where Bernie was also providing food services and catering. Some years later, Bernie brought his younger brother, Abraham to Philadelphia. Abraham Goldman, who everyone knew as Bunya, was the youngest of the eight Goldman/Glantz children of Minna and Yehuda Goldman. Bunya and his wife, Yetta, or Goldie, as we all knew her, were both refugees after the war and lived for some years in and near a displaced persons (DP) camp in Ulm, Germany, where their two sons were born. Ben sponsored them and brought them to Philadelphia.

Bunya, born in 1917, was the only one of his siblings left in Poland by the time the war broke out. Even his own sons, Jules and Joel, don't know how Bunya survived. Their mother, Goldie, talked to them more about her saga, surviving by her wits. Goldie was still a young child named Yetta when she was orphaned. She was raised by her grandparents, along with her thirteen siblings. After the war broke out, Russian soldiers killed her grandparents. It was only because she fled her home that she survived. Her fiancé and thirteen siblings all were killed, as well.

Goldie survived by using her skills as a seamstress and her wits trading ration cards, on the black market. Then someone stole her coat, in which she kept her identity papers, cut the lining, stole her identity papers, and then turned her in to the Russians, who were occupying eastern Poland and the Ukraine. The Russians sent her off to Siberia. Somehow, she got out and made her way back to Poland, where she met Bunya.

How Bunya survived is a good question. Like many of those who lived through the Holocaust, he didn't talk much in the first years after the war about what he saw and experienced. His son, Joel, says that when he and his brother Jules would ask, all their dad ever said was that he lived in a tree. He probably did, at some point. He hid and lived in the woods of eastern Poland, perhaps near where, just a few years earlier, his older brother, Ben, was bringing goods and folks across the Polish border with Austria and Hungary.

There were quite a few Jews, and many others, as well, who fled to the shelter of the forest. Some were organized into partisans, like the **Bielski partisans**, and both fought the Nazis and organized shelter for the homeless, which include women, children and the elderly. Bunya was likely connected to the local partisans where he was. It is unfortunate that he did not live long enough to tell this part of his story.

The partisan groups in the forests were primarily concerned with survival. Poorly trained and lacking sufficient arms and equipment, their first and main task was not fighting the Nazis but survival. This meant obtaining food and other supplies from the local population. Partisan group members operated field kitchens, hospitals, and bakeries. One source of revenue was providing tailoring, cobbling, and similar services for Soviet soldiers. This was how Goldie, then known as Yetta, survived.

At some point, somewhere on the run and in the forest, Bunya and Yetta met. Together they made it to Ulm, Germany, as did many other refugees. It is over a thousand miles from the area of Galicia south of Lvov to Ulm. Bunya and Yetta went from Galicia through southern Poland and across the Carpathians, into and across Czechoslovakia and then into American occupied Germany, between Munich, Nuremberg, and Stuttgart.

That was a long way to travel, on foot and penniless, but it was well worth the trip to end up in the DP camp in the American Zone instead of Soviet occupied Poland. Bunya and Yetta knew that life would be better in the American zone, but so did many others. The Americans used former Wermacht barracks to house the many refugees, mostly Jews, but also Poles, Ukraines and even Arabs. When the barracks and other public buildings, including the Donaubastion, a part of an ancient fortress on the Danube (Donau) River, were filled, the Americans began placing refugees in private homes which had been vacated by fleeing Germans. When more space was needed for refugees, Germans were displaced from their homes.

Documents of the Vaad Hatzalah rescue organization from 1947-1948 show that some 6,000 to 7,000 persons were living in the Ulm camps at that time. Bunya and Yetta were married in Ulm. Their first son, named Yehuda, after Bunya's father, Yehuda Goldman, was born there in 1947. He became Jules when he came to America. Their second son, named Joel, after Yetta's father, was born there in 1949. Joel was sickly as an infant. He had a lung disease, likely tuberculosis, and was in a sanitarium for quite a long period of time, perhaps a year, quarantined for much that time. But this does not account for all the many years Bunya and Goldie spent in the camp, with their two sons, before Ben Goldman was able to bring his younger brother to join him in Philadelphia in 1953. Neither Jules nor Joel knows why they remained in the DP camp until 1953.

The Philadelphia family Vivian and I knew as children all were in Philadelphia because of Ben Goldman. This included not just Ben, whom we knew as Uncle Bernie and his wife, whom we knew as Aunt Helen, and their three children, Jackie, Betty and Stevie, but also Bernie's younger brother Abraham, or Bunya, and his wife, Goldie, and their two boys, Jules and Joel. It also included Herman, and Clara Glantz and their daughters, Marsha and Elaine. This was the family that Vivian and I knew growing up in Philadelphia.

There were other Goldmans in Philadelphia that I did not know existed when I was growing up. Besides Sol Goldman and his wife and daughter, there were Hilda Frumer and Rose Kornfeld. They were Bernie's nieces, the daughters of Bernie's brother, Chaim Goldman, who lived his whole life in Brussels. I am not sure how or when Hilda and Rose came to the states. Hilda and Rose and their husbands and perhaps even children likely attended many of the family *simchas* that I also attended. Growing up I knew their names and probably met them, but I didn't really know then who they were or how they were related.

I attended Jackie Goldman's wedding to his wife, Joan Lerro in 1965. I was at Betty Goldman's wedding, to Jerry Markopoulos in 1967. Before that, I went to Steve Goldman's bar mitzvah. It was a double bar mitzvah with Jules Goldman. The next year I went to the bar mitzvah of Jules' younger brother, Joel. Then, in February 1963, they all came to my bar mitzah, at Temple Emanuel, and heard me read from parsha Yithro.

The Goldman bar mitzvahs were at Davis Caterers, at the corner of Broad and Girard Streets in center city Philadelphia, where Bernie was a *macher*, a manager, and where Bunya worked as a waiter. Herman sometimes worked there, too, on weekends, picking up extra work in addition to his regular job at Hesbe's. My bar mitzvah was not at Davis Caterers, but in Jersey. It was at Temple Emanuel, now on Springdale Road in Cherry Hill, but which was then on Cooper River Parkway, just off Cuthbert Avenue, near the Garden State Racetrack, the Latin Casino and the drive-in on Rte. 70. None of these establishments are still there. The bar mitzvah reception afterwards was in our home in Woodcrest. Bernie catered the bar mitzvah, of course.

In those bar mitzvah years, I spent a fair amount of time with my three Goldman cousins. I was like D'Artagnan, the fourth musketeer to the three Goldman boys. The four of us were together not just at the weddings and bar mitzvahs but for high holidays and other religious services and other family occasions. I was especially close to Steve. Cousin Stevie was the older brother I never had. I remember Steve taking me trick or treating on the streets neighboring the Goldman home on 38th Street near Locust Street, and telling me which houses to skip and where

I could get the good candy. I remember many visits to the Goldman home, playing with Steve, or watching TV there on Saturday afternoons. This was in the fifties.

It was from Steve that I discovered rock and roll. In the early sixties, Steve was a regular on American Bandstand, which started as a local teenage dance show in Philadelphia in 1952 but became the first nationally syndicated teenage dance show in 1957, after Dick Clark became the host the year before. It was where many baby boomers first saw Little Richard, Chuck Berry, the Beach Boys, and Motown stars like Little Stevie Wonder, who played the harmonica on Bandstand as a twelve-year-old on his first hit, Fingertips.

I remember Steve's big sister, Betty, tall, blonde and beautiful as a teenager, dancing the jitterbug. The was a far cry from the Polish folk dances, the mazurkas and polkas Nana taught me and a group of my sixth-grade classmates for our World of Nations show or from the tap dancing and ballroom dancing classes I took or the ballet classes Vivian took at Disken's Dance Studio, around the corner from our home on Nature Drive in Woodcrest. This was rock and roll!

Betty taught Steve to dance and then encouraged him to try out for American Bandstand, which every teenager in Philly watched even before it went national. The show was on Channel 6 every Saturday afternoon for years, even before Dick Clark went national in 1957. It was pre-recorded, taped during weekday afternoons at the Philadelphia Arena, at 46th and Market Street, not far from West Philadelphia High School, where Steve was a student, like his brother and sister before him. By the time he got there, Steve was one of only two white boys in his class. He played sports, but was not so interested in academics. He couldn't wait to go home, change into a tie and jacket and head to the Arena for Bandstand.

Steve wasn't the only dancer of notoriety in the family. Cousin Joel danced on what was perhaps a hipper circuit, if not as well known a circuit. Joel lived in Olney, in North Philadelphia, where he attended Central High School, an exam school, the Philadelphia equivalent of Boston Latin School. Wagner's Ballroom, near Broad and Olney, and the original Chez Vous, which was in the same neighborhood, was where the "hippest" Philly teens could dance, on the Jerry Blavat show. **Jerry Blavat**, was the "Geator with the Heater". He and **Hy Lit**, a/k/a/ Hyman Litman both Jewish, were the two top deejays on Philly's main AM rock and roll station, WIBG. They were Philadelphia's **Cousin Brucie** and **Wolfman Jack**, the nationally known radio DJs from New York and LA in those days before the Beatles.

Joel recalls that the Blavat shows, local Philly shows, often featured more rhythm and blues and soul music and less top-forty pop music than Dick Clark's Bandstand, which became American Bandstand when it became a national ABC network show. Joel was at a 1965 Blavat show that featured a "Special Appearance by Little Richard with Great Guitarist Jimi Hendrix". Joel would also dance on Bandstand, but it was at the Blavat shows where Joel learned the newest steps and moves that he would later show off on Bandstand.

When Joel's dad Bunya worked as a waiter in Atlantic City during the summer and on weekends in the winter, he rented an inexpensive studio apartment to sleep in. His wife Goldie and their two boys stayed at home, except for a few weeks or a month in the summer, when Bunya brought them to Atlantic City. Like so many summer "residents", they would do little more than sleep in the crowded one-room apartment, spending their days outside at the beach, and their evenings on the boardwalk.

In 1963, after Joel's bar mitzvah, tragedy struck. Bunya was driving back home to Philadelphia after a shift waitering in Atlantic City and was killed in a late night automobile crash. His wife, Goldie, was left a widow with two teenaged boys. It was a shocking loss for Goldie and her two sons.

Joel was still attracted to the Jersey Shore, and to the music scene. As a young teenager, Joel would go back to Atlantic City in the summers of 1964 and 1965, to dance on a seasonal teenage dance show that aired Saturdays live on WCAU TV, Summertime at the Pier. Joel would take an early morning subway from his Olney home downtown. From there he would take what was then a long bus ride from Philadelphia to Atlantic City, spend the afternoon doing the show and then spend the evening on the pier.

It was in those days that my cousin Steve took me to my first "teenage" parties, my first parties with girls. This is where I discovered rock and roll, soul music and rhythm and blues. This was where I learned the difference between ballroom dancing and "slow dancing". I was just learning about the world of rock and roll when, in February, 1964, the Beatles played on the Ed Sullivan Show.

This was before cable television and before the internet. There were only three networks, three channels, and the whole country watched the Walt Disney Show, the same westerns and the Ed Sullivan Show at the same time. Like so many other American families, we watched together in our recreation room as the Beatles took America by storm in 1963. That first Sunday night on Ed Sullivan they played five songs, including "She Loves You", "I Saw her Standing there" and "I Want to Hold Your Hand". Vivian and I went nuts, but our dad did not understand. With disdain, he shrugged and said they were just a fad and would not last three months.

I don't know how my Uncle Bernie felt about the Beatles' music, but Ben Goldman always looked out for his family and took care of what was needed. When the Beatles toured the U.S. for the first time that summer, they played a show at Convention Hall in Philadelphia. The show sold out, like all the Beatles shows, in minutes. But Uncle Bernie knew somebody. It seemed Uncle Bernie always knew somebody. Through a friend, Uncle Bernie got tickets for Steve.

Stevie had one ticket for me. I was going to see the Beatles! The show was scheduled for September 2, 1964, but I never got to go. We were in Florida that summer, staying with Nana's Aunt Tola, whom Nana hadn't seen since 1939. My father would not let me fly back early to see the Beatles. I pleaded. He said I couldn't stay by myself and I argued I could stay with Uncle Bernie and Aunt Helen. He said I should be with the family for Rosh Hashanah, and I should go to services. I argued that Uncle Bernie and Aunt Helen were family and that I could go to services with them. I had a ticket to see the Beatles and did not get to go because of my father, and I never forgave him for that.

How or when Zalman, or Sol, the oldest Goldman brother, found his way to Philadelphia is not clear, but he was already established in Philadelphia in 1940 when Bernie arrived. Chaim was the next brother.

Chaim had a store in Brussels, where he was established well before the war with his wife, Malka, the mother of his five children. Chaim and Malka had four daughters and a son, Bernard, who became a Chassid.

When Bunya's son, Jules, was in the army in the sixties, he was stationed in Germany for some time. This gave him the opportunity to visit his Uncle Chaim in Brussels, where Chaim still had the store in the center of the city, across the main square from the train station. Jules told me that it was a small department store or general store. By this time, Chaim was an old man and his Chassidic son, Bernard, was running the store.

Chaim had done well before the Shoah, and managed to hide his wealth from the Nazis, burying bars of gold bullion, which he later recovered. He did not believe in banks, perhaps because of what he lived through, and sold the bullion during an inflationary cycle. This allowed him to retire a wealthy man in the mid-sixties. Jules remembers that the store did have some jewelry, and his Uncle Chaim gave him some watches and bracelets to bring home for Chaim's brothers, Ben and Bunya, and their wives. Betty Goldman also remembers the gold watches and bracelets. She also remembers stories of Uncle Chaim having bricks of gold bullion in the basement of his Brussels home.

The two older of Chaim's four daughters, Hilda and Rose, ended up in the Philadelphia area. Like my father, Jan Bernard, Hilda had a way with languages, and worked at the United Nations as a translator when she came to the Unites States. She married Morris Frumer. Morris also escaped from the Nazis, fleeing after they killed his father. Morris became Marshall Frumer in the United States, where he had a successful law practice in Philadelphia. Hilda and Marshall raised two sons, Marc and Richard, both of whom joined their father's law practice, after following their father into the law. Marc, who passed away in 2019, had two daughters, Alexa Frumer and Lindsay Frumer.

Rose, Chaim's second daughter, followed Hilda to the States and then to Philadelphia, where she married Morris Kornfeld and had a daughter, Julie.

Chaim's third daughter, Jennie, married Roland Matthew. The last daughter, Bella, married Edgar Goldstein and they had three children, Alan, Therry and Danielle, who would be the same generation as I. I do not know where the Matthews or Goldsteins live. Chaim's son, Bernard, may still be living in Brussels, as a black hat Chasidic Jew. Chaim apparently married a second time, as Betty Goldman remembers her Uncle Chaim coming to visit with his wife, who she remembers was Black, probably in the late sixties or early seventies, certainly after Jules' tour of duty in Germany and visit to Uncle Chaim. This may have been a second wife.

The third Goldman brother, Maiche, or Moshe, seems to have disappeared. Little appears to be known about him or what happened to him. We know that he was not left behind in Poland and my father's notes show him as having had two sons. Next was Bernie, then Joshua. In Yiddish, he was Yossel Munya. He also appears to have disappeared, although by some accounts, he settled in Australia before the war. Finally, was Bunya, the youngest.

In addition to their six sons, Minna and Yehuda had two daughters, Sarah and Bertha. They were Bunya's two oldest siblings. Sarah married a doctor named Stauber. Next was Bertha, who married Mundek Groebel. Bertha and Mundek had two sons. I remember my father talking about Sarah Stauber and his notes in a partial family tree he sketched [See Appendix 1] say "died" under her name, so from this we might surmise that she died in Poland. That is likely not accurate, however, as Joel Goldman remembers that his two aunts, his father Bunya's two sisters, survived. According to Joel, one went to Argentina, the other to Australia. This is corroborated by things my father said about maybe having a distant cousin in Australia.

Sometime in the late 1960s, an Australian Goldman cousin, Geoffrey, showed up at Ben Goldman's home on Locust Street in Philadelphia. According to both Steve and Jules Goldman, this Geoffrey was named Goldman, not Stauber or Groebel. Thus it would seem he was the son of Jules' Uncle Joshua, his father's brother, Yossel Munya, who had left for Australia in the 1930s. However, Jules was not sure if it was his Uncle Joshua or his Uncle Maiche who left to Australia in the 1930s, and later concluded that it must have been Uncle Maiche, as Uncle Joshua would later appear and then disappear in the Dominican Republic.

Steve Goldman remembers that his dad, Ben, had brought the

Australian cousin Geoffrey to the kitchen at York Road Home for the Jewish Aged, where Ben ran the food services. This was another source of jobs for Bernie's family. I worked there washing pots and dishes when I was in high school. Cousin Steve, also worked there, both still while in school and then after his return from the service in Vietnam, but Geoffrey's visit was before Steve was drafted.

Steve remembers this cousin, Geoffrey Goldman, staying at their house, as well as visiting the York House kitchens. Geoffrey had long dark hair and a beard. He looked like a hippie, but, to the other kitchen employees, almost all African-American, Geoffrey looked "like Jesus". This was not so unusual in the late sixties, when he visited. Joel Goldman also remembers cousin Geoffrey's visit. Joel remembers Geoffrey staying at his house for a few days after visiting their Uncle Bernie. Joel says that Geoffrey then headed to the western United States and "was never heard from again".

Based on what Jules told me, that Geoffrey was the son of Uncle Maiche Goldman, I did some internet searches and found a Geoffrey Elidge Goldman listed on the Australian voter rolls in the 1970s with an address at 12 Malton Road, Beechcroft Berowra, New South Wales, which is near Sydney. He was born in 1939 and died 2017. This was the right age for him to have been Maiche Goldman's son, but I found no record that indicated who were Geoffrey's parents.

I did learn, from his obituary, that Geoffrey Elidge Goldman and his wife, Margaret Goldman, had a daughter, Lisa, and a son, Bradley. Bradley died in an accident at the age of 18 in 1986. However, this Geoffrey Elidge Goldman may not be the right one, as it is unlikely, although possible, that he got married and fathered a child in 1968, around the time he was traveling in America. Further, his profession is listed in the 1977 New South Wales Australian voter rolls as a plumber and Jules remembers that his cousin Geoffrey who visited Philadelphia was a therapist. So Geoffrey Elidge Goldman is probably not our distant cousin.

In any event, aside from Lisa Goldman, who would have been born in the sixties, this would seem to be the end of these Goldmans in Australia. Except for the two Goldman sisters. One of them, whether Sarah Stauber or Bertha Groebel, may have had children after settling in Australia. I don't know which of the sisters went to Argentina and which to Australia, but my father's notes, on his family tree, are that Bertha had two sons. Maybe one of them was Geoffrey Groebel. It is possible Jules had his two uncles confused and it was his Uncle Maiche, or Moishe, who went to Australia and that Geoffrey Goldman was the son of Maiche or Moishe Goldman, and not of Joshua Goldman. After all, we do not know what happened to either of these two Goldman brothers.

As for the Philadelphia Goldmans, Bernie and Helen had three children. First was Jackie, who was born in 1940, shortly after his parents arrived in the U. S. Jackie attended West Philadelphia High School, where he played guard on the West Philly High School basketball team. While still in high school, his dad got Jackie a job working after school at Davis Caterers. After school and on weekends, Jackie would head to Davis Caterers, where he would cut potatoes, wash vegetables and do other prep work. He worked with two other high school students, two African-American cousins from the Overbrook neighborhood in West Philly. These two cousin got jobs at Davis because one of their fathers was a cook for Bernie at one of the Penn fraternities. It seemed Bernie Goldman got jobs for everybody.

One of these two African-Americans cousins was a tall young man named Wilt, Wilt Chamberlain, then already a big basketball star at Overbrook High School. West Philly High and Overbrook High were big rivals and Jackie and Wilt had played against each other. Now, working together cutting vegetables in the Davis Caterers kitchen, they got to know each other and started playing basketball together on weekends. Jackie started going with 7' Wilt to the pick-up games at the full court at Cobbs Creek Parkway. Soon they were playing together not just on the same team in playground games, but in youth leagues across the city, the 5'6" guard, Jackie Goldman, feeding the big man, 7-foot-tall Wilt the Stilt.

Not long after graduating high School, Jackie went to work at Leventhal's, a store in downtown Philadelphia which sold pocketbooks and leather goods. After many years there, Jackie retired when the Leventhals sold the business.

In 1965, Jackie married Joan Lerro, an attractive dark haired girl from South Philly. They had three daughters, all of whom are grown and married and live near their parents, who now live in Willow Grove, a little north of Philadelphia. The oldest is Felicia. Her twin sisters, Tara and Tiffany were born on May 7, 1970. Felicia married Kevin Meakim and they live in Downington, Pennsylvania, near Jackie and Joan in Willow Grove. They have three children, Kevin, Jessica and Allie Meakim. Tara lives in Hatboro, with her husband, Mike Clark and two children. Her son, Ben, is named after his great-grandfather, Ben "Bernie" Goldman. Ben Clark was born May 7, 2002. He has an older sister, Maya, born in 2000. Tara's twin, Tiffany lives with her husband, Ed Emmell, two blocks away from her parents. Tara has a daughter, Kasey, and a son, Alex, also born on May 7, so the twins, Tiffany and Tara, born on May 7, each had a baby boy on May 7, two years apart. That tops the double birthday that my granddaughters Dalia and Avigail share.

Betty followed her brother to West Philadelphia High School. She was blonde and attractive and married her high school sweetheart, the very handsome Jerry Markopoulos. Betty was Jewish and Jerry was Greek and their families did not approve. But unlike Romeo and Juliet, they were married in 1967 and lived together happily until Gerry died in 2012, the day before their 45th wedding anniversary. Gerry was in the restaurant business until he went to work for his father-in-law, Ben, helping to manage the kitchen at the Home for the Jewish Aged. They had two children, Robbie and Missie, and two granddaughters, Nicole and Samantha Fiuore, Missie's daughters. Jerry passed away in 2011, leaving Betty to live alone in West Chester, outside of Philadelphia.

Steve Goldman was the only white boy and one of only two white students to graduate from West Philadelphia High School in 1966. Steve was drafted into the army after graduating, serving from 1966-1968. He was sent to Vietnam after basic training, and was back and forth between Vietnam and Okinawa. He was in Vietnam for about nine months, from the end of 1967 until his discharge in September, 1968. In the family tradition, he was a chef cooking for the troops. He says he never had a problem getting a seat on a flight, because he was a mess sergeant, a popular position, as he fed the hungry troops.

After his discharge, Steve did not go to work for his father, Bernie, as everyone expected. Instead, he went to work for Pep Boys, the Philadelphia area auto parts company. Anyone who grew up in Philadelphia remembers the Pep Boys logo, with the cartoon caricatures of the three

Pep Boys, Mannie, Moe and Jack, with oversized heads, looking like an R. Crumb cartoon. Steve spent a good eight to ten years with Pep Boys, rising from his initial entry level position to become a store manager.

Steve left Pep Boys to go out on his own, becoming manager of a transmission shop franchise, and soon thereafter opening his own franchise, in South Jersey. After some initial success, making good money, the franchise ran into problems, and failed. By this time casinos had come to Atlantic City, making three promises, none of which came true: that gambling would save Atlantic City, that gambling would provide taxes and fund the schools and that gambling would provide plenty of good jobs. Steve trained for and obtained a dealer's license, and worked for ten, maybe more years at the Playboy Casino, but that did not make him rich and he returned to the restaurant business, where he made more money waiting tables.

Steve was the last of Bernie's three children to marry, but he was the only one to marry a Jewish wife, and he did it twice. His first wife was Anita. Steve adopted her then two-year-old daughter, Jeannie. Steve and Anita had three children, Jeffrey, born in 1976, Eric, born in 1977, and Samantha, born in 1980. In the struggles that followed from the demise of Steve's franchise business, he and Anita divorced.

Jeffrey lives in Novato, California, with his wife Heather and they have two daughters, Taylor, born in 2008, and Abbie, born in 2010. His wife, Heather, is an executive for The Gap. Jeffrey finished law school, but does not practice law. He works for a company that develops commercial real estate and leases the developed space.

Eric was in the travel business for some years, which is what brought him to Florida, where he married the former Stacey Holtzman. Eric now works as the sales manager and has become part owner of his father-in-law's bottled water business, Mountain Valley Water Company. Eric and Stacey have two children, a son, Finn, born in 2014 and a daughter, Magnolia, or "Nollie", born in 2015. Steve's greatest pleasure at this point in his life is the time he spends with these two grandchildren.

Steve's daughter, Samantha, married Brian Davidson, with whom she has two children, a daughter born in 2011 and a son born in 2013. She lives at the Jersey shore, in the Atlantic City area, where she works in a doctor's office.

Steve retired after he was badly injured in a car accident, and in intensive care for several days. Steve has lived a long time with his current wife, Eleanor, first in Ventnor, next to Atlantic City, where he would sometimes help make the morning minyan at the local shul. He and Eleanor now live in Delray Beach, Florida. Eleanor is more involved in the Jewish life than Steve. She may be the reason he occasionally joins the morning minyan.

Eleanor has two daughters, Terry Goldberg and Rhonda Kotzen, and a son, Matt Hartman. They all live in the Philadelphia area. Both daughters are actively involved in their temples, and Eleanor will proudly tell you that both her sons-in-law were presidents of their temples. Eleanor speaks most proudly of her five grandchildren, especially the Goldberg twins. One of them, Ethan, is a cantor at the Westchester Jewish Center, in Mamaroneck. He is married to a cantor and rabbi, Shoshana Levin Goldberg, who works at Temple Israel Center in White Plains. The other twin, Ben, is a rabbi in Port Chester, New York.

The other Goldman cousins, Jules and Joel, had a tougher time after their father died. Joel describes his dad as "the glue that held our family together". Their mother, Goldie, had her hands more than full after Bunya, died in the 1963 car accident, just a few years after the bar mitzvahs of her two boys. Goldie was left a widow, with two pretty wild teenage boys, 14 and 16 years old. The two boys were left without a father.

Fortunately, Bunya had a good life insurance policy that not only paid for the car that was destroyed in the crash, but also paid off the mortgage on their house. Herman Glantz used to say "what do you need life insurance for? It's just throwing your money away." That's true, until you need it.

The insurance could not replace a husband or a father. Joel also says that the loss of their father is what led to his brother, Jules, dropping out of Olney High School. After leaving high school, Jules ended up drafted and in uniform. The Vietnam war was escalating and, like his cousin, Steve, Jules' service also included a stint in Vietnam, which he served in 1964 before he completed his service and returned to Philadelphia.

Joel also went into the service, but via a much different and better route. Joel was a precocious child, who stood out from the start. When he started elementary school, he was immediately moved to third grade, once the school discovered that this bright new first grader not only spoke English fluently, but German, Yiddish and Polish as well. Joel then was accepted to and attended Central High School, which was Philadelphia's exam school, comparable to Boston Latin School.

Joel started college at Temple University, but Temple, a commuter school down Broad Street from his Olney home, did not inspire him and he soon dropped out. This cost him his student deferment and he joined the Air Force to avoid being drafted. It was a provident choice that turned out to be a wise career move, as the Air Force provided Joel with an education in computer programming that he would not have gotten at Temple University or most other colleges in the sixties. The computer training he received in the Air Force provided him the foundation for a career writing software and designing complex software systems.

Moreover, it kept him safe. Joel learned computer programming on some of the original Univac and IBM computers. He soon became such a good programmer that instead of shipping out to Vietnam, like his brother, Jules, and his cousin, Steve, Joel was sent to Langley and then to McConnell Air Force Base, which at the time was the central command for SAC missile silos.

After his discharge, Joel began writing computer software for hospital systems, the start of a decades-long career. Joel worked on the original DRG (Diagnosis Related Group) project created in the early 1970s at Yale University. Later, Joel did database design for SPARKS, a program that allowed Rochester Hospitals to compare patient complaints with actual treatment, allowing medical facilities to improve both medical care and cost management. Joel's name is on many patents, although he is quick to clarify that he does not own any of these many patents.

Over the years, Joel has lived in Colorado, California, Michigan, Georgia, and elsewhere, moving to where he needed to fulfill contracts to write software for hospital systems. He spent eight years in Puerto Rico in the 1980s and spent time in the Dominican Republic, returning several times for periods of months in 2002 and 2003. During these stays in the Dominican Republic he spent time looking for his ephemeral missing uncle, Jose Goldman.

Joel chuckles when he talks about doing business in the Dominican Republic, saying if you want to get paid, after you estimate the cost of the work, you need to double it, then ask for half the money up front. This is a necessary strategy for getting paid doing business not just in the Dominican Republic but in many developing countries. There may be a coup before the job is done, and the new dictator may refuse to recognize the contract. Or the dictator that hired you may just refuse to pay you.

In the end, Joel has done well. He lives in Hollywood Florida, where he still does a little consulting, but is mostly retired. His house is close to the beach and he drives an electric Jaguar. He was married twice, first to Jeanine McCoy, with whom he had a daughter, Michelle. He cared for his second wife, Jamie neé Larsen, for seven years that she suffered with cancer, until she died in 1999. He then had a partner for many years, Susan Barnes, who became ill after her mother passed in 2008. Susan passed in 2019.

Joel's daughter Michelle's first husband was an Englishman with a most English name, Alan Eltringham. Michelle and Alan were married in a destination wedding in the Dominican Republic in 2002, before destination weddings became popular. The marriage did not last long. Michelle then married Jonathan Knox and became Michelle Knox. Michelle and Jonathan had two boys, Jackson, born on September 6, 2014, and Parker, a year and a half younger, born April 11, 2016. These two great-grandsons of Holocaust survivors Bunya and Goldie Goldman attend Tarbut V'Torah Community Day School in southern Irvine, in Orange County, California, a Jewish day school founded by a Holocaust survivor, Irving Gelman.

Joel's older brother, Jules, also suffered the loss of multiple partners. He separated from his first wife, Gloria Winnick, the mother of his son, Abraham, named after Jules' father. She left Jules when Abraham was small, and then gave up their child when he was young. Jules spent many years fighting legal battles to regain contact with his son, while spending more time caring for his mother, Goldie, whom he increasingly cared for in her last days and years. Goldie lived until the age of 93, but her long life was not an easy life.

Many Jews moved out of the Olney North Philadelphia neighborhood in the late sixties and early seventies, as Olney became a much tougher urban neighborhood. Goldie followed the Jewish flight to the "Great Northeast", the section of Philadelphia that was then the center of a large and bustling Jewish community. It was where Clara and Herman had moved, when urban renewal razed their Eastwick Avenue home in the sixties and where both Elaine and Marsha lived after they each were married.

Elaine and her husband Irv anticipated the next Jewish flight out from the city, moving in the mid 1980s from their modest Northeast Philly duplex to a much larger and more luxurious suburban home in Huntington Valley, further north of the city limits. It had a swimming pool and cabana where Irv was able to show off his financial success with Northeast Aluminum Windows, the business he had started in the mid-1970s and successfully grown. Elaine and Irv raised their two children, Alisa and Alan in that Huntington Valley home.

Alan, already working at his father's business while still in school, started working there full time when he graduated high school. His wife, Fran, then still his girlfriend, Fran Burstein, joined him there, as did his cousin, Scott, Marsha's older son. Alan took over the business when Irv retired. In 2018, Alan sold the business and also retired, saying that at age 53, he "wants to be young enough to enjoy retirement". Alan and Fran have a large compound at the Jersey Shore, as well as a house in Aruba. Alan and Fran have two children, Sydney and Austin. Austin is planning a destination wedding in Aruba.

Alisa has sought her own path. While still working as a social worker, Alisa began investing in real estate. She now owns some 40 rental properties as well as a number of air B&B's across the country. She had four children with her then husband, Fred Glickstein, three daughters, Denylle, born in 1998, Mikena, born in 2000, and Holland, born in 2005, and a son Harrison, 2002. Alisa is a physical fitness buff, and like me, likes to bicycle.

Marsha and her husband, Harvey Goldberg, stayed in the Northeast much longer. Marsha worked for many years as a clerk for the Navy in its large purchasing and supply facility in northeast Philadelphia. Harvey, a Boston native who attended the Baldwin School at the corner of Washington Street and Corey Road, near our house, met Marsha when he was in the service. He drove a school bus after retiring as a mailman, but was better known for his jovial manner. When we, or other family, came to visit, he preferred to joke with the children than talk with the adults, and the children always liked him. Marsha and Harvey raised two sons, Scott and Jason. Scott worked at Northeast Aluminum and continued to work there, on the production floor, even though his uncle and cousin have sold the business and retired. He lives with his wife, Dianne in Marlton, New Jersey, just past Cherry Hill. They have two daughters, Jessica and Sarah.

Jason lives in Horsham, where he and his then wife Jennifer raised three daughters, Carli, Haley and Madison. Horsham is another of the Montgomery County towns north of Philadelphia to where the Jews from the Northeast Philly have been migrating, but Jason lives in a much more modest neighborhood than where Elaine and Irv or Alan and Fran live. Jason manages to cobble together a living as a Jewish educator, teaching Hebrew school, tutoring and working in Jewish camps and after school programs. Linda and I met up with his daughter, Haley, when we were in Israel in 2022. At the time, Haley was studying at an Orthodox girls seminary in Yafne, a little town between Rishon leTzion and Ashdod and doing volunteer work in Jerusalem.

After Alisa and Alan left home, Elaine and Irv sold their large home and downsized to a single level condo. At the time, they bought another condo just across the street in the same complex for Marsha and Harvey. Elaine and Marsha were close all of their lives, speaking to each other on the phone most every day. They remained close until Marsha died in 2016, even despite the economic disparities between their two husbands.

Elaine and Marsha, but more frequently Marsha, who was still living in the Northeast, would both run into Goldie, who remained quite a character, full of stories about her latest boyfriend as she went from her seventies into her eighties. When I would visit Marsha, or when we would speak on the phone, Marsha always had a story about running into Goldie, at shul or at the kosher butcher or at some simcha or event.

After reaching retirement age, Goldie told Marsha that she "had enough work" in her long career as a seamstress, but retirement did not slow her down. Indeed she did her best to enjoy her last years and she remained full of energy. She was always doing something new and always had a story to tell Marsha, about going dancing or what she was doing at the Russian synagogue or about her latest new boyfriend. Despite the hardships she endured during the war, when she and Bunya hid in the forests with partisans and then their long years in the refugee camp outside Ulm, Germany, Goldie managed to live her life fully. When she died, at the age of 93, she was one of the last holocaust survivors in what until not so long ago was a large Jewish neighborhood, Northeast Philadelphia, known as "The Great Northeast".

In her last years, Goldie's health deteriorated, and her son Jules quietly cared for her as she developed heart problems. These years were hard years for Jules. After his first wife, Gloria left him, taking their son, Abe, Jules lost his companion of over ten years, Liz Kushner, to cancer. In 2009, Jules lost his second wife, Rene Roth, to whom he was married ten years. Shortly thereafter, that same year, Jules lost his mother, Goldie.

From the time his father died, in 1963, Jules has not had an easy life. After the army, he worked at various jobs, doing accounting, and maintaining inventories for different companies. He was not happy with these jobs and started buying and selling antiques. This grew into buying and reselling old books and then to buying and selling art. Since around the time of his mother, Goldie's death, he has lived in a three story storefront and townhouse at 29 North Second Street, near Independence Hall. Jules had been living in center city Philadelphia since the early 1970s, first on Walnut Street, then South Street, and eventually in the place he calls home on North Second Street.

As of early 2023, Jules is still alive and well, living in Philadelphia. He has been in business selling antiques and buying and selling used and rare books. He runs these businesses from the first floor of his Second Street home near Independence Hall, in historic old Philadelphia. The first floor of Jules' building houses the antiques shop and used bookstore. On the second floor, Jules has an art gallery, which features, among other showings, the works of some artists he has discovered and promotes. He and his companion, Larice Learn McCann, live on the third floor. He is still hustling, always out looking to buy or sell a lot of old books, antique furniture or works of modern art.

Jules is the last of the Goldmans still living in Philadelphia. His son, Abe Winstin, lives in California, as does Michelle, his brother Joel's daughter. Joel is happily ensconced in Hollywood, Florida. Steve Goldman also lives in Florida, in Del Ray, although he and Eleanor still spend time in Atlantic City. Steve's sister and brother, Betty and Jackie both live in Philadelphia suburbs. But for some thirty years after he arrived in Philadelphia, Bernie Goldman was like the godfather of the family. Herman Glantz came to Philadelphia because his cousin Bernie Goldman had work for him. Then Bernie brought his younger brother Abe "Bunya" to Philadelphia, and he always had work for him. Most important to me, Bernie Goldman took care of his cousin, Jan Bernard, my father.

First, Ben Goldman gave Jan his first work in America, as the cashier at the White Manor Country Club, where Ben did catering and ran the cafeteria. Initially, Jan protested. He said that, despite his extensive formal education, "what do I know about the restaurant business?"

"I know one thing", Bernie answered. "When you're done for the day and go home, all the money will still be in the cash register."

When my parents, Jan Bernard and Litka moved into their first apartment, Ben Goldman again took care of things. I was still an infant, sleeping in the drawer of Herman and Clara's dining room cabinet. Jan and Litka did not have a crib for me. They did not have a bed for themselves. They did not have any furniture. When they moved out of Uncle Herman's house and arrived at their own apartment, on Powelton Avenue, there was a crib for me and a bed for Jan and Litka, the first bed of their own in America. There was also a kitchen table and some chairs and other basic furnishings. Ben Goldman saw to it that the apartment was furnished for his cousin Jan Bernard. He never asked, he just did it.

Ben Goldman catered my bar mitzvah, at our home in Cherry Hill. I don't think my parents, Jan and Litka, could have afforded something expensive in a fancy restaurant, but I couldn't have had a better bar mitzvah party. Elaine Levin remembers my bar mitzvah in Cherry Hill, also, as it was the first time she brought her then soon to be fiancé and then husband, Irv Levin to meet the family.

Ben Goldman took care of a lot things, besides my bar mitzvah. He found jobs not just for his sons and son-in-law, but for his brother, Bunya, and his cousins, Herman and Jan Bernard. He even found a job for a young Wilt Chamberlain.

CHAPTER 20
The Mystery of Jose Goldman

I first heard about Jose Goldman from my cousin Joel Goldman. According to Joel, his Uncle Joshua went to the Dominican Republic while it was still possible in the late 1930s. At the time, Allied countries attempted to negotiate the resettlement of European Jews who were under threat from the Nazis. In July 1938, the international community, led by Churchill and Roosevelt, convened a conference in Évian-les-Baines, France. It would later be known as the Évian Conference. This conference was an effort to address the refugee crisis caused by the rise of Nazism in Europe and the threat it posed to Europe's Jews, many of whom eagerly sought but were unable to flee Europe.

The conference included representatives from thirty-two nations and sixty-three organizations. There were several hundred journalists covering the event. Everyone there was well aware of the Nazis' desire to expel all Jews from Germany and Austria, and somewhat aware that the fate that awaited those who could not leave was likely death.

The Évian Conference failed. It failed for one reason, a lack of leadership. Neither Roosevelt nor Churchill were willing to take Jewish refugees when Hitler was still willing to let Jews leave Nazi-occupied Europe.[24] All the countries represented at the conference looked to the United States and Great Britain, and all but two small countries, the Dominican Republic and Costa Rica, followed their lead. As Evian Conference Australian delegate T. W. White said, "as we have no real

---

24 David Swanson, "WWII was not fought to save anyone from death camps", September 21, 2020, https://davidswanson.org/wwii-was-not-fought-to-save-anyone-from-death-camps/#_edn7

racial problem, we are not desirous of importing one."[25] He could have been speaking for any of thirty countries, including the United States and Great Britain.

Only the Dominican Republic and Costa Rica opened their ports. The Dominican Republic was then ruled by the military dictator, Rafael Trujillo. Trujillo came to power in 1930 with the backing of the United States and ruled the Dominican Republic until his assassination in May 1961. Trujillo viewed Jews as "racially desirable", for they would bring more "whiteness" to the country. Trujillo set aside enough land for 100,000 Jews. Fewer than a thousand ever actually ever arrived.[26] Perhaps as many as 5,000 visas were actually issued, but the vast majority of the recipients did not reach the Caribbean nation because of how hard it was to get out of occupied Europe.

Those who came settled in an area on the northern shoreline of the Dominican Republic, near Puerto Plata, in a town that was built for these Jewish immigrants called Sosua. Initially the settlement prospered. At one point, Productos Sosúa dairy company supplied dairy products for the whole island. Between the dairy company, the various inns, and the bed and breakfasts they established, the Jewish settlers laid the groundwork for Sosúa to become a major international tourist destination in the 1980s, a trend that has continued into the present.

In the post-war years, most of the Jewish immigrants left the Dominican Republic to pursue business opportunities or to reunite with families in the US and Israel, returning to their pre-war non-agrarian lives. My children Shira, Miriam and Teddy probably remember visiting what was left of the Jewish community in Sosúa during our 2005 winter vacation to the Dominican Republic when we saw the old synagogue building, the graveyard, and other remnants of Jewish life there. Very few Jews remained.

Could one of the Jews who came to the Dominican Republic in the 1930s have been Joshua Goldman, who may well have changed his name

---

25 Holocaust Educational Trust, 70 Voices: Victims, Perpetrators, and Bystanders, "As We Have No Racial Problem," January 27, 2015, http://www.70voices.org.uk/content/day55, as quoted by David Swanson

26 Lauren Levy, Jewish Virtual Library, a Project of American-Israeli Cooperative Enterprise, "Dominican Republic Provides Sosua as a Haven for Jewish Refugees". See also Jason Margolis, The World, "The Dominican Republic took in Jewish refugees fleeing Hitler while 31 nations looked away", November 9, 2018, both also cited by David Swanson.

and become Jose Goldman in a Spanish speaking country? Did he stay in the Dominican Republic? Joel Goldman seemed to think so.

Joel insisted to me that he has been looking for his lost Uncle Jose since his work setting up medical billing systems sent him to the Dominican Republic in the 1980s. He had no luck. Joel first told me this story over a number of conversations we had in 2020, when I first sought him out for information for this family history.

His brother Jules remembers meeting their Uncle Jose, and offered to show me his Uncle Jose's business card. Jules said he had the card from when his Uncle Jose came to Philadelphia in the early 1960s, when his father, Bunya, and his father's two brothers, his Uncle Ben and Uncle Jose, were making plans to open a casino in the Dominican Republic. Fidel Castro had taken over in Cuba and closed all the casinos in Havana. This was an opportunity

Joel said that their father Bunya and his brother Ben Goldman, neither of whom had the money or resources to do so, planned to finance a casino in the Dominican Republic. Their brother Jose would be the local contact. Supposedly, Jose, who knew some government officials and had some connections in Santo Domingo, would be the grease that made it happen. That was why brother Jose came to Philadelphia. Ben and Bunya flew to the Dominican Republic after their brother Jose's visit, but the plan never came to fruition. Jules told me he would send me a copy of Jose's business card, but then he could not find it among his papers. Somehow all the evidence of Jose Goldman seems to disappear.

Joel said he went looking for this lost uncle when he was working in the Dominican Republic, both in the 1980s or 1990s, speaking to the government contacts he had from his work setting up computer billing programs for the government health system. Joel had no success. Joel heard that there was a Jose Goldman who was minister of finance or a minister in finance under Trujillo. According to what Joel told me he learned, this Jose Goldman did quite well. Joel thought that this Jose Goldman fit with the stories he and his brother Jules had heard from their father and might have been their elusive Uncle Joshua possibly escaping from Europe to Latin America, perhaps to the Dominican Republic. He tried to track him down, but never found him.

In some ways Joel's story made sense, so I did some research. I googled Jose Goldman, but could find no treasury minister or any Dominican official at all. The only thing that came up was two articles from the archives of *The Jewish Journal*, a weekly Jewish community newspaper on Boston's North Shore. These two stories were about the Red Sox and two Jews from the Lowell area who were involved in setting up a sports center for Dominican kids in Sosua. One of them was Elihu "Hugh" Baver, a former college player who had a short stint in the minor leagues. The other was named Jose Goldman. Here was a connection, Jose Goldman and Sosua, in the Dominican Republic.

According to the first of the Jewish Journal articles, this Jose Goldman was involved with the Red Sox, as a scout or some sort of a part-time Red Sox employee. The article said he was from the North Shore, not the Dominican Republic, but maybe there was something there. Maybe there was a connection.

So I called Steve Goldman. He didn't know anything about any Uncle Jose coming to Philadelphia or of any trip to the Dominican Republic by his father, Ben, and his Uncle Bunya. Steve said to talk to his older sister Betty.

Betty didn't know anything either. She said she never heard of any Uncle Jose. She said that she would have known if her father and Uncle Bunya flew to the Dominican Republic and laughed, saying she didn't know where he would have gotten the money for such a trip. She suggested I speak to her older brother Jackie. Maybe he would know something.

There was another problem. Joel's story of Joshua Goldman going to the Dominican Republic meant that Joshua Goldman most likely could not have been the Goldman brother who went to Australia, who could have been the father of Geoffrey Goldman, the hippie looking cousin who showed up in Philadelphia in the 1960s.

There was one other piece of evidence that Joshua Goldman was the Goldman brother who went to Australia. In addition to the family trees drawn in my father's hand, there was an another family tree I referred to for the family trees I drew. It was an old computer printout of the Glantz family tree that Elaine Glantz Levin, Herman's daughter, put together, based on what her father told her. It listed Yossel Munya Glantz as the father of Geoff Goldman, the Australian cousin. While it is possible that Joshua went first to Australia and then to the Dominican Republic, it was not very probable or likely.

In my frustration, I deleted the whole chapter on the mystery of Jose Goldman. I went to work on the chapters on Adolphe and Solange and Maurice and Charles. It was a year later, perhaps as much as two years before I called Joel Goldman again. I had a question about his daughter's last name and her husband's name. We started talking again, about her wedding. Joel reminisced about the destination wedding in the Dominican Republic that he was pleased to pay for. Michelle was his only child and Joel was working in the Dominican Republic at the time, the early 2000s, and doing well.

Then Joel switched the subject to his Uncle Jose. I was surprised.

"That's when I was looking for him," Joel said. "It must have been 2002 or 2003."

Joel said he had come across other leads. He heard other stories. He wanted to know what I had found. It seemed he was hoping I could succeed where he didn't, that maybe I could find his missing uncle.

I tried again, but had to start from scratch, as I had deleted what I had written. I went back to my notes and tried to reconstruct my research. I went back to *The Jewish Times* archives, only to discover that the other Jose Goldman had disappeared. Now there was only one article, the second one, about "Hugh" Baver. That article never mentioned the younger Jose Goldman. It seems that all the evidence about Jose Goldman disappears. Hugh Baver was living in Sosua, where he was running a baseball camp, and was involved in the history of Sosua, starting with the Evian Conference. He was no help in tracing either of the now two missing Jose Goldmans, either the missing Goldman brother or the missing Jewish baseball player and later Red Sox scout.

I went back to my father's family tree, with the two Goldman sisters, Sarah and Bertha and then six Goldman brothers, in order, in my father's handwriting, Solomon/Zalman, Chaim, Maiche/Moishe, Bernie, Joshe/Yossel and Bunya/Abraham. I compared it to Elaine's computer printout: it only listed five brothers, leaving out Moishe, but showing Yossel as Geoffrey's father. I called Elaine and asked if she could be mistaken, if she left out Moishe by mistake, if Moishe could have been Geoffrey's father. Elaine said, she was certain what she had was right, because everything she had was what her father, Herman, had told her.

I called Steve again and then I called Betty again. Once again Betty said to call Jackie, that he would know. This time I did. It was a short conversation. Jackie said that his father never went to the Dominican Republic, that there was no Jose Goldman, and that none of this was true and I shouldn't include anything about him in what I was writing.

Yet despite Jackie's harsh warning, I could not resist. I could not delete the story of Jose Goldman a second time. The story was too good and I did not want to leave it out. Is it true? Did Jose Goldman even exist? There's an old Irish saying that is also attributed to Mark Twain. Never let the truth get in the way of a good story.

CHAPTER 21
Saying Kaddish

Even before I became a teenager, my father and I increasingly clashed and our clashes increased as I grew older. Maybe it was me, becoming more rebellious. It started long before the fight over letting me go to see the Beatles. It seemed to me that he never found time for me. Other dads came to their son's Little League baseball games. My dad never did. He wasn't interested in baseball. He never came to my swimming meets, either. He said he wasn't interested in sports and that he was too busy with his work and his studies. That made me feel like he wasn't interested in me.

Strauss's dad took him to Phillies games, and to Rutgers football games, and to see the Camden Bullets, a minor league basketball team that featured aging former Philadelphia Warriors stars Paul Arizin and Tom Gola, who had played with Wilt Chamberlain, all players whom I admired from secretly listening to games in bed on my transistor radio after the lights were out. Strauss got to bring a friend to these games, and that friend often was me.

Nana didn't know much about sports either. She didn't come to any of my Little League games, either, or very many of my swimming meets. But she tried to show an interest in what I was interested. Nana knew who Stan Musial was, not because he was a great baseball player, like Mickey Mantle or Willie Mays or Roberto Clemente, which he certainly was, but because he was Polish-American, like Nana, like us. When I was reading the sports page of the Philadelphia Bulletin or Camden Courier Post, as

I did every afternoon, she would often ask me "How did Moo-shel do?" That's how she pronounced his name.

My father did take me to the U.S. - U.S.S.R track meet once, at Penn's Franklin Field. For me, a track meet was not a real American sporting event, like a baseball game or a football game. My father just did not get it. I wanted him to be an American dad, my American dad, but that's not who he was. He loved America, the country where he found freedom, the country that fought the Soviets, the Russians who had imprisoned him in a Siberian labor camp, but he had no interest in behaving in ways that I thought were American.

I knew about Siberia, and about the labor camp, but I did not know about a wife. I did not know about a son. I only learned about my father's first wife and son many years later, from Willie Heller's gaffe, shortly before my father died. There were lots of things I did not know about. Despite the stories my father did tell, about the eye and the *shema*, as with many others who survived, there was much that my father did not talk about, did not want to remember, perhaps that he could not talk about.

Like many other survivors, it was hard for my father to love, to trust, or to show his feelings. It was not until much later, after he died, after I had children, perhaps not until after I started writing this family history, that I came to realize how hard it must have been for him to carry the memories that he had, and how much harder it was when he could not talk about them. The one thing he said, though, was that the reason that he had a son was so that he would have someone to say Kaddish for him.

Growing up in Woodcrest, in Cherry Hill, New Jersey, baseball and American sports were important to me. I felt that my father never thought about what was important to me, only what was important to him, what he wanted me to be. He made me go to summer school after ninth grade, which prevented me from returning to the Woodcrest Pool summer league swimming team. I did not want to spend my summer mornings in a classroom. I wanted to be at the Woodcrest Recreation Association Pool, around the corner from our house, in the swimming pool with all the other kids from the neighborhood. Instead I had to ride to the high school every morning, with my father, who was teaching summer school himself by that time.

I took a writing course in summer school that summer, with too much homework for a summer class. The teacher was dad's best friend, Burk Sullivan, later Dr. Sullivan, the chair of the CHHS (Cherry Hill High School) English department. Like my father, Mr. Sullivan was a scholar and an intellectual and when my father came to CHHS they immediately bonded. My class with Mr. Sullivan was my first writing class and the beginning of my aspirations to be a writer. Looking back, I am grateful for the class and for Mr. Sullivan as a teacher, but at the time, it was not where I wanted to be.

I don't think Jan Fischer ever thought he would be a teacher when he came to America, except for maybe being a university professor in international law. He soon learned that in America, as in England, his two degrees from Jan Casimir University did not mean anything. The law he studied was no longer the law, not in Great Britain, not in the United States, not even in Poland, where the pre-war legal system was destroyed by the Nazis and replaced by the Communist government that the Soviet Union had installed. When he came to the United States in 1950, Jan wrote to the American Bar Association and to United States government agencies asking about possible employment as a lawyer. He also wrote to universities seeking academic positions in comparative law, his field of study at Jan Casimir University, to no avail.

After settling into the apartment in Powelton Village, Jan was ready to move on from being a cashier for his cousin Ben Goldman. He began doing translation work for Francis Botelho Translations, in an office in downtown Philadelphia. Doing translations full time, Jan had soon saved enough money to buy a car. He was on his way to the American dream. After all, owning a car was proof that you had made it in America.

His boss, Dr. Botelho, had other advice for my father. Dr. Botelho asked him "why do you need a car?"

Dr. Botelho reminded my father that he could easily come to work on the streetcar or the Market Street subway. Then he ask my father how much the car cost.

My father told him.

Then Dr. Botelho said "Put the money in the bank", and asked him "How much is the insurance? And the maintenance? And how much does it cost you each week to take the streetcar to work?"

They added up all the other costs, and then Dr. Botelho told him not to buy the car but to put the money in the bank, instead, and take the streetcar to work. He told him to take cabs when he needed. This would be cheaper than the monthly insurance and maintenance.

My father, Jan, did not take his boss's advice and bought the car, but he used to love to tell that story. I like to tell it, too, when I am arguing for bicycles, complete streets and the environment. In many ways, Jan Bernard Fischer was a visionary ahead of his time.

It was not long before Jan left Dr. Botelho to work for Maurice Jacobs Publishing. If you look at older **Jewish Publication Society** (JPS) publications, some of which are in our family libraries, you will see the name Maurice Jacobs Publishing. Maurice Jacobs was a small printing company that in the middle years of the twentieth century specialized in printing books not just in multiple languages but in languages with different alphabets, mostly Cyrillic, Hebrew and Arabic. The company had a nice niche market, printing both Jewish prayer books, with English and Hebrew, and scholarly works that quoted from non-Roman texts.

At this time, in the early fifties, books were still printed on printing presses, with cold type, in which the letters were each separate pieces of metal that were put together to form words and lines of print that were coated with ink and then stamped onto paper pages in large printing presses. Most printing companies only had Roman type, as they only printed in English. They could print something in French or Spanish, but Maurice Jacobs had metal types for a variety of non-Roman alphabets.

I remember my father taking me to his job, as fathers do with their sons, and I remember seeing the presses and the rows of metal letters in rows of cubbies and watching the presses run. I also remember the first black hat Orthodox Jew I ever saw was there, Menahem Glen. Father explained to me that Dr. Glen, who had a PhD from **Dropsie College for Hebrew Learning** in Philadelphia, was a pious Jew (I think that was the word my father used), a scholar and an author, perhaps the author mentioned in this blog, **Yiddish Leksikon**. Most important, some years older than my father, he was a mentor to my father, Jan.

I also remember Bud and Charlie Vanos, father and son. They were typesetters and ran the presses, but my father and Dr. Glen proofread everything for typos and misspellings and grammatical errors. I understood that this was an important job my father had. When Maurice Jacobs Publishing received a big contract to publish a number of books in Arabic, father, who knew a little Arabic from his war years in North Africa and the Middle East, was sent to study Arabic, so he would know it well enough to proofread the texts.

Father had already returned to school, as a graduate student at the University of Pennsylvania. He received his MA in Classical Studies in 1955, a second master degree to replace the one from Jan Casimir University in Lvov, one that was no longer recognized. In 1961, he completed his PhD in Classical Studies from Dropsie College, whose academic programs has since merged with Gratz College and whose library has been managed by the **University of Pennsylvania libraries** since Dropsie closed its doors in the early 1980s.

Jan's thesis, <u>*The Arabic Transmission of the Poetics of Aristotle*</u>, dealt with the tripartite division of Semitic grammar in Aristotle's poetics. It was exactly the type of work in which Maurice Jacobs specialized, with both Hebrew and Arabic in its text, in addition to English. It could only have been published by the likes of Maurice Jacobs Publishing.

Mr. Jacobs, the Maurice of Maurice Jacobs, was not just the name of the company but the owner of the company. He liked my father a lot, treating him like a son, and for some time, my father had a reasonable expectation that he might take over the company when Jacobs retired. That was not to be. At some point, Mr. Jacobs' daughter, his only child, got engaged. After the marriage, her husband become the heir apparent successor to the company. My father knew then that there was no longer a future for him with Maurice Jacobs.

By then, the Fischer family was settling in happily in newly suburban South Jersey. Father began taking me to Friday night services at the recently formed Temple Emanuel. Among the new friends Father and I met at Friday night services at the Haddon Fortnightly were Sam Strauss and his son Robert, then just eight or nine years old. Robert and I are still friends, but Jan and Sam were good friends, too.

Formed in 1950, Temple Emanuel met at the impressive building on King's Highway at Grove Street in downtown Haddonfield, known as the Haddon Fortnightly a beautiful old building, originally a Methodist church, that belonged to the Haddon Fortnightly Club. **The Haddon Fortnightly** was very waspy organization, a "civic and social club for women", with an elegant hall that still stands on Kings Highway in Haddonfield. I never knew it was a women's club, as I saw mostly just men there at the Friday Shabbat services my father took me to as a boy.

As is often the case for new Jewish immigrants or "greeners" like Jan and Litka, now Lidia, the synagogue was a place to meet new people, and my father and I did. A young rabbi, Herbert Yarrish, led the synagogue throughout my youth. He had a son, Robert, whom we knew as Bobbie. My father quite appropriately saw Bobbie as a role model for me. He was two years older than me and a year ahead of me in school. He was always a top student, and a courteous boy who never got into trouble. He went to Harvard and Penn and became a doctor, served in the military treating the wounded, in the Iraq War and in Afghanistan, and returned to work as an attending physician in New Rochelle, New York, until his death in 2012.

Under Rabbi Yarrish, who had been hired in 1956, the congregation grew. In 1959 ground was broken for its first building off of Cuthbert Road, on Park Drive, facing the Cooper River. I went to the stone setting when the building was completed. Everyone there shared the feeling of accomplishment that morning. That building was where Vivian and I went to Hebrew School and to Sunday School and where I had my bar mitzvah and where Vivian and I were confirmed.

Rabbi Yarrish retired in 1975. The congregation moved that same year to a new building in east Cherry Hill, near the then new Cherry Hill East High School that Vivian attended. As in many American cities, Jewish communities that were once in the inner city would first move to the suburbs and slowly move further out into newer suburbs. When my wife Linda and I were at the bat mitzvah of one of Strauss' two daughters, in the new Temple Emanuel building, Strauss took me to a row of photos in one hallway and showed me the picture of our confirmation class. The site where the original Temple Emanuel building stood, where I had my bar mitzvah, is now at the edge of the cloverleaf intersection of Cuthbert Road and Route 70, the building long gone.

The building may be gone, but the friendship was strong and lasted. Robert has been a life-long friend. Robert was an only child that Sam and his wife, Edna, had late in life. Unlike my father, Sam was always looking for things to do with his son, activities in addition to just baseball and football, going to Connie Mack Stadium to see the Phillies, or New Brunswick to see Rutgers College football. There were historic events and places as well.

One of the places Sam took us was to the reading of the Declaration of Independence at Independence Hall on July 4th. Sam Strauss took his son, Robert, there a number of times, and I came along at least once that I remember. It may have been in 1960, when I was ten years old. Pennsylvania's two senators were there, Hugh Scott, a Republican and Joe Clark, a Democrat. I met and shook the hands of both these two senators as well as some of the other important officials and dignitaries. The reading of the Declaration of Independence made an impression on me and that is why we read it aloud each year on the Fourth of July in our house.

Hearing the Declaration of Independence read at Independence Hall was only part of the reason I credit Sam Strauss for my decision to become a lawyer. Sam Strauss was the first lawyer I knew. Like my father, he filled his downstairs "recreation room" with bookshelves. Only in the Strauss house the shelves were filled with law books and history books. In addition to Independence Hall, Sam Strauss took us to other historic sites, as did my father, that contributed to my admiration for the American system of government that I admire and have strived to protect.

My father had his own admiration for America, but I don't think he appreciated my admiration for a country we both loved. Our most difficult times were during the Vietnam War. I don't think my father ever saw how much of my values came from him. What I saw was a father who was not interested in me or in listening to what I thought. As a result, we argued a lot. Years later, when I had children, I began to see how much I was like him, both the good and the bad, but in my teens, in the sixties I only saw his frustration, and his anger and did not understand why he treated me the way he did.

I saw in Sam Strauss not just a father who, unlike my father, looked to do things with his son. I also saw Sam Strauss as a lawyer who was always looking to do things to help people. He was a big help to my mother, your Nana, when she formed the LARCS, the League to Aid Retarded Children. So, Sam Strauss was the image of what I thought a lawyer should be. He was the image of what I wanted to be when I decided to become a lawyer.

My Father was not happy when I became a lawyer. He wanted me to be a teacher like him. I thought he wanted me to stay a teacher, like him, because he wasn't able to practice law and resented that I was able to do what he wanted to be but wasn't able to be. I was hurt that he couldn't be proud that I was able to succeed. This would have allowed me to share my achievement with him, to hear him say that my success allowed him to have succeeded, in the end, by surviving and having a son do what antisemitism kept him from doing. But that was not to be.

Sam Strauss suggested to my father that they start a translation business. Strauss did a fair amount of immigration work, where he encountered passports, visas and other legal documents in various foreign languages. He had a general practice where he saw foreign documents in other contexts, such as witness statements, wills, divorce and marriage records, even trust documents. He thought that he could drum up the business and my father would do the translations, and they could make a few dollars on the side.

Unfortunately, there was not as much translating work as Sam Strauss thought there might be and their venture never made much money. In fact, despite their learning and scholarship and their ability in their respective professions, neither Sam Strauss nor my dad were very good businessmen

Sam Strauss' efforts to help to my mother yielded much greater success. It began with the LARCs and the LARCs began with Gert Schneider. Gert Schneider was a Woodcrest neighbor and friend of Nana's, who had a very sweet down syndrome daughter, Amy. Nana adored the baby Amy and felt a great deal of sympathy. This led her to form a local equivalent of the national association for aid to retarded children, still known as ARC, despite the fact that "retard" is now viewed as pejorative and is no longer used to refer to what are now known as people with Down's Syndrome.

Nana thought LARCs would be a bright and light name. Nana had a vision to open a nursery school for young Down's Syndrome children on the lovely grounds of the Bancroft School, a well-established school for children with mental limitations and challenges. Nana succeeded in opening a nursery school for developmentally delayed children, like Gert Schneider's daughter, Amy, but it took perseverance and building an organization.

Sam Strauss was a big help to Nana and the organization she was founding. Most important, Sam introduced her to a number of people who not only helped her. Two of them, Henry Leiner and San Angell, turned into close and life-long friends. Henry Leiner was the local Republican Party chair and knew many people in various positions throughout Cherry Hill and Camden County. San Angell was the executive director of the Camden County United Fund.

Mr. Leiner and Uncle San, as Vivian and I called him, helped Nana find the location for the LARCs nursery school and negotiate the arrangements with the **Bancroft School** to rent space. This was only the beginning, not just for the nursery school and the LARCs, but for two long friendships. Henry Leiner and his wife, Grace, become close family friends and Henry helped Nana with many personal favors over the years.

Being a Republican was different in those days, especially in New Jersey and Pennsylvania. In the 1950s and 1960s, the Republican party in the northeast was the party of the Saltonstalls, of Eliot Richardson, and of Henry Cabot Lodge of Massachusetts. For these New England Republicans, "conservative" meant conservation, creating and protecting state forests and wildland, as well as fiscal conservatism. It was the party of Rockefeller Republicans like New York City's dashing young mayor, John Lindsay, and New York's liberal Jewish senator, Jacob Javits. It was the party of Senator Hugh Scott and later Arlen Spector in Pennsylvania. In South Jersey, it was the party of Henry Leiner, San Angell, and Sam Strauss. This was why Lidia Fischer and then Jan Fischer became Republicans.

When my mother, Lidia, was trying to find a job in Jersey, Henry Leiner helped her get a secretarial job at Cooper Hospital in Camden. Henry Leiner helped find Vivian get a summer job in Tacoma Washington, as a forest ranger with Weyerhauser Corporation, again through someone he knew. This later would lead to Lidia getting a job at Weyerhauser's Barrington, New Jersey office, with better pay and a shorter commute. It was a job she held for many years and led to me getting a summer job in a Weyerhauser warehouse.

This use of influence might sound like what Democratic politicians do in big cities, but as Tip O'Neill said, "All politics is local." Henry Leiner and his wife, Grace became close family friends, a friendship that lasted for decades. The relationship with San Angell and his wife, Tiny became even more.

Tiny Angell became my mother's best friend. Vivian and I soon came to call her Aunt Tiny, because she was close to our mother like a sister. They spoke regularly and often. They became frequent bridge partners, playing with a group of women that played bridge together regularly. In addition, the Angells would come over or mother and father would go the Angells' house to play bridge, father often a bit reluctant to interrupt his work but also joining in what was for him a rare regular social engagement. There was also a monthly bridge party with two other couples, who would change over time, but always the Angells and the Fischers.

The Angells had one daughter, Faith, a few years older than me. She was a social worker for some years before going to law school, graduating in 1971, the same year I graduated Penn. In 1990, she was appointed a Federal Magistrate Judge by the first President Bush. Nana, playing matchmaker, tried hard to fix her up with Romic (Roman) Lasota, the older of two sons of Franic (Frank) and Bronya Lasota, friends of Jan and Lidia from the war years.

Like Jan and Litka, Frank and Bronya were saved by deportation, Polish refugees who ended up in British camps in Kazakhstan or somewhere north of what was then Persia. Their two sons, Romic (Roman) and Yurik (George), were born in the refugee camps. I think Jan may have met Franic when they were both in Polish uniform in North Africa, with the British.

I have very fond memories of spending Christmas Day every year at the Lasota's. We would drive Christmas morning over the Tacony-Palmyra Bridge, where my father always joked about saving the five-cent toll because it was Christmas Day. Then we spent the day with the Lasotas, eating an afternoon Christmas dinner. There were always gifts for Vivian and me under the tree. When we got bored, Romic and Yurik took us upstairs to their bedroom and let us read their Pogo and Peanuts comic books until Bronya called us down for the multi-course mid-afternoon Christmas dinner.

I remember the chicken soup and boiled potatoes and the smell of ginger ale, like a Proustian madeleine. Bronya Lasota grew the parsley that garnished the potatoes in her small backyard garden, along with other herbs. Her garden was the model for our herb garden at 21 Bartlett Crescent.

Bubcha, Bronya Lasota's mother, was the grandmother of the house. She and I would sit on the backstairs that let into the kitchen and talk for hours, although she spoke no English and, as a little boy, I knew no Polish, yet somehow we communicated. I remember Bronya and my mother smiling at me, when I asked Bubcha to be my grandmother, explaining that I didn't have one, and Bubcha smiled and agreed to be my grandmother. Maybe this was during the time Vivian and I stayed with the Lasotas for several days as little kids when Nana was in the hospital.

Before the meal, my father Jan would drink a shot of whiskey with his friend Franic, maybe two shots. As they got older Romic and Yurik would join them. I was too young to drink whiskey, so they gave me a glass of ginger ale. The smell of ginger ale still reminds me of Christmas day at the Lasotas. I don't have many memories of my father smiling, but one of the few times he did smile was when he was drinking with Pan Franic. It is also one of the few times I can remember my father drinking. The other times I remember him drinking alcohol was when he drank liqueurs from Uncle San's collection on Christmas Eve and other special occasions.

Just as we spent Christmas Day at the Lasota's home, we would later come to spend Christmas Eve every year at the Angell's and San and Tiny, and often Faith, would join us for Passover seders every spring at our house. The Angells held an open house every Christmas Eve that started early and would last until and sometimes past midnight, when my father would join San for midnight mass at the nearby neighborhood parish church. I sometimes joined them.

In the end, Lidia's efforts to match Faith with Romic Lasota did not succeed. They dated for a while, perhaps not wanting to disappoint my mother, a close family friend to both of their mothers, but the spark wasn't there. Faith would eventually marry Ken Carobus, and they had two sons, Alex, who lives in the Bay area, where he works for Google, and Andrew, an assistant district attorney in Philadelphia. Both Vivian and I stayed in touch with Faith for a long time. Linda and I even attended her son, Andrew's wedding.

Romic, a chemist who graduated from Drexel and then worked for Dupont, never married. He ended up buying a house in the Pennsylvania country outside Doylestown, near the **Our Lady of Czestochowa shrine** where he lived by himself until his father died and he brought his mother there, where she lived with him until her death. She spent her time there growing herbs and vegetables and picking fresh mushrooms in the woods. His younger brother, Yurik, or George, graduated Jefferson Medical College in Philadelphia and become a neurologist/psychiatrist.

Their father, Pan Franic, worked as a banker in Poland before the war. When he came to Americas, as a refugee, he also worked in a bank. He put on a tie and jacket every day when he went to work, but in the bank, he was only a custodian. Like his wife, he came to America speaking very little English and never really learned to speak English very well.

As they made friends with Sam Strauss, the Angells and the Leiners, Lidia and Jan were making a new life in South Jersey. South Jersey was farther away from the Goldmans or Uncle Herman in those days, before the Walt Whitman Bridge or the interstate. For cousins Elaine and Marsha Glantz, it was a big trip, almost as far as going to their Uncle Jack, who had a farm in Audubon, New Jersey. Indeed, when we moved to Nature Drive in Woodcrest, in 1957, Nature Drive was only paved to the house after our house. There the street ended and there were woods, where I would go to play, often with our dog, Rusty. One time, Rusty took on a skunk and got sprayed. I remember the smell. Rusty had to stay in the garage for a week and my father had the unenviable chore of washing Rusty every day that week.

Marsha and Elaine came to my birthday party the first winter in our new house. It was in February, 1958, when I turned eight years old.

Marsha was twelve and Elaine about fourteen. It started snowing before the party and by the time the party had ended, we had a raging blizzard. The telephone pole in front of our house fell and I remember the wires blowing precariously back and forth close to my bedroom window.

The roads were impassable for several days after the snow stopped and Marsha and Elaine, who had no clothes other than their party dresses they were wearing, were stuck at our house for several days before the roads were clear and the Woodcrest bus to Haddonfield, where they could catch a bus back to Philadelphia, began running again. That turned out to be a real unexpected adventure for Marsha and Elaine that we talked about for years afterwards. It was the biggest snowstorm I had been in until the blizzard of 1978 in Boston.

The house next to ours, on a corner lot, was built after ours. It was bigger than any of the houses on the street. It was built for Harold Sarshik and his family. His father, Morris, was the developer who bought the farmland and started the development. Three streets in the development, Randy Lane, Barby Lane and Carol Drive, are named after Harold's three daughters, Randy, Barbara, who was known as Barby, and Carol. When Harold took over as developer from his father, building the more upscale Country Club Estates section of Woodcrest, he named the main street Morris Drive, after his father.

When the Sarshiks moved in, they knocked on our door and Mr. or Mrs. Sarshik introduced their three daughters. I answered the door as Rusty came to greet them. My father was right behind me and when the three girls were introduced, my father, pointing to the dog and me said "This is Andy, and Rusty."

Barby thought that I was Rusty and the dog was Andy, but we still became friends and spent many afternoons and evenings playing kickball and wiffleball on a field that began with home plate at the corner of their back patio and second and third base between the two yards and left field in our backyard. Woodcrest was a comfortable neighborhood for kids to grow up. There were lots of kids to play with outside every day. My best friends, Tommy Milner and Denny Flacco lived across the street and in the house one up behind me. The Woodcrest Pool was just around the corner.

After the Sarshiks moved in, Aster Drive, the street on the other side of their house, was paved. Then we had to cross the street to get to the woods. In 1958, the Woodcrest School was built and opened. I went there through sixth grade, having attended Sharp School for second grade, until I was skipped to the third grade, and moved to the Stafford School. These two schools have both long since closed but both buildings still stand. The Stafford School, on Berlin Road just the other side of the turnpike and Rte. 295 overpass from Woodcrest is now used for school department or town offices.

I loved to go traipsing through the woods beyond Aster Drive or to the apple orchard behind the Woodcrest Pool, and to the meadows and fields beyond. I would play that I was an explorer or fur trapper, exploring America. Mostly I loved being in the woods or laying in an open field gazing at the clouds, at one with nature. But after Woodcrest school was built, the woods were further away. Behind the school there was the playing field and then the woods. Then houses were built there as Woodcrest grew. Eventually, the streets of Woodcrest joined the streets of Willowdale, the next development, built off of Springdale Road, on what had been a farm. My father admired the way America was growing, but, as I became a teenager, I began to regret the loss of the American countryside to the suburbs, to what would later be called the "urban sprawl" that Cherry Hill came to embody.

When we first moved to Woodcrest, Lidia continued to work in Philadelphia at her job at the Benjamin Franklin Hotel, then one of Philadelphia's classic traditional hotels. Lidia worked as a secretary in the offices at the front desk. She was able to work evening hours when Jan was home and could watch Vivian and me. She took the bus from Haddonfield to downtown Philadelphia, and father would pick her up when she got off in Haddonfield.

The Benjamin Franklin Hotel was where Lidia met Lucy Parrish, a stylish and attractive single woman whom I knew as a young boy. Lidia and Lucy became good friends, even after Lucy left the hotel to work in the book department at Wanamaker's Department Store. After we moved to Woodcrest, they remained friends and Lucy continued to visit Lidia. Lucy always bringing me a book, which she would often inscribe. Some of the books she gave me, such as *Toby Tyler* and *The Jolly Tailor*, still sit on our bookshelves.

I think of Lucy when I visit my parents in the cemetery in the Mt Lebanon Cemetery in Collingdale, just south of Philadelphia, as I would drive through Folcroft to get to the cemetery. Lucy married into a wealthy WASP family, but she stayed in touch with Nana even after she moved from her home in Folcroft to her new husband's horse farm in Devon, Pennsylvania.

More than my father, Nana had many friends who were not Jewish. I think she was more interested in being American than in being Jewish. She did not go to synagogue often. I don't remember her ever lighting candles on Friday night or doing anything to observe shabbat. The only time we lit candles was when Vivian, who was more interested in Hebrew school than I ever was, insisted on lighting candles.

Father put together the seder plate and organized the Passover seders. The seder guests were often not Jewish. Besides the Angells, we would have Burk Sullivan and his family or other non-Jews to whom Father could show a Jewish home, in a spirit of American ecumenism. It was as if mother resented being Jewish. After all, what did being Jewish do for her except kill her first husband, kill her brothers and sister, kill her parents and make her an orphan without any family?

In suburban Jersey in the 1950s, she built a community through her volunteer work. Once the LARC nursery school opened, she raised money for the school. Every summer, she rented the Camden County Music Fair for a night. It was a 2500-seat in-the-round theater under a big tent that featured musicals like *Oklahoma*, *South Pacific* and *Annie Get Your Gun*. She organized a one-night show and the ticket sales for a LARC fundraiser, a project that took up a month of her time every summer.

Nana also volunteered for my sixth grade "World of Nations". Sixth grade was when we studied world history and cultures in social studies. At the end of the year, there was a World of Nations celebration. There was food from different cultures and music and dance, and Nana taught two Polish folk dances, a polka and a mazurka. I had to dance with Ricki Gottlieb as my partner. I was not happy about that at the time. She was the smartest girl in the class and the teacher's pet. Eventually I got over it.

There would soon be another big change. Around 1960, my father, now Dr. Fischer following completion of his PhD from Dropsie College, in a great coup for the school system, was hired as the chair of the Foreign Languages Department at Cherry Hill High School. He had already pioneered an after school foreign language program at the Woodcrest Elementary School, with French, Spanish, and sometimes German taught by volunteer Woodcrest School parents. The after-school program spread to several other elementary schools, so Dr. Fischer had developed a reputation for organizing foreign language instruction. When it became clear that he was not going to be the successor to the owner at Maurice Jacobs Publishing, he realized it was time to move on, and he took the new position.

By the time I started high school in 1964, Dr. Fischer had already become a legend. With bow-ties and his pipe, a noticeable foreign accent, and a set of eccentricities, he stood out with distinction in this still new high school in a rapidly growing but still semi-rural township. He brought a state-of-the-art language laboratory to the school. Students each sat at a desk with a build-in tape recorder and repeated the language instruction from tape recorded lessons.

This was a coup for the school. These were the days before the computer revolution. Only the government had computers and an IBM was not a laptop but a large machine that filled a room and had less memory than an iPhone. Delaware Township had not yet become Cherry Hill, and Cherry Hill High School was still Delaware Township High School. Delaware Township was still mostly rural. Most of the dairy farms had not yet been converted into tract housing developments, but Delaware Township High School, not yet ten years old, had a language lab and an eccentric European professor to run it.

In 1960, the Latin Casino, the top night club in the Philadelphia area, moved from downtown Philadelphia to a new location, on Route 70, across from the Garden State Racetrack. The Latin Casino featured not just old fifties acts like Frank Sinatra, Joey Bishop and Dean Martin, but the Temptations, Smoky Robinson and Diana Ross and the Supremes, the big Motown acts. Then, in 1964, the Cherry Hill Mall opened. It was on the other side of the racetrack, across from the Cherry Hill Inn. The

Cherry Hill Mall was touted as the first enclosed shopping mall east of the Mississippi.[27] This was a big deal in a township of truck farms striving to become not more urban but more urbane, the essence of suburbia in the 1960s. When the Cherry Hill Mall opened, most everyone was proud.

Delaware Township was no longer a backwater, consisting of small farms outside of Haddonfield. Everyone wanted to come to the mall, the first mall, the Cherry Hill Mall. That's how the movement to change the name from Delaware Township to Cherry Hill started. I did not understand why people were so proud of a shopping center, but I was just a kid, rapidly becoming a rebellious kid. The argument went like this: there are lots of places named Delaware. Our township wasn't in Delaware. It wasn't on the Delaware River. Nor was it in Delaware County, and there were three Delaware counties in three different states, and Delaware Townships in several other states, too, but everybody knows the Cherry Hill Mall.

Even my father, never a fan of shopping, was swept up in the Cherry Hill Mall name change hysteria. That's how the high school I attended as a freshman, Delaware Township High School, became Cherry Hill High School in my sophomore year. It would become Cherry Hill West my senior year, 1966-1967, the year Cherry Hill East High School, the second high school opened, where Vivian went. This was a measure of how fast suburbanization was swallowing up the South Jersey farmlands and mostly pine forests, that the township required a second high school when the first one was barely a decade old.

Until the 1950s, high school students from Delaware Township attended Haddonfield High School in historic colonial Haddonfield. Haddonfield High School had an enrollment of well under a thousand students, even with a few hundred farm kids coming from neighboring rural Delaware Township. By 1954, there were 760 "guest students" from Delaware Township, a number that became so overwhelming that Haddonfield stopped accepting Delaware Township students. Delaware Township High School, the school that would become Cherry Hill High School and then Cherry Hill High School West, opened in 1956.

When I got to the high school, I was the son of the imminent and eccentric European professor. Everyone knew me as Dr. Fischer's son. It

---

27 The first modern indoor "climate controlled" shopping mall was the Southdale Center in Edina, Minnesota. The Cherry Hill Mall was the second.

was a role I did not want to play. I was no Bobby Yarrish. I did not want to be the rabbi's son or the teacher's son.

To the rest of the school, Dr. Fischer was viewed as a visionary who foresaw a future driven by technology, the technology that inspired America. Those were the days of the response to Sputnik, of the first space flights by Alan Shepard and John Glenn, and John Kennedy's challenge to the American people on May 25, 1961 to put a man on the moon. I saw my father as the man who got the Beatles wrong, dismissing them as "just a fad" and walking out of the room when we saw them for the first time on TV on the Ed Sullivan Show.

Father said the Beatles wouldn't last six months. It wasn't that he was wrong about the Beatles. It was that he was so dismissive, once again, of what was important to me. My response was to lose respect for him. I did not want to go to Hebrew School and I was never a very good Hebrew student. I was not interested, like my sister Vivian was. After school I wanted to be playing baseball and going to practice for Little League, not sitting in a classroom at Temple Emanuel. Instead, I was stuck in a Hebrew School class, sometimes with my father as the teacher. That was even worse than having him be the eccentric Dr. Fischer at my high school.

In order to have a bar mitzvah at Temple Emanuel in those days, we were required to attend a certain number of Shabbat services. Religious school ran from 9 to 11 Saturday mornings and the Shabbat morning services began right after beginning around 11:15. After services, the parents' carpools would pick us up. Most of the parents, including my parents, did not attend the services they required their children to attend. The religious school teachers had to maintain discipline the same way our teachers needed to police a study hall.

Some of us would slip out of the building, skip the services, and go to the coffeeshop in the motel next door to the temple. We called it "motel services". We knew what time services were over and knew when to be back, at the temple parking lot, where the carpools were picking us up. Even then I thought that it was hypocritical for parents to tell us it was important for us to go to services when they didn't go themselves, and I resented having to go. For many years, I harbored a real hostility to Jewish religious observance, feeling much like the boy who climbed onto the roof of synagogue in Philip Roth's short story "The Conversion of the Jews".

Not until I met Linda and began going to shul with her did I begin to change. The real change came when my father died, in 1986. As I've mentioned he always had said that the reason he had a son was so that he would have someone to say kaddish for him. I never thought much about that until he died. I said kaddish for him for the first time at the graveside at his funeral. I said it again that evening at sunset, stopped by the side of the road along the New Jersey Turnpike.

When I got home to Brookline, Linda told me that there were lots of places where I could say kaddish, and I should try them and see where I felt comfortable. I went to the Rebbe's, to Young Israel and to a few other places. I felt most welcomed at two places. One was Temple Beth Zion, which was nicknamed the Cake Shul by Shira and Miriam, who would sometimes join me. The other was Kadimah-Toras Moshe, where Jeffrey Houben greeted me when I came, introduced himself, and showed me how to put on tefillin, which I then did for the first time.

At Kadimah, which Shira and Miriam dubbed the Candy Shul, because of Meyer Hack,[28] I also came under the wing of **Rabbi Abraham Halbfinger**. He soon invited Linda and me to a shabbat lunch. He and Linda established a family connection: his daughter was married to David Reisman, the son of Itzik Reisman, a cousin of Linda's cousin, Gloria. That made us "family".

Before long Rabbi Halbfinger had me doing a legal brief for the shul. That case led to an appeal to the Supreme Judicial Court. I was a young lawyer then and that case was the first time I appeared before the Massachusetts state supreme court. It is my only reported case in the state Supreme Judicial Court in my forty years of active practice, *Kadimah-Toras Moshe v. DeLeo*.

Rabbi Halbfinger was also the chief rabbi of the Vaad HaRabbonim, the Beit Din, or Jewish religious court, for the Boston area. Rabbi Halbfinger

---

28 Meyer Hack, a Kadimah regular, was a Holocaust survivor who had his own story, documented by my friend and colleague Susie Davidson in her book *I Refused to Die* [https://www.amazon.com/ Refused-Die-Holocaust-Survivors-Concentration/dp/0972460144] recounting the stories of thirty Boston area holocaust survivor. Meyer was, for many years, the "candyman" at Kadimah-Toras Moshe. All the children in the shul knew where to find the "candyman", who kept a stash of candy in his tallit bag, which he would open to offer candy to children when they arrived at shul for shabbat services.

soon had me doing other legal work for the Vaad HaRabbonim. I represented the Vaad in a dispute over who owned several old torah scrolls
that were found behind a wall when the then run-down and abandoned
Vilna Shul building on Beacon Hill was renovated and restored. Rabbi
Halbfinger accepted every Jew as who they were. It did not matter to him
how religious or knowledgeable you were. Rabbi Halbfinger's attitude
was that it was his job, as a rabbi, to make it easier to be Jewish. He
made me feel comfortable not just in his shul, Kadimah-Toras Moshe,
but in any shul.

I ended up saying kaddish every day for my father every day. Every day.
Over the course of the eleven months that followed, I said kaddish in a
variety of places, from the shtiebel down the street from my cousin Stanley
Glantz' Brooklyn home, to the conservative synagogue in Burlington,
Vermont, whose members gathered a minyan for me when I was visiting
my friend, David Barrington.

Saying kaddish for my father every day made me think about him
every day, bringing me closer to him than I had been in many years.
Saying kaddish also taught me the daily prayers, something I had never
learned or done, and taught me the cycle of the Jewish holidays. I came
to understand the Jewish calendar and its relationship to the natural cycle
of the seasons and the rhythm of the changes of the moon. My father
tried to teach me to be a Jew, but our relationship did not allow him to
finish that job. Saying Kaddish allowed my father to complete his job
of teaching me to be a Jew. It also allowed me to begin rebuilding my
relationship with him.

When my mother, your Nana died, I said kaddish for her. When
Abe Fischer died, he no longer had a son to say kaddish for him, so I
said kaddish for him. After Solange died, I did not say kaddish for her
every day, but, in the year after her death, I said kaddish for her on
shabbat and holidays and at other times I was with a minyan for *tefillot*.
Now I say kaddish on my parents' yahrzeits and on the yahrzeits of Abe
and Solange and Maurice and Charles. I do not claim to be a religious
or observant Jew, but I do believe that not only is saying kaddish a way
of keeping alive the memories of my parents and family, but that I am
rewarded, that I gain something from saying kaddish.

CHAPTER 22

The Aftermath – Lodz and the Szylberstajn Family. "Don't Ask", but Your Good Deeds Will Be Rewarded

After the fighting had ended, and Litka had settled in her first home in London, Litka soon tried to track down and locate any family she had that may have still been alive. This was a difficult task. She did not know of any family that she might have had anywhere. She did not think that Myetek Kantor, whom she had married just days before the war started, could be alive. He was hot headed and had a quick temper. She was certain that he could not have survived the Soviet prisons and labor camps. Yet, she did not know for sure.

More than Myetek, to whom she had only been married for two weeks, Litka missed her family: her parents, her two brothers, Henry and Abram, and her sister, Manousha, "little Manya". Litka also had aunts and uncles, her father's nine siblings. She was very close to the younger ones, like Tola, and to her cousins, like Zlata. She had no idea what happened to any of them, the ones that were in Lodz, or the uncles who had left for Vienna, Harry and Adolphe. Litka truly felt like an orphan.

Later on she would warmly embrace her husband's family as if it could replace the family she had lost. In the meantime, she did what she could do to find anyone. Lidia felt like an orphan, with no family, which perhaps explains why she was so eager to reach out to Jan's family, Clara and Herman Glantz and Bernie and Helen Goldman, in Philadelphia and especially Jan's aunt, Ruth Glantz and cousin, Selma Heller, who generously taught Lidia American dress and fashion and so much more about American life. Generosity and kindness to others, basic *tzedakah*, was something she did not need to be taught.

In London, Litka had tried to locate any family. She wrote to friends and neighbors, anyone for whom she had an address in Lodz. The only person who responded was a Polish woman, Lola Servich, who lived in the same apartment building on Wschodnia Street. Lola wrote back in 1947. Lola's response was discouraging.

"Don't come back. There's nothing to come back to. Don't ask anything else."

Lidia did not know where else she could look.

As a child growing up, I knew about Nana's Polish friend, Lola, although I did not know her name then. I knew who Lola was because she had a son a little bit younger than me, perhaps a year or two. Nana would save my clothes and shoes when I outgrew them and she would send them to her friend, Lola, in Poland, for Lola's son, perhaps a couple of times a year. Nana would always send a package before Christmas. Nana did not send these things with any hope of a reward, but in the early 1960s, Lola became the link between Litka and her Uncle Adolphe when Lola ran into Sol Rusziewicz and told him that Litka was alive in America. Once again, despite all the suffering, all the losses, all the tragedy, good deeds do get rewarded, as my father would say, only you never know where or when.

CHAPTER 23

Nana's Uncles Find Her

The hero of this chapter is Sal Rusziewicz. He was married to Nana's aunt, Ruzia, or Rachel. Ruzia had one young son, Monyek, or Maurice, and perhaps a second son. They were killed in the Shoah, but Ruzia's husband, Sal Rusziewicz survived. After the war, Sal, Sol, or "Salek", now a widower, returned to Lodz and remarried, this time to another Jewish woman from Lodz. She was from the Abramowitz family, a well-known family in Lodz before the war, and Nana knew her before the war. In fact Nana dated and almost married her brother. Sal and his new wife were moving to Brussels, where they would live for many years, and where they had two sons. Before leaving Lodz for Brussels, Sal either sought out Lola Servich or just ran into her while still in Lodz. Sal knew her because she had lived on Wschodnia Street, near the Szylberstajns, and had been a friend of his first wife, Ruzia, Nana's Aunt Ruzia.

Sal and Lola exchanged pleasantries and chatted during the meeting. Lola congratulated Sal on his new marriage and Sal told her that he and his new wife would be moving to Belgium, where they planned to live in Brussels. In the course of the conversation, Lola then made an offhanded remark about someday visiting Litka, Ruzia's niece. Sal's face must have brightened up at this mention of Litka and he inquired further. Lola then explained that she was in touch with Ruzia's niece, Litka, who was alive in America.

Sometime later, perhaps years later, after 1960, Sal Rusziewicz was in Paris where he saw a poster for a concert of Viennese music, featuring the conductor Adolphe Sibert. He recognized the photo of "Adolphe Sibert" as his first wife's brother, Adolphe Szylberstajn. Sol went to the concert, and after the concert, he went backstage and met with his former brother-in-law. He and Adolphe chatted, and in the course of the conversation, he told Adolphe that his niece, Litka, was alive and living in America.

Ruzia Szylberstajn Rusziewicz

After getting Litka's married name and address, Adolphe contacted his brother, Harry, in Miami. He gave Harry Nana's married name and address, which he had obtained from Lola Servich. Harry started composing a letter asking "Are you the daughter of my brother Joseph", but his younger sister, Tola, could not wait. Thus came the phone call Vivian and I will never forget.

There are very few earthshaking events that we remember where we were when we heard. If you were born before 1992, you know where you were when you learned that planes had crashed into the World Trade Center on September 11, 2001. Likewise, every one of us old enough to remember can tell you where we were on November 22, 1963, when we heard that John F. Kennedy was shot. The third such earthshattering event that I remember was the phone call that evening after dinner one day in 1962.

We were sitting at the kitchen table after dinner and the phone rang. Nana was sitting at her usual spot and picked up the receiver from the wall when it rang. There was no caller ID back then. Nana said hello and listened to the reply. I will never forget the look of shocked surprise, followed by a smile of joy on Nana's face when she heard who it was. I had never seen her smile like that. She was no longer an orphan. It was like her family had come back from the dead.

Within a few months, in August 1962, Adolphe's two children, Jean Claude and Lilian, came to visit. They came by boat, landing in New York, and then traveled to Cherry Hill. It was very special for all of us. For Nana, she was no longer an orphan: she now had her own family. For me, I had always felt a little different. I was not born in America, and my parents were not American, and I felt different, even from the other Jewish kids. Now I not only had newly discovered cousins, but they were European. Jean Claude was young and handsome and Lilian was young and beautiful and a singer, a chanteuse. They were French, charming and a bit exotic.

Jean Claude and Anna 1962

I remember the first dinner we had when Jean Claude and Lilian arrived. We wanted to show Jean Claude and Lilian a real American meal. Nana made hamburgers and corn on the cob. It was going well until Jan passed the corn on the cob to Jean Claude. Jean Claude's smile turned to an odd look of amazement and disgust. We were confused at what was happening until Jean Claude managed to ask why we were serving him pig food. In France, we learned, corn on the cob is considered a food for pigs, not humans.

Despite that faux pas, the visit was wonderful. Vivian and I, young kids as we were at the time, were enchanted with these new sophisticated French cousins and Nana could not have been happier. Now she had family, too. I can still picture the way her face glowed with the broad smile that appeared when she had answered the phone a few months earlier.

Soon after Jean Claude and Lilian's visit, Nana flew to Miami to see her Uncle Harry. She was amazed that she recognized him immediately as she got off the plane, even though she had not seen him since he left Lodz for Vienna before the war. I think Nana also saw Tola then for the first time since 1939. I am not sure of this, as she flew to Miami to see Harry and Tola was living in Orlando. My memory is that Tola drove to Miami to see Nana. This was a much longer drive in 1962 or 1963 than it is now.

Nana first learned from Tola that her father and younger brother Abram were shot and killed in the street of the ghetto, in Radom or Lodz. She would soon hear confirmation from Solange that her brother and father were both shot in the street in Radom. But she never learned what happened to mother, or her younger sister, or her older half-brother, Henry. She only knew that they died. They died like all the other Szylberstajns who had also perished.

CHAPTER 24
The Sad, Sad Tale of Tola and Martin

Tola was the eighth of the ten Sylberstajn siblings, the much younger sister of her older brothers, Joseph and Maurice, Nana's father and Solange's father. Tola was closer in age to her two nieces, Litka and Zlata, than to her older siblings. Growing up she lived in her parents' apartment, downstairs from Litka and across the courtyard from Zlata. She was more like another sister than an aunt to them, just as Herman was more like an older brother than an uncle to Jan. Both Nana and Solange were very close to Tola growing up and they both always spoke very fondly of her. When they remembered Tola in our conversations around Solange's kitchen table, it was always with both affection and great sadness.

Tola

Nana was very pleased to have her Aunt Tola back in her life in the early 1960s. Aunt Tola's presence gave Nana a piece of her family that she had sorely missed for over twenty years. Nana had grown up with Tola. Spending time with her again, after so many years, made her feel that she was no longer an orphan, that she had her own family again. Although Tola's brothers Harry and Adolphe found Nana, they had left Lodz for Vienna around the time Nana was born, so she barely knew them. It was Tola whom Nana knew so well growing up. Nana had been close to Solange as well, but Solange was far away, across the ocean in Europe.

Tola was in the United States, in Orlando, Florida, just a phone call away, not across the ocean, in a foreign country. In those days before the internet, cell phones, and WhatsApp, the world was not yet a global village. International travel was not cheap or easy and overseas phone calls were unusual and expensive. Nana could talk to Tola on the phone, albeit long-distance, and she was where they were able to visit and see each other more easily.

The first time that Vivian and I flew on an airplane was when we visited Tola for the first time. It was something special, not just because we were meeting this long lost and newly discovered family. Air travel in the early sixties was not like it is today. Flying was still new, unusual and expensive. In those days, people dressed up in a suit and tie or a nice dress to fly. The meals were not frozen TV dinners, either, and the silverware was not plastic and the glasses were glass. Flying was still special.

Vivian and I both remember Tola well. We remember fondly the times we spent staying in her Orlando home. Those were special vacations. The first time, when Vivian and I first met Tola and Martin, the whole family flew down to Orlando together, but after that, we sometimes flew down with Nana and father stayed home to work and joined us later.

All in all, we spent several summers in Orlando. During these visits, we had the chance to watch Nana and Tola together. It was Tola's two brothers, Adolphe and Harry, who found Nana, but it was from Tola that Nana learned what had happened in Lodz to their family. More important, Nana again had someone from her past. They talked about their life in Lodz and about their family and growing up, much as Nana would later talk with Solange. At the time I did not realize how important that was to Nana, but, even as children, Vivian and I could feel the joy the two of them felt from being with each other again.

Tola doted on us. She learned what our favorite foods were and cooked especially what we liked. While we appreciated her warmth, we were children and did not realize at that time how important this re-connection was to Tola, as well as to Nana. It was Tola whom Vivian and I knew as our mother's family. We met Harry, and both his first wife Gustie, and his second wife, Mayme, from Cuba, whom he married after Gustie died. Mayme was from Cuba and had been his secretary for many years.

Harry gave his attention to his newly rediscovered niece, Litka, more than her two little children, Vivian and me. Later his time would be pre-occupied with Martin. So we never really got to know Harry. For Vivian and me, the face of the new family our mother had reclaimed was Tola.

Tola had a newer and fancier home than our modest Woodcrest home. The living room had large picture windows and sliding glass doors that opened to the patio and the swimming pool. The pool took up much of the back yard. Tola's son, Martin, Vivian and I spent many hours of the hot and muggy Florida summer days in and out of the pool.

Martin, like Steve Goldman, was just a few years older than me, and in the same way that I looked up to Steve as an older brother, I came to look up to Martin. He was joyful, irreverent, and always fun to be with. We spent quite a bit of time together, with Martin and Tola coming to our Woodcrest home for extended visits as well, but Tola's Orlando home, with the pool, was a measure of greater financial success than we knew in Woodcrest. At the time, it seemed that Tola had a happy and successful life.

Orlando was a very different place then in the 1960s, before Disney World, which would transform what was more of a southern redneck town than a Florida resort. Orlando was the largest city in Orange County, but that was not saying much, as pre-Disney, Orange County was aptly named, consisting largely of orange groves that had once been plantations. Like much of northern Florida, Orlando was rooted in the plantation culture of the south. Nonetheless, it was Florida, and there were tourist attractions, although the tourist attractions in Orlando were somewhat tackier than the hotels and beaches in Miami Beach, Ft. Lauderdale, or Tampa.

Tola and her husband Henry took us to all the tourist sites. We saw the mermaid shows at nearby Weeki Wachee Springs and the glass-bottom boats, underwater ballet, and water-skiing shows at Sanlando Springs.

Orlando in those days was more like the deep south. Orlando was a typical southern town like Valdosta or Waycross in Georgia, Tuscaloosa in Alabama or Hattiesburg, Mississippi, with a hot and dusty main street where many of the stores were owned by Jews, who had arrived as peddlers, and who then grew their businesses into successful brick and mortar stores and settled down. These merchants built a small Jewish community in Orlando, as in other similar towns.

Tola had opened just such a store. Stephens Clothing Store was a haberdashery, a clothing store, in downtown Orlando. It was small and the aisles were crowded, filled with shirts, slacks, shoes, and other items of apparel. In those days of racial segregation, the store catered to an African-American clientele. Sometime in the 1950s, Tola married Henry Lishner, her third husband. She became Tola Lishner and he helped her run the store. While it appeared that Tola had found a happy life after her struggles, this period of success and happiness was short-lived and illusory.

Tola had been married the first time in Poland, shortly before the war but before "going to the camps", as Jean Claude would later recount to me, but this was not a marriage of love. It was a marriage the family wanted. This older husband was taken by the Nazis first. According to Jean Claude, he died, not surviving very long in the camps. As best I know, Tola remained in Lodz, and was still there when her older brothers, Maurice and Joseph, fled with their spouses and children to Radom. According to Solange, at some point Tola jumped off a train on the way to Treblinka, probably one of the trains that transported close to two hundred thousand victims from the train station at the edge of the Lodz ghetto to the camps.

Perhaps the train was going to Chelmno and not Treblinka, as the transports taking Jews and others from the Lodz ghetto, went mostly to Chelmno, the first of the Nazi death camps, located only some 35 miles from Lodz, and not to the Auschwitz complex where Treblinka was located. The transports to Treblinka were mostly from the Warsaw Ghetto. So the train to Treblinka from which Tola jumped likely was not the train from Lodz. Maybe it was not the train to Treblinka but the train from Treblinka? To where?

In any event, after Tola jumped out of the train through an open window, she was captured. As I understood the story, she was naked when she jumped, although this may not be accurate, as clothes were usually not removed until victims entered the gas chamber "showers". After she was recaptured, she jumped from a train a second time, only to be captured again. Tola was a gutsy woman.

Somehow, Tola not only survived her time in the camps, but in the camps, Tola met the true love of her life, Shlomo Gasior. Tola and Shlomo were married. When the Nazis surrendered and they got to a DP camp, a Displaced Person camp, Tola was pregnant. Once again she showed how gutsy she was. She asked to use the phone, and called 911, Information, and asked for the listing for her older brother, Harry, whom she knew was in the United States. She said something like "I am pregnant and in a DP camp, but I have family. I have a brother in America. Can you give me his phone number?"

Tola knew her brother, Harry, and his wife, Gustie, had come to the United States. Gustie had family somewhere in the United States, an uncle or cousin, maybe in Pennsylvania. Did Tola know this? Did she know that her brother Harry was, by then, in Miami? Or that he had Anglicized his name from Szylberstajn to Silby? Harry Szylberstajn had anglicized his surname to Silby, but the Red Cross found the listing for Harry Silby in Miami, gave Tola his number, and allowed her to call him in the United States. Harry immediately made arrangements for her and her new husband to come to the United States.

The newlyweds sailed from Bremen on May 29, 1947, on a ship named the Marine Marlin. They are listed in the Ellis Island Alien Passenger manifest as Sewer Gasior and Tola Gasior, husband and wife, with her brother Harry's address in Miami. They landed at Ellis Island on June 7, 1947. Tola's son, Martin, was born a few months later, on August 31, 1947. Just as life began looking up for Tola, her husband Shlomo, the true love of her life, died of an illness he contracted shortly after they arrived in America, about the time that their son, Martin, was born.

Tola never overcame the loss of her beloved Shlomo Gasior. Her brother, Harry, helped her establish herself, financially, so that she could open her store and make a living. In the early 1950s, as a widow with a small child, she sailed to France to visit Adolphe, her other surviving brother. Jean Claude remembers Tola visiting twice in the early 1950s, when he was still a boy. He also remembers his father, Adolphe, taking everyone for a holiday to Néris le Bain. Jean Claude remembers fondly his aunt who adored her little boy, Martin. He also remembers Martin, his American cousin, whom he first met when they were both small boys.

Over the years, Jean Claude would often ask me about Martin, and if I knew what happened to Martin. It was Jean Claude who prompted me, in 2013, after many years, to ask my investigator, to find out what had happened to Martin. That is how I found out that Martin had died, June 27, 1981. Jean Claude asking me is what finally got me to find out the answer to a question that had been troubling me, too.

Martin was already troubled by the time I met him, although I did not realize it at the time. Martin was having problems in school, he did not get along with his stepfather Henry, and Tola was having a hard time controlling him. Martin was beginning high school and Tola was worried. She turned to Jan for advice. In fact, I later realized that one of the reasons Martin was spending time with us was so Jan could identify Martin's needs and address them.

At the time, I was in Boy Scouts. I not only enjoyed being a scout. I also I learned many valuable life skills in the scouts: how to start a fire, how to tie knots, how to gauge heights and distances. The two or three one week sessions of Boy Scout Camp, at the Pine Hill Boy Scout Reservation were the only summer camps I ever attended, and I loved them. Father wanted Martin to attend boy scout camp with me, but Martin was not interested. Martin was interested in professional wrestling, which was as phony then as it is now. He and I both were big fans of a professional wrestler named Antonino Rocco. My father made a deal with Martin: He agreed to take us (Martin and me) to a professional wrestling match, if Martin would go to Boy Scout camp.

There was talk about Martin staying with us and going to Cherry Hill High School, where my father could watch over him in a way that his stepfather would not. I would have loved that. It would have been like having a big brother move in. But my father thought that sending Martin to a military academy would be better for him: that it would instill in Martin the discipline that he needed. My father and Martin visited several military academies in Connecticut and New York State. I think Martin may have attended one very briefly, but he was not happy with the idea of a military academy. He returned to Orlando where he attended Boone High School.

After graduating high school, Martin attended college in St. Louis, but left after a while, returning to Florida. He was clearly troubled. He was not staying with his mother, as Henry accused Martin of assaulting him. Unable to keep him at home, Tola again sent Martin to Cherry Hill, to my parents, again hoping Jan could help. I did not see him then, as by then I was away at college.

I did not know much about what was going on with Martin at that time. My father did not talk to me much about Martin. My father was already too worried about me becoming a "hippie" and "dropping out" like Martin. My father was convinced that Martin's problems were from smoking pot and taking LSD and he was afraid Martin would be a bad influence on me. It was the 1960s, the era of "tune in, turn on and drop out". It was easy to blame Martin's problems on "drugs", and miss Martin's deeper problems.

When Martin attacked my father in our living room, the police came. Martin was arrested but there were no criminal charges. Instead, Martin was committed to a mental hospital, rather than jailed, although there may not have been much of a difference, given what we know today of conditions in mental hospitals at that time. I don't know if this was the first, but it certainly was not the only time that Martin was committed to a mental hospital. I found, among my father's papers, an undated letter Martin wrote to me from Florida State Hospital in Chattahoochee, Florida. I don't know whether this was before or after Martin was committed to Ancora State Psychiatric Hospital, in New Jersey. The last time I saw Martin was when I visited him in Ancora. He was in a locked cell, behind a heavy steel door, with a small window about face high, with bars, through which we talked.

In 1969, Tola committed suicide by jumping from a window. After losing her one love, she put all her hopes and dreams into their one son. Tola's need for him may have been more than she could handle. In the end, this strong and courageous woman, who was able to survive Auschwitz, could not survive her broken heart.

Martin died June 27, 1981. Like Jean Claude, I still think of him with sadness.

CHAPTER 25

Reunion in Paris

In 1965, Nana went to London and Paris, with Vivian, then eleven years old, and saw Adolphe, his family, and Salonge and her husband, Albert. After Nana and Vivian visited Nana's post war friends Ellen Butler and Stella Hoskins in London, they joined my father, in Paris. My father, still head of the language department at what had just become Cherry Hill High School, had taken a job consulting with the Foreign Language League, a Utah company that operated summer language programs in France and other European countries. This job paid for him to fly to Europe, where he oversaw the language instruction at the various student campuses, which were at French schools that were otherwise closed for the summer, and at other European locations, as well.

I was able to attend the program as his son. This way, I spent six weeks that summer, 1965, in France. The first three weeks were in a school in Villard-de-Lans, a small town in the French Alps, close to Grenoble. I attended French classes there with a group of American high school students, all of us away from home and from our parents rules for the first time.

After the three weeks in Villard-de-Lans, we visited Paris on the way to Rheims, where we would study French for another three weeks. Rheims presented quite a contrast to the rural campus in Villard-de-Lans, a small village in the French Alps. Rheims, a major city not very far from Paris, was the home of one of the great French Gothic cathedrals. The cathedral, the centerpiece of the city, was truly awesome.

My first time in Paris was at the end of that summer program. My father, Jan, met me in Rheims, and brought me to Paris, where we joined Nana and Vivian. I met Adolphe and his French wife, Maggie, visiting them at their apartment on Rue Félicien David. By this time Adolphe was no longer a young man and had grown shorter, but he still radiated an energy, a passionate creative energy. You could feel the creativity overflowing from him. He was a brilliant man that we all admired.

I was not there when Nana and Adolphe saw each other, for the first time after so many years, but I have heard from Lilian and from Solange that it was quite a memorable event. Adolphe looked at Litka and recognized his niece instantly. Then he broke into tears. He was taken aback at how much his niece looked like his mother, Nana's grandmother, and he could not hold back the tears as he cried "Mama, Mama". Based on this reaction, Solange thought that this was the first time Nana had ever seen Adolphe.

It is easy to understand why Solange may have thought, from his response, that Adolphe was seeing Litka for the first time. Adolphe had left Lodz to seek his fortune as a musician in Vienna, not long after Nana was born, in 1916, certainly before Solange was born in 1922. By the time Solange was old enough to remember Adolphe, he was well settled in Vienna, and her early memories of Adolphe must have been from visiting him in Vienna with her mother. Jean Claude also did not think that Nana knew Adolphe in Lodz, as she was still a small child when Abram left Lodz to become Adolphe in Vienna and he did not think his father ever returned to Lodz, after leaving for Vienna.

Solange and Jean Claude were mistaken. Nana spoke often of knowing Adolphe when she was growing up in Lodz. Adolphe returned home frequently to visit his mother. His niece Litka, first as a child aspiring to be a dancer, and then as a young lady who had become the dancer, looked forward to these visits from her uncle, the violinist and band leader who was already on the road to becoming the master of Viennese waltzes.

It was on this visit that I met Adolphe and Maggie for the first time. When Adolphe met me for the first time, he broke into tears, saying "Joseph, Joseph". His reaction confirmed what Solange has said so many times: I look like my grandfather, Nana's father Joseph. I am very proud of this, as he was quite a handsome and dignified man, according to everyone who knew him, and from the picture of him that hangs in our home.

In the few days I was in Paris on that first visit, we had several big family meals together at Adolphe and Maggie's apartment, at 14 Rue Félicien-David, where I saw both Lilian and Jean Claude. It was also on that trip at Adolphe and Maggie's apartment where I met Solange for the first time.

We did not go to Solange's house on that visit. Much to my disappointment, I did not meet her sons Maurice or Charles on that trip. That would not come until many years later. Nana did not explain why. I suspected and Solange later confirmed that my father feared that Solange's husband, Albert, would be a bad influence on me, because he was a communist.

I would return to Adolphe's apartment for many more visits. The discussions were always lively and stimulating and the subjects philosophical and controversial. Multi-lingual conversations were a necessity as there was no language everyone knew. French was always the principal language, but there was usually someone who knew no French, such as Nana. She would speak in Polish, and Solange would answer in Polish or Yiddish. This left out Maggie, who spoke only French, Lilian, who spoke French and some English, and Jean Claude, who spoke French and English. None of them understood either Polish or Yiddish. Jan Bernard was in his milieu in this setting, as only he understood everything that was said.

Like Adolphe, who was so overjoyed to host his niece, Solange also hosted a dinner for Litka, her long lost cousin. I was not there, so it must have been either before or after my few days in Paris. I think it was before I was in Paris. Solange seated her cousin, Litka, with her husband, Jan at head of table, but Nana refused to sit there, declining the honor and insisting that Adolphe deserved to be seated at the head of table. Solange's mother, Manya, objected.

This was not the first time that Manya slighted Adolphe in Paris. Four of Manya's brothers, the Luxembourgs, had settled in Paris before the war and had brought Manya, and her daughter, Zlata, to Paris. The Luxembourg brothers were quite successful financially. They had built several businesses, including a clothing store. Some years before my mother's visit, in the early 1950s, when Adolphe, with a wife and two young children, was still struggling financially, with two young children, he had asked Manya if she or her brothers could help him get a suit for Jean Claude's first communion. They refused.

Jean Claude has told me this story more than once, which I take as a measure of how hurt he was by this slight. The slight was not to him, however. It was to his father. Nor did the slight involve Solange, whom Adolphe did not really know until he came to Paris.

According to Nana, Solange's four uncles, the Luxembourgs, the four brothers of Chacha Manya, Solange's mother, Miriam, were not willing to give a confirmation suit to Adolphe's Christian son. This is the way that Jean Claude tells the story, as well. Was that the real reason for this slight? Perhaps it was not about a communion suit. Perhaps Manya still remembered Adolphe's involvement in her husband's affairs in Vienna.

CHAPTER 26
Adolphe the Philosopher

Over the next years, both Vivian and I had the great pleasure of spending time with Adolphe in the country cottage in a small village, Bridoire, in the province of Savoie, in the French Alps, near the Swiss and Italian borders. The cottage had been in Maggie's family for over a century. It was a quiet cottage in the country, a short walk from the village center. Vivian spent two weeks there, with Adolphe and Maggie in the summer of 1971, after a week in Paris. It was French immersion for her, as neither Adolphe nor Maggie spoke any English. Nor did Solange. Vivian's French was much improved after this trip that summer.

My time with Uncle Adolphe came in the summer of 1976, when I was returning from my first trip to Israel. I had arrived in France but my luggage had not. It had gone to Iran instead of France. I don't think I ever recovered the luggage, but Uncle Adolphe, who first came to Paris in a much more precarious situation than mine, told me not to worry about the luggage.

"You can always buy new clothes. You can replace your underwear," he said, smiling.

Those few days in Savoie were wonderful. Each morning Uncle Adolphe, then well into his seventies, picked up his walking cane and put on his hat. Then he turned to me and said "come, we are going walking."

We would walk to the market where the farmers were selling their fresh produce in the village center and bought fruit and vegetables for dinner. The main purpose of the walk was for Adolphe to talk with me, about life, music, art, politics, family and anything else relevant to the times, our lives and my life. The walk, the exercise, and the shopping were secondary.

Adolphe was a musician, but he was also a philosopher and an artist. He was a thinker and a true romantic. Not just Jean Claude and Lilian, but Nana, and Vivian and I, the more we got to know him, all saw this artist and intellect as the patriarch of the family. He was quite content to accept this role as the grand old man of the family. Aside from placing in proper context the loss of a suitcase of replaceable clothing, Adolphe wanted to know about me, my romance and this choice I was making to marry Linda. He was concerned with my life's plans and how I viewed myself and my future. I was grateful to Uncle Adolphe for his interest in me, his niece Litka's son, but more than that, I was awed with his thoughtfulness and his ability to put things in a perspective that was both personal but also reflected a broad and thoughtful philosophy of life and art.

This was something he passed on to his daughter, Lilian. After my several days with Uncle Adolphe and Aunt Maggie in Savoie, I took the train to Paris, where I stayed overnight with Lilian before flying home. That night, explaining why I was coming from Israel, I told Lilian about my romance with Linda, and this led to a long, all night, discussion, more in French than in English, about love and romance and passion and relationships, about our philosophies of love and life, much like the discussions with her father, Adolphe, except that this discussion took place over wine late into the night in an apartment in Paris, rather than while walking down the mountain to the market in the Savoie village of Bridoire.

In my subsequent visits to Paris after that, I have had many similar long and wonderful conversations with Lilian, who had become Anna. These conversations took place at her favorite cafes in her favorite neighborhoods of Paris, especially St. Germain de Prés, or in her small but charming apartment on 4 Rue Blumenthal, just a short walk from where her parents lived, at 14 Rue Félicien-David. Our conversations always covered a broad range of topics: from life to love, to art, to poetry, and to music.

CHAPTER 27

Adolphe's Escape, From Vienna to Paris

Upon his older brother Harry's invitation and urging, Adolphe, then still a teenager named Abram, came to Vienna perhaps as early as the beginning of World War I in1914. Lilian thought that her father came to Vienna at the age of twelve, with his older brother, Harry, who would have been fifteen at the time. Jean Claude was certain that their father came before Archduke Franz Ferdinand was shot, the event which was the beginning of World War I.

In Vienna, the young Abram Szylberstajn, still a teenager, gave up his given name, Abram, or Abraham, and became Adolphe, Adolphe Siberth. The two brothers, Harry and Adolphe, lived quite happily for some years in Vienna. There was even talk of Adolphe marrying Harry's wife Gustave's sister. It turned out to be Adolphe's misfortune that he did not do so.

In the1920s, before the rise of Nazism, Vienna was a good place for Jews. A beautiful old city, Vienna had been the capital of the powerful multi-national Habsburg dynasty for five centuries. After the fall of the Habsburg Empire at the end of the First World War, in 1918, Vienna became the capital of the new but much smaller Republic of Austria. The Jewish population of Vienna in the 1930s, was more than 180,000. It may have been as high as 200,000. It was more than 10 percent of Vienna's total population of 1,900,000 and Vienna was an important center of Jewish culture and education. Many Viennese Jews were well-integrated into urban society and culture. Jews made up significant percentages of the city's doctors and lawyers, businessmen and bankers, artists and journalists.

This was why Harry and Adolphe had migrated to Vienna from Lodz. Harry, while unable to become a doctor, was quite successful as a pharmacist and chemist. His younger brother, who had become Adolphe in Vienna, was also doing well, having begun his way down the road to becoming the maestro of Viennese waltzes, operettas and what is known as *"musique légère"*, or "light" classical music.

When he first arrived in Vienna, the teenaged Adolphe made a living as a busker, a street musician, playing his violin mostly at outdoor sidewalk cafes. He earned enough for tuition at the National Academy for Music and Art, where he was a private student of Bronislav Hubermann.[29]

In 1923, Adolphe was awarded a first prize for his violin performances, while completing studies in piano, counterpoint, harmony and composition, and then second level piano. He was also conducting the school orchestra, together with Wilhelm Furtwängler and Clement Krauss, who both went on to fame as conductors. While a student at the National Academy, Adolphe audited courses at the University of Vienna in philosophy, literature, and anatomy, and most notably, courses with Sigmund Freud.

Adolphe played violin for tips in sidewalk cafes while attending the Academy. Soon he was leading small ensembles of five, six, or seven musicians playing Viennese waltzes and other light classical music in larger cafes. Adolphe continued to perform this style over his long career of some sixty years. Between 1929 and 1931, he performed in numerous concerts as a violinist and also assembled a jazz orchestra, with which he made a number of recordings.

Adolphe graduated from the Academy of Music in 1930, receiving his diploma as an orchestra conductor. In 1932, he obtained, with the assistance of Richard Strauss, a position as a conductor with Vienna Radio, a position he would hold until he fled Vienna in 1938. Adolphe's social circle in Vienna included the writers Thomas Mann and Arthur Schnitzler and he was friends with the composers Franz Lehár, Emmerich Kálmán, and Robert Stolz, in addition to Richard Strauss. Adolphe earned a reputation as a tireless worker and dedicated musician in Vienna.

---

29 Hubermann would later emigrate to Palestine, where, in 1936 he founded the Palestine Symphony Orchestra. In 1948 it became the Israel Philharmonic Orchestra.

This world changed dramatically in March 1938, when Nazi Germany incorporated the Austrian Republic in what became known as the *Anschluss*. Harry had seen the writing on the wall and had left for America in 1933 or 1934, where Harry's wife, Gustave, had family. They may have returned to Vienna briefly before the war, but they were settled in the States by March 1938 and thus did not face the *Anschluss* and its aftermath in Vienna.

Adolphe did not fare so well. Instead of marrying Gustave's sister, Adolphe had married an Austrian Catholic, the marriage he had hidden from his mother, Bronya Poznanski Szylberstajn. This marriage did not last. Adolphe stayed in Vienna with his Catholic wife too long, not leaving until 1938, when he crossed the border into Switzerland with little other than a valise with some clothes, his passport, his violin, and some money. He had left his savings and all his other belongings with his wife. The plan was that she would settle his affairs, sell off everything and then join him after he found a place to settle down. Instead she sold all Adolphe's possessions, took the money, then asked the Nazis to annul the marriage. Then she married Adolphe's best friend.

Switzerland was not taking Jewish refugees. Adolphe passed from Switzerland through Italy and found his way to Nice, where he was in touch with a Poznanski cousin, also married to a Catholic. This cousin had fled Vienna ahead of Adolphe and passed through Nice before moving on to Morocco, and eventually to the United States. This Poznanski cousin was a dentist, but he had to retake his exams to practice in the United States. After he died, his wife returned to Vienna, where Jean Claude visited her. She was living in a small apartment, very poor after having been quite wealthy when they lived in Vienna before the war.

Through his Poznanski cousin, Adolphe was put into contact with a Frenchman who had a cousin, Maggie, who kept what Jean Claude described as "not exactly a small hotel". It must have been something more modest and less formal than a hotel, perhaps better described in English as a rooming house or an inn, or a house with rooms and breakfast rented to boarders. It was something less formal than a hotel. At great risk to herself, this young lady, Maggie took in Jewish boarders.

Born around 1910, Maggie was somewhere between 28 and 30 years old at the time Adolphe knocked at her door. Maggie was born in Lyons but grew up in Bridoire. She was raised by her grandparents in a small cottage built by her grandfather in 1840. Her mother worked making wire in a factory in Lyons and was unable to care for her. Maggie's mother died of cancer in 1935, a year after her father died. In the late 1930s, Maggie left the cottage in Bridoire and joined her brother, her only sibling, in Nice. There she found work at the "hotel" or rooming house. By1938, she was managing it.

At risk to herself, Maggie was sheltering Jewish refugees, some passing through quickly and other staying longer. She was rewarded when a short but handsome and quite charming Viennese violinist, Adolphe Sibert, sought shelter at the inn. They were immediately attracted to each other. They met in 1939. She soon was pregnant. They were married in February 1940 and Jean Claude was born the next month, in March 1940. Jean Claude's godmother was the wife of Adolphe's Poznanski dentist cousin.

Adolphe and Maggie remained very happily married for the next fifty years, the rest of their long lives. One would hardly have predicted, from the way things started and the challenges they faced and overcame in the first years of their marriage, it would be such a long happy marriage.

While he was in Nice, Adolphe became active in the French Resistance. This led to his being arrested in 1942 and taken to the Camp de Milles. Although the **Camp de Milles** was in Vichy France it was operated by the Nazis. The camp was located near Aix, within Archbishop Paul Remond's jurisdiction. Most of the Jews taken to the Camp des Milles were deported to concentration camps, but Adolphe was among those who escaped this fate due to the efforts of Monsignor Remond. Then the Archbishop of Nice, Monsignor Remond would later become Cardinal Remond.

Upon his release, Adolphe was sheltered by and then became active in CAR (the *Comité d'Accueil des Réfugiés*, or Committee to Welcome Refuges). CAR was an organization that aided Jewish refugees arriving in Nice, both those staying and those passing through, out of Europe. It was through CAR that Adolphe met Monsignor Remond, who was responsible for Adolphe's rescue, among many others, as well.

Archbishop Remond, has been recognized at Yad Vashem as a righteous gentile, for the work he did rescuing many Jews, but most famously for his rescue of many Jewish children, whose parents had been deported from the Camp de Milles. After Odette Rosenstock and Moussa Abadi, two Parisian Jews who had fled to Nice, informed the Archbishop about these orphaned Jewish children in 1943, **Archbishop Remond** arranged for the rescue of over 500 Jewish children from the Camp de Milles. On good terms with the Vichy French government under Marshall Petain, Archbishop Remond was able to take these children from the Camp de Milles and hide them in convents and other church facilities. These children were then scattered and placed in the homes of Catholic parishioners.

Many other Jews were also kept hidden in Nice through the grace of CAR and of Archbishop Remond. These included Adolphe Sibert, according to the AJPN, a French/Jewish organization whose name is an acronym for "Anonymous, Just and Persecuted by the Nazi". The AJPN described Adolphe on its website as *"chef d'orchestre Viennois, qui deviendra agent de liaison et secrétaire"*, which in English is "Viennese conductor who would become the liaison and secretary" to Archbishop Remond.

Although the AJPN does not directly say so, the implication is that Adolphe was the Archbishop's liaison to the French underground, quite an important role. In his other role, as "secretary" to the Archbishop, Adolphe was protected from arrest, at least while in the sanctuary of church buildings, but this did not protect him from all danger of arrest.

While Maggie was still in the hospital with newborn Lilian Anna and Adolphe was home, caring for Jean Claude, the local butcher turned him over to the police. Adolphe was arrested with his two-year-old son, Jean Claude, in his arms. Adolphe and Jean Claude were taken to the *commissariat*, the local police station. The sergeant in charge looked at Adolphe and recognized the maestro of Viennese waltzes. The sergeant said that he loved classical music and asked, "Are you Adolphe Sibert, the musician from Vienna?" He then went on about how much he adored Adolphe's music.

Adolphe said, "Let me go home and I will bring you some of my recordings."

The sergeant answered, "Why should I believe you?" but he let Adolphe go.

Adolphe returned with some of his recordings and gave them to the sergeant, who pointed to the back door, saying "Tonight this door will be unlocked. If you don't go, I can't do anything more for you."

He then got up and left the room. Adolphe exited quickly. He never looked back.

This was when Adolphe decided it was time to leave Nice. Nice is not far from the border of Italy, then controlled by the Fascist leader Mussolini, an ally of Hitler. Nice, which had been a safe refuge, was becoming more dangerous as Italian soldiers massed on the border. The arrest by the Vichy French was too close a call. Adolphe and Maggie locked the flat where they were living, left everything behind and hastily fled. They got out just in time. The Germans occupied Nice on September 9, 1943, and Gestapo agents commanded by Alois Brunner launched a brutal manhunt for Jews.

Maggie took Adolphe and their two little children to Savoie. For the duration of the war, they rented a cottage near the small cottage in Bridoire that Maggie's grandfather had built in Savoie, then occupied by Maggie's uncle and brother. With Adolphe unable to work, these years were hard, but they were safe in the small cottage, tucked away in the Alps. There were few German or Italian soldiers that far from the urban centers, off the beaten path.

In 1945, at the end of the war, Adolphe and Maggie returned to their apartment in Nice. Everything was just as they had left it. They spent the next five years in Nice. Adolphe became the Conductor for Viennese Music at Radio Nice, but this was not a full-time position and Adolphe had a hard time supporting a wife and two children. Viennese waltz music had gone out of style. In the winters of 1946 and 1947, Adolphe found some work playing in casinos during the winter ski season in Savoie-Chamonix, but that was not enough work. After five years of struggling, the family left Nice for good in 1950.

CHAPTER 28
Adolphe in Paris

Adolphe's brother, Harry, had settled in Miami with his wife, Gustie, and he was doing well there, after starting his own small business developing chemical products. Harry and Gustie had been sponsored by his wife Gustie's family, but they did not stay for long with Gustie's uncle or cousins, who were in Pennsylvania or somewhere further north. It is not clear how or why Harry and Gustie ended up in Miami. Harry set up a chemistry lab there and before long, he had his first American patent, for a skin cream. This was the first of several patents he registered, including patents for a tobacco filter and for a liqueur made from milk.

Harry encouraged his younger brother Adolphe to join him in Miami, as he had once encouraged him to join him in Vienna. Adolphe arrived in Miami in October, 1950, with Maggie, ten-year-old Jean Claude, and eight-year-old Lilian, all hoping for a new start. But Miami was enthralled with Cuban dance music. There was no salsa music yet, but the cha-chas of Desi Arnaz and Latin rhythms like the samba and the rhumba were the craze in Miami. There was little interest in Viennese operettas and waltzes.

Adolphe had a hard time finding any place to play music, and the whole family had a hard time with the hot and muggy Miami climate. Maggie could not tolerate the heat, even in the relatively cooler months of October and November. By Christmas, they had returned to France, where Adolphe stayed for the rest of his life. After disembarking the boat at le Havre, they headed for Paris.

<table>
<tr>
<td colspan="2">United States Patent [19]
Silby, deceased</td>
<td colspan="2">[11] 3,753,724
[45] Aug. 21, 1973</td>
</tr>
</table>

[54] **LIQUEUR PREPARATION FROM MILK**

[75] Inventor: **Harry Silby, deceased**, late of Miami, Fla. by Mayme Silby, executrix

[73] Assignee: **Wire Sales Company**, Chicago, Ill.

[22] Filed: **May 5, 1971**

[21] Appl. No.: **140,370**

Related U.S. Application Data

[63] Continuation-in-part of Ser. No. 32,438, April 27, 1970, abandoned.

[52] **U.S. Cl.**.............................. **99/30, 99/34, 99/38**
[51] **Int. Cl.**... **C12g 3/04**
[58] **Field of Search** 99/29, 30, 34, 38

[56] **References Cited**
UNITED STATES PATENTS

2,783,147   2/1957   Pauls et al. 99/38
3,050,397   8/1962   Carroll.................................... 99/30

FOREIGN PATENTS OR APPLICATIONS

1,942   1870   Great Britain......................... 99/34

OTHER PUBLICATIONS

Heinstein et al.; Chemistry and Technology of Wines and Liquors, D. Van Nostrand Company, Inc. N.Y., 2nd Ed., 1948, pp 53–55 and 217–225

Primary Examiner—David M. Naff
Attorney—Beveridge & De Grandi

[57]   **ABSTRACT**

A liqueur is prepared by fermenting a mixture of uncooked milk, alcohol, sugar, lemon and vanilla. No distillation is involved and all pure flavorings and colorings are utilized. After fermentation and filtration of solids, additional uncooked milk is added to the filtrate for a second fermentation step. The solids recovered after the filtration contain fat from the milk and may be used for other purposes.

12 Claims, No Drawings

One Silby patent

Adolphe hoped Paris would be a place where he could make a living playing and conducting his *"musique légère"*, the light classical Viennese music for which he had become known from his days in Vienna before the war. Eventually, he was able to do so, but it took eight years in Paris before Adolphe found a musical home and financial security with the Radio Orchestra de France. In the meantime, the family continued to struggle financially.

Adolphe was now in his fifties, a married man with a family. He needed more secure work and a more reliable income than playing cafes and busking on the street. They stayed first in a flat belonging to a friend of Maggie's in St. Denis, before moving into their first apartment in Paris, a small one room apartment, not adequate for a family of four. Jean Claude and Lilian slept in the bathroom. Jean Claude slept on a bed that folded up during the day. He put a flat surface on the folded bed to make a writing surface on which he did his homework. Lilian, who was still quite small, slept on bedding in the bathtub that they folded up during the day. Adolphe and Maggie slept in a Murphy bed that folded up into the wall to give the family living space in the one-room apartment.

It was during these hard times that Adolphe went to his sister-in-law Manya, to ask for the confirmation suit for his son, Jean Claude. Always a proud man, it must have been very humbling for Adolphe to do so. That he did so was a real measure of how hard these first years in Paris truly were for him and his young, struggling family.

Adolphe finally found steady work in the 1950s playing Viennese music with a dance orchestra he led in Néris-les-Bains, a resort town in central France long famous for its hot springs. It has been a popular resort at least since Roman times, perhaps even before, because of the curative and healing effects of the mineral waters there. Close to Paris, it was still a popular resort destination two thousand years later.

Adolphe began playing at a casino there and the work soon became both regular and lucrative. Adolphe was finding musical success for the first time since he came to France. Jean Claude and Lilian both enjoyed going to the resort as children, as it provided a wonderful escape from the cramped one room flat in Paris. Life seemed to begin improving. When Harry and his wife, Gustie, came to France to visit his younger brother, Adolphe took them to the resort of Néris-les-Bains. Adolphe also took his younger sister, Tola, to Néris-les-Bains both times that she came to visit in the early 1950s. Tola was then a young widow with her young son, Martin. It was where Adolphe, still living in tiny quarters and struggling financially, could show the first steps of success.

Sometime still in the early 1950s, the owners of the casino in Néris-les-Bains opened a venue in Paris. It was in the center of Paris, on Boulevard Bonne Nouvelles, not far from the Follies Bergère. It was also not far from what was then the Jewish neighborhood and where Solange would live for many years.

By the end of the 1950s, Adolphe was making a name for himself in Paris. He began releasing the first of what would be many recordings of the Viennese operettas and Austrian waltzes that he loved so much. Over time he developed a reputation as a "maestro" of the "*musique légère*", as this style of light classical music was called. In 1958, Adolphe began a relationship with Radio France that would last the rest of his life, conducting the Orchestre Radio Lyrique de la radiodiffusion française, l'ORTF. In 1963 he became the chief conductor of the Orchestre Radio Lyrique de la Radiodiffusion Francaise, a position he held until 1975. During these years, the radio programming included both live radio broadcasts and broadcasts of recorded performances.

Adolphe conducting

In 1959 or 1960, now established with Radio France, Adolphe moved into his home for many years at 14 Rue Felicien David, a short walk to the Radio France tower along the Seine. This was the home that Nana, Vivian and I came to know.

After Adolphe's 1975 retirement as chief conductor, he continued to conduct the orchestra as a "senior" conductor and remained a radio presence, hosting a daily show of his Viennese *"musique légère"*, entitled *"Du Danube à la Seine"*, "from the Danube to the Seine". The half hour show ran during the day and was rerun later at night, so that it was broadcast as many as twenty hours a week during the 1970s. Adolphe also hosted a show entitled "Concert Promenade", which aired Sunday mornings from 6 to 8 AM and another radio program called "Un Café Viennois".

Adolphe continued theses radio programs, playing his own recordings as well as those of others, until his death, at the age of 92, in 1991. In the later years, Adolphe's daughter, Anna, assisted him. After Adolph died, Anna continued to produce the radio shows that played his music for some years, together with Marie-Paul Levy, who had been her father Adolphe's assistant for many years. Anna has also kept her father's music alive and in print, through re-issues of his recordings.

Adolphe's music was originally recorded on vinyl records. Nana never had very many records, but her small collection included a number of her Uncle Adolphe's records and not much else. Then Adolphe recorded audio tape cassettes, and eventually CDs. Radio France has continued to repackage and reissue collections of Adolphe's recordings, marketing them much like the Time Life re-issues of rock-and-roll classics from the fifties and sixties that are still sold through late night television advertisements in the United States.

Two of Adolphe's CDs

Adolphe lived a long and full life, maintaining his creativity and wit and self-confidence as an artist and as a philosopher until the very end. I remember a boisterous afternoon over tea and pastries at Uncle Adolphe and Aunt Maggie's apartment during my last visit to Paris with Nana. Jean Claude and Anna were there with Nana and me, as was Solange. There was a long discussion about whether men should tell their wives when they have affairs, with Solange and Adolphe arguing and interrupting each other. Although the discussion was posed as a hypothetical, it seemed that Adolphe was talking about himself and Maggie. Perhaps this should not have been as surprising to Nana and me as it was, for everyone else there seemed to assume Adolphe's affairs.

At one point, Adolphe said that it was important to be honest in a marriage. A man should never hide anything from his wife and should always tell his wife the truth. Especially, he said, a man should always tell his wife about an affair because it was important to be honest in a marriage. Then, he continued, it was up to the wife to choose whether to divorce him or to accept the situation. At this point Maggie, who, as usual, had been quiet most of the afternoon, responded. Her answer was not clear to me. Perhaps it was because the conversation was in French and she spoke so quickly, but it seemed that she knew much more about her husband of close to fifty years than she was willing to reveal.

Adolphe pontificating, with Anna, Nana et al

That trip was the last time we saw Uncle Adolphe, who died November 10, 1991, not long after losing his dear Maggie, who had died the year before, on May 26, 1990. Like my memories of the long walks at their country home in Bridoire, I have fond memories of joining Adolphe for lunches at one of his favorite Paris cafés. We would walk to the café from his home on Rue Félicien-David, sometimes with his pet dachshund, Crac. We would have a long leisurely lunch and talk. At the end of the meal he would have an expresso, drinking the strong black coffee through a cube of sugar that he would hold between his teeth. The last time we lunched together was in 1990, when Adolphe was ninety or ninety-one, but as sharp mentally as ever, the philosopher and thinker to his last day.

There was a reason Nana admired Adolphe so much. It was not just that her uncle adored her as well. For Nana, Adolphe was the living evidence of the genius, wit, and creativity of her family, the Szylberstajns of Lodz. There was an elegance and gentleness to this wonderful man, traits that he passed on to his two children, Jean Claude and Anna. For all the years we knew Adolphe, from the time when he found Nana in 1962, until his death in 1991, Adolphe was truly the patriarch of the reassembled remnants of the Szylberstajn family, loved and respected by all who knew him.

CHAPTER 29

Jean Claude and Anna

Adolphe was very proud of his two children. How proud? He returned to Vienna to show them off to his pre-Shoah Austrian wife. One might see this trip an act of vengeance. On the other hand, it might have been no more than a measure of how comfortable Adolphe had become with his life in Paris, not just as an artist and as a musician, but as a father, as well. I am not sure when he took this trip, or exactly why, but, according to Anna, he took no luggage, only photos of her and her brother, no longer little children but not yet adults. She smiled with pride when she told the story.

Adolphe arrived in Vienna and proceeded straight to the house of his first wife, the Austrian Catholic who never followed him, as she had promised him she would when he fled Vienna for Marseilles. Instead, she sold off the belongings Adolphe left behind and married his friend. The years had passed, this husband died, and she was left a widow, without children, living alone in a small apartment. Adolphe knocked on her door. When she answered, he took out his pictures of Jean Claude and Anna and showed them to her. He said "I just wanted you to see what I have." Then he left and returned to Paris.

Adolphe was proud of his two children, both of whom were close to their parents even as adults. Lilian, as we first knew her, followed her father into a career in music. Like her father, she was always exuberant and full of life, creative, a bit of a romantic, a bit of a philosopher and always a performer. I first thought of her as Chaplinesque, from her walk and waddling mannerisms. Over time I began to realize her sense of mime and timing, despite her self-avowed love of Chaplin, were more rooted in her French upbringing, in French mime. The roots of her physical behavior, of her mannerisms and her expressions, even her facial expressions, were in Marcel Marceau[30], and the French culture of Pierrots and harlequins.

Lilian aspired to be not just a singer, but a chanteuse, in the French tradition of **Edith Piaf** and **Jacques Bre**l. In 1968, Lilian arrived in Quebec where she first stopped going by her first name, Lilian, instead using her middle name Anna. She pursued a singing career, under the name Anna Sibert, supported by the Decca record label. After five years in Quebec struggling to make it as a French singer, she returned to Paris in 1973 and did not sing again for many years. Yet when I stopped in Paris to see her, in 1975, after the several days with her father in Savoie, she took me to the artists' quarters in **Montmartre**, then a neighborhood where she spent time and which she always loved.

In 1976, Montmartre was still an artists' colony. Since the 1800s, it was a neighborhood full of artists' studios. Modigliani, Monet, Renoir, Degas, Picasso, Pissarro and Van Gogh were among the many artists, not all so well known, who lived or had studios in the Montmartre neighborhood. When Lilian and I walked through Montmartre then, we saw artists painting in studios, on the streets and in the squares.

Montmartre has since became overrun with tourists, tourist shops and tourist restaurants. The studios are gone and the cafes are now tourist traps. As the chanteuse and then painter, Anna was an "artist" comfortable in the Montmartre artists scene. But after it became a tourist trap, her favorite cafes had disappeared or changed and we no longer returned to Montmartre. Instead, we met at the front entrance to the **Eglise de St. Germaine** in what was her favorite neighborhood, St. Germain de Près.

The cathedral was across the street from **Les Deux Magots** , long famous as a meeting place of artists and intellectuals. Verlaine, Rimbaud and Mallarmé were regulars after the café opened in 1885 and the existentialist philosophers Albert Camus, Jean Paul Sartre, and Simone de Beauvoir

---

30 The world's most famous mime was born a French Jew in Strasbourg. He was both a Holocaust survivor and a hero of the French resistance. He rescued many Jewish children, using mime to teach the Jewish children he was smuggling out of France how to communicate silently. https://forward. com/culture/557546/marcel-marceau-mime-jewish-wwii-hero-entenary/?utm_source=Iterable&utm_medium=email&utm_campaign=afternoonedition_7498205

could be found there in the 1950s. Other patrons included Pablo Picasso, James Joyce, Berthold Brecht, and James Baldwin and Richard Wright, African-American writers in exile.

Anna Liber Decca Records poster

We occasionally had drinks at Les Deux Magots, but usually walked to other nearby brasseries, where all the waitstaff knew Anna. That evening we just went to Anna's apartment and stayed up most of the night talking and sharing a bottle of wine. I was eager to tell Anna about Linda, with whom I was madly in love, and this was the foundation of a night discussing love and romance, philosophy and life. In the early morning, I took a cab to the airport. The discussion would continue, for many years, as part of my trips to Paris.

When I visited Anna at her apartment, she would serve wine and something light to eat, maybe cheese and French bread, and some fruit, strawberries or slices of fresh pear. I loved her apartment, small but filled with interesting things, objets d'art. There were art books and music, always music. The apartment was small, so even the bathroom became part of the gallery. Prominent in the living room were photos and posters of her father, and copies of his recordings. In addition to her father, Adolphe's, she had recordings of classical and contemporary French music including that of French chanteurs like Jacques Brel.

On one of my visits, perhaps in the 1990s, Anna pulled out a CD that she wanted me to hear. She said it was new, a very recent recording. It was a compilation of *chansons* by different artists all in the style of Jacques Brel. Two or three of the tracks featured Anna Sibert. She also sang backup vocals on other tracks. She had not sung professionally since returning from Quebec and it was the first time she had recorded in some twenty or twenty five years. It was a reawakening for her.

On a subsequent trip, there were new wall decorations, a couple of dozen paintings hanging on the walls in her living room and in the halls. I could not figure out where she found room for them. Anna explained that around the time she started singing again, she also took up painting.

I was awestruck by the volume of work she had produced in a short time, several dozen works, all oils on canvass. They were all faces. Every one of the faces were dark and gloomy, every one of them. It was hard to imagine where the darkness and gloom came from. The Anna I knew, the Lilian I knew before that, was always full of life. She always had and effervescent smile and a joyful bounce to her walk. One would never know from Anna's many smiles and comical facial expressions, from her Chaplinesque walk and from her joyful miming that there was a hidden dark side. These paintings revealed another side of Anna, one that she did not show.

On occasion, we would meet at a museum, particularly if there was a special show or exhibit that Anna wanted to see or wanted to show me. This was a common practice on my visits to France, now sometimes with Linda or with one or all of the children. Jean Claude often suggested a special museum or exhibit. Solange's sons, Charles and Maurice, would also suggest an exhibit, and would join us, too.

Anna's paintings of faces

The most memorable of these exhibits was an exhibit at the Grand Palais entitled "Visages des Puissance". I no longer remember whether it was Jean Claude or Charles or Maurice who recommended this amazing exhibit to us. Visage means both "face" and "image" in French, so that the title of the exhibit, roughly translated as "Faces of Power" could also mean "Images of Power". The double meaning was a play on words that revealed the subtleties of the show.

There were portraits of kings, princes, popes, politicians, generals and other persons of power, mostly European, from the middle ages through the nineteenth century. Sometimes the person of power would be both a nobleman and a military leader, or both a cleric and a politician. There was also a room with just women, duchesses, queens, and other women of power. By far the most interesting thing in this fascinating exhibit were three portraits of a cleric. One was when he was a young bishop. The second was when he was a cardinal and the third after he became pope. The differences were remarkable, revealing not just how the man had aged, but how his visage changed as he became more powerful and more self-confident but also acquired the burdens of greater power.

I saw exhibits of Gauguin and of Cezanne's landscapes and country villages with Jean Claude at the Grand Palais, Palais. Jean Claude also introduced Linda and me to the Musée Jacquemart-André. This museum, on Rue Hausman, was a gorgeous and elegant mansion built as the residence of Èdouard André and his wife Nélie Jacquemart. It now houses the extensive collection of art that the two of them collected.

One of the most humorous excursions was to the Pompidou, where Solange's son, Charlie, took us when Teddy was still little but old enough to appreciate art. Charles, although he never had children of his own, knew how bored a boy could be in the somber halls of a grand museum like the Louvre. So Charles, who could be quite the comic, took us to the Pompidou, which housed modern art. There he was able to vamp and clown, using the contemporary artwork as props. Teddy was not the only one amused by Charles' performance.

By far the most revealing exhibit I saw in my many trips to Paris was a short time after I first saw Anna's own paintings, the collection of grim faces she had painted. Anna was excited about an exhibit at the Palais Royal of **Oskar Kokoschka**, a twentieth century Austrian painter and writer best known as a painter for his portraits and landscapes, although he was also known for his theories on vision that influenced the Viennese authors and visual artists and especially the Viennese Expressionist movement.

As I looked at Kokoschka's paintings, I saw the same dark colors, the same thick brush strokes, the same somber faces Anna had used in the portraits she painted. I understood why Anna wanted me to see Kokoschka's portraits, as it was clear his style had influenced her. But the powerful emotions in Anna's paintings were Anna's alone. Her paintings revealed a sadness well hidden by Anna's usual vivacious personality and ebullient mannerisms.

As a boy, I did not really know Anna, or Lilian, as I called her then. I was just thirteen when I first met her, and she was eight years older. After her first visit with Jean Claude to the states I did not see her for many years, knowing her only as an exotic French chanteuse, in far off Quebec City. I only first got to know her after my stop in Paris on the way back from that first trip to Israel, when we had that all night conversation about "amour", love.

Anna was always quite attractive, with her short, cropped hair and ever-present charming smile, but she never married. Over time, she developed a strong relationship with Marie-Paul Levy, who had been her father Adolphe's assistant for many years. Anna and Marie-Paul had a close and very special relationship that only grew stronger after Adolphe died. The two of them were inseparable. Marie-Paul lived in the same apartment building, in an apartment on a different floor. The two of them travelled together. Although their travel was limited by the fact that Anna would not fly, they would vacation on the beaches of Normandy and Spain, and in other places to which they could travel by train.

When I was in Paris and met Anna in St. Germain de Près, Marie-Paul would usually stop by, sometimes joining us, sometimes just to see me long enough to say hello. Marie-Paul always asked about my children and, in later years, about the grandchildren, and about Vivian, whom she also knew, and Vivian's children, whom she also knew. Like Anna and Jean Claude, Marie-Paul was born Jewish, as Marie-Paul Levy, but she was raised French and secular.

Her parents had also come to France for refuge but her father fled to Italy where he hid. When Marie-Paul's mother, still in Paris and pregnant with Marie-Paul, learned that the Nazis were coming for her, she managed to escape to Algiers. When Marie-Paul was born, she was baptized. Her father was not happy to learn this when her parents reunited. Marie-Paul considered herself French and knew little about Judaism or her Jewish past, but she was always curious about it.

Anna and Marie-Paul cared for each other, through various injuries and illnesses. In their later years, Anna, despite her cancer, nursed Marie-Paul when she was recovering from back surgery. Marie-Paul sought to recover quickly because she knew that Anna was deferring her cancer treatment until Marie-Paul no longer needed caretaking assistance, and she did not want Anna to delay the treatment she needed.

Nana was always very fond of Marie-Paul and accepted her almost as family. For Nana, family was important. She saw how Marie-Paul cared for and took care of Adolphe: he was not just her boss, but someone she cared for like he was her father. Likewise, Nana saw the bonds between

Marie-Paul and Anna, whom Nana also adored. For Nana, it was always a treat to see or talk to Marie-Paul, as well as to Anna.

By the time Maggie died in May, 1990, Anna and Marie-Paul, who had worked for years as Adolphe's assistant, had taken over managing and preserving Adolphe's musical legacy. When her mother Maggie died, Anna took over the remaining responsibilities of caring for her father, who was then over 90 years old. She took on this added task happy to have each remaining day with her father. Years later Anna told me that she was glad she did not have children, because she did not want to die and leave them with no mother. I don't think she really meant what she was saying. Rather, I think she never got over losing her own parents, especially her father.

Nana used to say that Jean Claude was like his mother and Anna was like her father. I think this was true. Anna was a musician like her father. She was also a romantic, like her father, and an artist in the broadest sense.

Jean Claude was more practical, like his mother. He was reserved and quieter than his effervescent sister, often keeping his thoughts to himself. Jean Claude was scholarly and academic, an intellectual who enjoyed art and fine objects. He loved opera and traveled regularly to Italy during opera season, both for the operas and to enjoy the museums and art there. He traveled elsewhere as well, and he traveled often. He read prolifically, assembling a collection of some five thousand books. He was particularly interested in works about the Holocaust and the rise and history of the Nazis.

While he has always been reserved about his private life, Jean Claude has always cared about family. When his father, Adolphe died, Jean Claude was happy to let his sister, Anna, take control of the legal rights to their father's music. This not only assured that Adolphe's recordings would remain in print and available: it also provided Anna with some extra income from the royalties, income that Jean Claude did not need.

Jean Claude was always very fond of his American cousin, your Nana. He has repeated to me a promise he made to Nana before she died that he would stay in touch with her children and grandchildren, a promise that he has faithfully kept. He has always been warm, welcoming and very generous to me, often coming to meet me at the airport, even though he never had a car.

Visiting him once, I picked up a book that caught my eye, a history of Jews in occupied North Africa. Jean Claude immediately insisted that I keep it. I still have it. Jean Claude often had gifts for me and for the family. When I would tell him the gifts were not necessary, he demurred, saying that he wanted there to be things from him in our home that we would see regularly, as it would assure we would be thinking of him.

These gifts from Jean Claude are visible throughout our home. They include two framed pieces of paper money from the time of the French revolution, a pair of portraits of Danton and Robespierre, a photo book of the chateaus of the Loire Valley that he gave us after my daughter Shira and I took our bike trip there, and another set of picture books, that he gave my son Teddy, with engineering drawings of buildings and monuments in Paris. He gave Teddy some other books, as well, a book on Napoleon and another of French soldiers.

I loved to walk Paris streets with Jean Claude. Walking the streets of Paris with him was always a pleasure, a cultural experience that no tour guide could provide. As we strolled the streets, he pointed out buildings and other items of interest, told when and by whom they were built, explained who lived in them, often adding some historical, architectural or cultural details and context. He did the same for the streets, squares, monuments, bridges and other public structures. He always had some place new to explore, like the hidden park in the Vosges, near the now Jewish Marais quarter of Paris. The homes in the Vosges were one of the first planned neighborhoods build outside the older city.

Jean Claude had his own method for visiting the Louvre, too. He wasn't interested in seeing the Mona Lisa and the other tourist highlights. To do that, you would have to rush from one end to another of a huge building and spend your time in the most crowded spots. Instead, he liked to pick a medium and a period.

After saying "We're going to the Louvre, today," Jean Claud might suggest "Would you like to see sculpture? We could see classical Greek and Roman sculpture, or neoclassical French sculpture of the 17th and 18th century. If we did that, we'd see quite a bit of Houdon."

We might spend another visit viewing just Renaissance painting, or

Dutch masters, or Italian religious art. Jean Claude knew other interesting places, as well, such as the Musée Jacquemart-André. When Teddy was still a boy, Jean Claude took us to Les Invalides and the Naval Museum at the Trocadero. Jean Claude wisely concluded that a young boy would be more interested in soldiers, Napoleon, and naval history than Italian renaissance religious art. On that trip, Jean Claude also took us to Fontainebleau, rather than Versailles.

Jean Claude attended a prestigious secondary school, the Lycée Charlemagne,[31] near the Place de Vosges in the Marais. As Jean Claude and I walked past the school, he would have filled me in on the background. He would have noted, for example, that the lycée was founded by Napoléon Bonaparte in 1812, in buildings originally constructed by the Jesuits centuries earlier. He would have explained that the Jesuits were given the property by the Cardinal de Bourbon, who had bought it from the Duchess of Montmorency in 1580. The Jesuits demolished the duchess' "hotel", or home, which was standing on the site at the time. They replaced it with a chapel dedicated to St. Louis, which they completed in 1582. Between 1627 and 1647, the Jesuits constructed the buildings that would be their home in Paris. The only other experience I have had of walking through a city that is comparable to walking through Paris with Jean Claude is walking in Jerusalem with Hila Kobliner, who is the fifth or sixth generation of her family born in Jerusalem. Jean Claude, on the other hand, is the first Szylberstajn born in France.

One of the first places to which Jean Claude ever took me, in 1976, was the Comédie Française. Jean Claude explained that the theater was established by Louis XIV in 1680 and noted that it is the oldest operating theatre in the world. Its history extends back to the French playwright Molière's acting company, and the Comédie Française still presents Molière's works. Going there was incidental, however. It was on the way to Jean Claude's business at the time. By that time, Jean Claude was already in business with his lifelong partner, both in life and in business, Jean Gabriel Peyre.

When Jean Claude finished lycée at the Lycée Charlemagne, he went

---

31 The school is known as Charlemagne Magnus in Latin, or Charlemagne the Great. It is well known for preparing young men for the top universities in France.

directly to University. After he graduated, he went into the French Army. He began his service in November, 1965. Fortunately, this was three years after the Algerian War had ended. Jean Claude served in the army until April or May, 1967, stationed in Strasbourg. From 1967 to 1971 Jean Claude taught English in a lycée.

It was around that time, in the early seventies, that Jean Claude and his partner, Jean-Gabriel, began buying and selling antique furniture and other rare items in their space in the Palais Royale courtyard around the corner from the Comédie Française. By the end of the 1980s, Jean Claude and Jean-Gabriel had a new business, selling patterns to clothing factories in India. The factory proprietors would use the patterns to design the shirts, blouses, skirts and dresses that were made in the factories and marketed throughout the world.

This new business obliged Jean Claude and Jean-Gabriel to travel to India several times a year during the several years they had this business. It also gave them the opportunity to explore other places in Asia by extending their business trips to India. Unlike his sister, Anna, who did not fly, Jean Claude loved to travel and he and Jean-Gabriel continued to travel extensively, even after they gave up the business in India, not just to Italy, for the opera season, but throughout Europe and to Africa, Asia and even the Americas.

Jean Claude and Jean-Gabriel next opened another store on the Rue de Bac, a block or two from the Seine on the Left Bank, not far from the Louvre and the Palais Royale. They maintained this shop for many years, with their business focusing not just on antiques and furniture but more and more on porcelain pottery, cups, plates, pitchers, serving pieces and other "objets". Much of what they bought and sold was centuries old, collectors' items that were rare and quite expensive.

Their specialty was painted porcelain and faience pottery. Faience is tin-glazed earthenware plates, cups, and saucers. Made in France from the late sixteenth century until the end of the eighteenth century, faience pottery is considered a technical triumph noted for its richly colored decoration. Faience is explained in a little more detail in this explanation of a past **Frick Museum exhibition.**

Many of Jean Claude and Jean-Gabriel's customers were wealthy collectors. Jean Claude and Jean-Gabriel, like other rare art dealers, developed relationships with some customers that sometimes became friendships, as well. Jean Claude and Jean-Gabriel again were obliged to travel, either attending auctions throughout Europe or otherwise searching for particular items, a burden that they enjoyed. Jean Claude and Jean-Gabriel acquired a reputation in this specialty and they were often called upon to find a particular piece that completed a set or a collection for a wealthy customer.

In addition to their regular travels, Jean Claude and Jean-Gabriel acquired a second home in Aix-en-Provence, in a centuries-old building only a few minute walk to the former Théâtre de l'Archevêché, now home to the **Festival d'Aix-en-Provence** a summer classical musical festival that features productions of the operas for Mozart, Verdi, and other composers and to the **Palais de l'Ancien Archevêché** the former palace of the Archbishop, now a theatre. **The Paroisse Cathédrale Saint Sauveur Aix-en-Provence** one of France's great cathedrals, is behind their home.

Linda and I visited Jean Claude in Aix in 2013. It was a wonderful visit to a beautiful part of the world, and Jean Claude was a gracious and welcoming host. We stayed with him in what had become his principal residence. It was large for a European residence, and he prepared breakfast and lunch for us, from fresh local produce each day. We marveled at the beautifully decorated apartment in a refurbished centuries old building. There were cabinets filled with beautiful cup and saucer sets and other porcelain, some hundreds of years old, as well as his collection of some five thousand books.

The book collection included classics and modern writing, fiction, drama and quite a number of works of history. Much of the history collection was about the rise of Hitler and the Nazis, the Holocaust and the history of the Jews in Europe. Always generous, Jean Claude gave me one of these books when I picked it up to look at because the title attracted me. It was *Le Juifs D'Afrique du Nord Sous Vichy*, a study of the Jews of North Africa under the Vichy French government, the puppet government of France during the Nazi occupation.

I don't think Jean Claude sees himself as Jewish. He quite clearly sees himself as French. To the extent that he and Anna had any religious upbringing, it was Catholic, not Jewish. Yet Jean Claude had a strong commitment to family and with that came an interest in family roots and history. His interest in the Holocaust was personal. It is consistent with his commitment to family. Despite the fact that he was always very private about his personal life, Jean Claude was always quite interested in his family. Over the years, during my visits to Paris, he told me about other Poznanski cousins he knew as a child, telling me what he knew about them. They were cousins of his father. What happened to them is another of the stories that still need to be explored.

Jean Claude and Nana were always very close. After Nana's death, Jean Claude has made it clear to me that he takes very seriously his promise to Nana to stay in touch with Vivian and me and he has always taken an interest in our children and, now, our grandchildren.

Likewise, after the death of his father and as Solange aged, Jean Claude has viewed Solange as the matriarch of the family. This has not been easy for Jean Claude, who still remembers the issue over his confirmation suit, even though that slight was not about him or about Solange, but between his father, Adolphe, and Solange's mother, Miriam. When I flew to Paris for Solange's funeral, Jean Claude met me at the airport and took me directly to the room in the hospital where Solange's body lay. Yet he did not attend the funeral.

At the end of our 2013 visit to Aix, Jean Claude took Linda and me to the museum that is now inside what was the Camp de Milles. Together we saw an exhibit of art from the camp, including the collection of children's art, the works of the children who were imprisoned there. Yet Jean Claude did not say anything at the time about his father's connection to the Camp de Milles or of his father's involvement with then Archbishop Remond. Perhaps he did not remember, or perhaps he did not realize the connection at the time.

There is much that Jean Claude never talked about. Handsome and quite accomplished, Jean Claude was always warm, gracious and generous, but Jean Claude could be very private. He rarely shared his own feelings. Perhaps this was why he was sometimes hesitant to talk about his father.

When I asked him questions about his father that he could not answer, I suspect that this did not embarrass Jean Claude as much as it led him to feel guilty about never asking his father the questions I was asking. I understand. There are so many unanswered questions that I still have about my own father.

CHAPTER 30

Solange in the Shoah, Part One, The Radom Ghetto

Like your Nana, her first cousin, Solange had a happy childhood growing up in her home in Lodz. Although her Jewish name was Zlata, she was called Sophie in Polish. Sophie later became Solange, but her Jewish name always remained Zlata, Zlata bat Moishe. Like Nana, Solange was very close to her brother, Abram, although her brother Abram was an older brother and Nana's was a younger brother. Like Nana, Solange had a father who adored her, and who was Jewish but not religious at all.

Like Nana's mother, Solange's mother was more religious and kept an observant home. On Friday evenings, Solange's mother, Miriam, or Manya, would have both Solange's friends and her brother Abram's friends over for Erev Shabbat. Mother Manya would serve them cakes and beverages. They would listen to music and dance, not exactly a traditional Kabbalat Shabbat, but, as Solange explained, their mother liked to have their friends to the house, so she would know who their friends were. "*Ses copains était mes copains et mes copines sont ses copines*", Solange explained: her brothers friends were her friends and her girl-friends were her friends.

Like Nana and her brother Abram, Solange and her brother, Abram, had both Jewish and Polish friends. They spoke Yiddish at home and Polish at school and in the streets. While Solange and Abram had both Jewish and non-Jewish friends, the two hundred people living in the apartment complex around their courtyard were mostly Jewish. The building, however, was owned by a German, whose name was Baumann, and he was as friendly with his tenants as landlords sometimes are with their tenants. Solange knew Mr. Baumann well enough to say "hello" and "how are you". While anti-Semitism was not unknown in Lodz, for Solange, life was good and she was happy growing up where she did.

Like Nana, Solange spoke fondly of her life growing up in Poland. While Solange described the general quality of life in Poland in the twenties and thirties as "*pas tellement magnifique*", or "not so great", life was good for the Szylberstajns who grew up on Wschodnia Street in what was then a mostly Jewish neighborhood in the center of Lodz. Solange grew up a favorite daughter in a warm and loving family. She was the apple of her father's eye. Like his older brother, Joseph, Nana's father Maurice was always bringing gifts for his daughter, Sophie, as she was known in Polish.[32] She went to school. She went to the skating rink. She had friends, Jewish and not Jewish. Mostly she looked up to her brother, Abram, whom she described as handsome on the outside and even more beautiful on the inside. Before the war he was attending the lycée to become an engineer.

Maurice Szylberstajn

---

32 In Yiddish Solange was Zlata.

Things changed rapidly when Hitler and Stalin invaded Poland on September 1, 1939. Lodz was occupied by the Nazis within a week. The Germans had long laid claim to Lodz, where many Germans had lived for a long time. The Nazis renamed the city Litzmannstadt, after the German general, Karl Litzmann, who had captured the city during World War I. Solange fled with her parents and her brother to Radom, where her mother's family was from.

They went to the home of Solange's aunt, her mother Manya's sister. This aunt lived in Radom with her stepfather. Solange's parents, Maurice and Manya, locked their apartment in Lodz and left, with their two by then grown children, Abram and Sophie. They took some money but left everything else behind. They did not expect to be gone for very long, even though Maurice was told "get out, the Lodz ghetto will be known as Litzmannstadt." In fact, the Germans would refer to both the city of Lodz and the ghetto within the city as Litzmannstadt. One would think that they would have known, that Maurice would have realized, that they would not be returning soon. Who knew what would soon come to pass?

The ghetto in Radom, a much smaller city than Lodz, was still not as bad as the Lodz ghetto, now already being called "Litzmannstadt", Solange explained. There were no crematoriums, no "ovens", or any of the other horrors that she would see later.

Solange, her brother and her parents arrived at the home of Solange's aunt, her mother's sister. The small apartment was on a street that was demarcated as a "ghetto" street, inside the area enclosed with barbed wire. "This was where the misery began", Solange lamented. Her aunt's apartment was adequate for her aunt's immediate family, but became crowded with four more adults. In the course of their stay in the Radom ghetto, two more families would join them in the two bedroom flat.

Under the new Nazis rules, Jews had to be home in the early evening, as there was a curfew. There was not much bread available, and very little to eat. There was soup with a lot of water, a few potatoes and not much else. If you had some money, you could go to the barbed wire fence and ask one of the local Poles to bring you some bread or other food. This was the start of a black market along the fences of the ghetto, with Jews on one side and Christian Poles on the other. The problem was that eventually the money would run out.

In the meantime, the Jews in the ghetto organized a small economy in the ghetto. In addition to the black market at the barbed wire fence, the craftsmen and professionals – what Solange called the "maestros", set up shop. In Lodz Solange's father, Maurice, had practiced as an orthodist, a medical professional who made braces and other devices to support an injured knee, leg, wrist, or foot. The orthotic device might be a cast, a shoe insert, or a brace.

Maurice set up shop in Radom, with the other tradesmen. He had enough business, but not all of his customers could pay. Some paid not at all and some paid what they could.

Solange found work with her new sister-in-law, Henya, who would later become Helène Alembic in France, after the war. Henya had already been Abram's girlfriend in Lodz, and so Nana knew her from Lodz. Henya became Solange's sister-in-law for the first time when she married Solange's older brother, Abram, in the Radom ghetto. Their wedding provided a brief moment of joy in an otherwise bleak time. Solange's father, Maurice, initially opposed the marriage, rightfully protesting that the ghetto was not a place to celebrate and it was not a time to be married.

"In the ghetto, you don't get married", Maurice lamented. "We don't know what will happen tomorrow and the day after tomorrow."

Solange remembers that her father did not protest too strongly, however. Her mother, Manya turned the argument around, saying that it was true, they did not know what would happen, so why not let them enjoy the pleasure the wedding would bring. Manya made some cakes, with flour and ingredients she bought on the black market, and there was a little celebration. Abram and Henya were in love and there was a brief moment of joy in the bleak darkness of their lives in the ghetto. This is how Solange and Helène became sisters-in-law for the first time. Solange and Helène would become double sisters-in-law later, in Paris, when Solange married Helène's brother Albert, in a more joyful celebration.

Helène was a seamstress. Like her new father-in-law, Maurice, she opened a shop, offering alterations and tailoring. Solange, then seventeen years old and without job skills, found work with Helène. Little did the two young women know where their bonds and friendship would take them or what they were destined to go through together. The two of them would be support for each other through the Shoah, through the deaths of parents, family, and friends, and through the deaths of their husbands and brothers and much more. They were literally friends for life. Much later, after the Shoah when life had returned to normal and they were both living in France, Solange's Shabbat ritual was to call Helène Friday evening before dinner. In 2018, a fragile but still very lucid nonagenarian Helène spoke at Solange's funeral.

In 1939, however, it was hard to get by, even if you had a small business, like Maurice or Henya. Making a living was very difficult because you had to work for the Germans. There were quite a few Germans who lived in eastern Poland. The one in charge of the Radom ghetto was a German named Schauvitski. As Solange explained, Schauvitski was neither a Nazi nor an SS. He was just a German living in what had become occupied eastern Poland. Schauvitski had been put in charge of the Radom ghetto. If a German wanted a dress, or a coat, or a pair of shoes, they went to Shauvistki and he would go to the Jewish dressmaker or the shoemaker and say "I need a dress" or "I need some shoes." He would take the products but he would not pay for them. So the Jewish tradespeople were forced to work for free for the Germans.

Before long, Solange, her father, Maurice, and brother, Abram, were working even more directly for the Germans. They were among the able-bodied who were put to work in a factory. The Nazis began shooting the others, those who couldn't work, the elderly, the sick, and children. Solange tells of mothers who hid their babies under piles of dresses and clothing when the Nazis began random searches to find Jews they could kill. Solange marveled that somehow the babies who were hidden under piles of clothing often seemed to know not to cry.

Solange's mother, Manya, did not have a work card because she did not have an official job, so she was at risk of being shot by these marauding Nazis. Solange begged and pleaded with the supervisor of the factory kitchen to give her mother a job. Ultimately, she convinced the supervisor, and her mother got a job in the kitchen.

Manya was peeling potatoes in the kitchen with other Jewish women when the SS raided. The supervisor looked at Manya, and from the look, Manya thought that his heart would stop. Did he fear for Manya, that Manya would be caught and shot, or was he afraid for himself, afraid what the Nazis would do to him? Most likely it was a bit of both.

The kitchen was a large industrial kitchen with an array of very large pots. Manya was small enough that she could fit inside one of the pots. For some reason, the supervisor put Manya inside one of the large pots and put the lid on the top before the Nazis reached the kitchen. There were a number of these large pots. The Nazis looked in one, then another, but they did not look in all the pots and they did not find Manya.

Solange was not there at the time. Her mother later told her what happened. When Solange told the story, she says that this is why she believes in the destiny of people. Solange saw mothers hiding their babies under the dresses in Henya's dress shop. Some of these babies survived and others did not, but somehow Solange's mother, Manya, survived. Was it because of the quick action of the frightened kitchen supervisor? Was it luck? Perhaps it was a little of each, but Manya survived. Solange survived and Henya survived. Others did not. What is the destiny of people?

CHAPTER 31

Never Judge Another, as You Never Know What You Would Have Done

In the years after my father, Jan, died, Nana grew even closer to Solange. Our trip to Paris in January 1990 would be the last time the two cousins, who grew up together, would spend time together. Looking back, I think they both knew that at the time, even though I didn't. Nana and I stayed with Solange for over a week, maybe for as much as two weeks. That's when I spoke and learned the most French since college. Every night after dinner Solange and I would watch "Dallas", the popular 1980s prime-time American soap that was then on French TV, dubbed in French. Solange would ask me questions about American life as she expressed her opinions about the characters in the TV series, about American life and about a host of other things.

That is when Solange and I began our special dialogue, a dialogue that lasted the next eighteen years until her death. We talked about a lot of things. I learned about Lodz. I learned about what was known as Nana's "ballet" school, which she let Solange attend, only because Solange was Nana's "special" cousin. That's when I first began to learn about some of Solange's experiences in the ghetto and later in the camps and when I began taking the notes that are the basis of what you are reading now.

The three of us, Nana, Solange and I sat around Solange's kitchen table and the two of them talked about life growing up and as young girls in

Lodz. They would laugh about these stories. How they would laugh! Then they would break into songs, more often Polish but sometimes Yiddish. It went back and forth, Solange and Nana in Polish, then they would look at me and Nana would translate into English, or Solange into French. Then they would start singing again, and laughing, and reminiscing.

Only once did I observe any tension between them. It was about their brothers, the two Abrams, also known as Adam or Adamik in Polish: Litka's younger brother and Solange's older brother. The two Abrams were the same age and grew up across the apartment complex courtyard from each other. From the time they played together as babies, they were inseparable, and they had remained inseparable all their lives.

Solange's brother Adam, two and a half years older than his sister, went to a lycée and studied to be an engineer. He was tall and broad shouldered. Solange adored him. Likewise, Nana adored her younger brother, the other Adam. Nana was separated from her family when the war broke out and only learned many years later what happened to her brother from Solange. Solange saw Nana's father, Joseph, shot in the back with a cigarette in his hand in the Radom ghetto. Later, she told us, Nana's brother Adam also was shot.

Solange told Nana that Nana's parents, Joseph and Bluma, had come to Radom, where Bluma, like Solange's mother, Miriam, had family. They came with their son, Adamik, and their younger daughter, Manousha, leaving Lodz in time to avoid being sent to the Ghetto there. Solange confirmed that Bluma and Manousha were killed, but could not tell Nana how her mother or her sister died. As for her older, half-brother, Henyik, Nana never learned how he died. She and Solange wondered together about what had becomes of their uncle, Henyik, the poet, whom both of them spoke of adoringly. That night in Solange's kitchen, I learned about how Nana's brother, Adam, betrayed Solange's brother and his lifelong friend, Adam.

In the ghetto, the Nazis enlisted young men to serve as ghetto police. These ghetto police were given lists of names of Jews in the ghetto, and it was their job to deliver the people on the list to the Nazi SS police, the people who enforced the Nazi racial policies. Those on the list did not come back. They were killed or sent to death camps like Auschwitz. The benefit to being a ghetto police officer was that you were given extra food and privileges and you might be able to keep your family members from being taken.

Solange's brother, Adam was recruited by the Nazis to be on the Jewish ghetto police, perhaps because he was a big and broad-shouldered young man. He refused. He did not want to be in a position of acting against his own people. Solange, in testimony which she gave later, said that her father encouraged her brother to accept the Nazi offer, saying that this was a way for him to protect and perhaps save the family. Solange's Adam refused, saying he was a Jew and he was not going to arrest and beat other Jews.

Solange said that she agreed with her brother's decision. She understood what the Nazis wanted, for the Jews to turn on each other. She saw the Jewish ghetto police as agents of the Nazi Gestapo, doing their bidding.

Nana's brother Abram saw things differently, perhaps feeling that being a ghetto police officer was the only way to survive and would enable him to help his family survive. Each morning, the Nazis gave Nana's brother Adam a list of names. It was his job to find each person on the list and bring them to the gate of the ghetto and deliver them to the Nazis by the end of the day. The Nazis took these people away, and they would never be seen again.

One day, Solange's brother, Adam, was on the list, as was their father. At the end of the day, Nana's brother, Adam, brought everyone on the list to the ghetto gate except for his cousin and his uncle. He may have told the Nazi officer that there was some confusion between the name Szylberstajn and the name Szylberberg. The drivers of the transport were eager to leave, as they did not want to be in trouble with the SS for being late, so they left, two Jews short.

The next day, Nana's Adam got his morning list and saw that his cousin, Adam, and his uncle were on the list again. Again, Nana's brother delivered everyone on the list, except his cousin and his uncle. Nana's brother again had an excuse for why he couldn't find this other "Adam Szylberstajn". The German officer looked at him and said "Tomorrow you will find this Adam Szylberstajn, or you will go in his place."

That was the end of the story of that night. Solange never said that her cousin turned in her brother, although we all knew that neither Adam survived. As with some of the other stories that Solange told, she stopped before the story was finished. There were things that she saw that she could not bear to remember, that she could not bear to speak.

Solange told a slightly different story when she gave testimony to the *Foundation pour la Memoire de la Shoah*,[33] which took video testimony from survivors, much like **Spielberg's recordings**. In her recorded testimony, Solange never mentioned that Nana's brother, Adam, was part of the Jewish ghetto police or that he had a role turning in her father and brother. Nor did Solange disclose that he and her brother, Adam, had been inseparable friends from the time they were born. Solange understood the position in which her cousin found himself.

In her video recordings, Solange said that when the ghetto police came for her brother and father, there was some confusion between the names, Szylberstajn and Szylberberg. They asked the ghetto police whether they were looking for the right persons. The ghetto police officer assured them that Adam and Maurice would return. They never did return. Solange never forgave her cousin for not warning her father and brother so that they could have tried to escape.

Nana had heard the story before, from Tola as well as from Solange. Later that night or the next morning, Nana finished the story for me. Nana said that her brother, Avram, couldn't turn in his dear cousin or his uncle, so someone else, other ghetto police, had to do it. The policeman who came to the Szylberstajn home that evening was not Solange's cousin, Avram. It was a stranger. That's why the police officer was confused about the names. I wonder whether the confusion over the names Szylberstajn and Szylberberg might not have been the result of something Nana's brother Adam may have done to try to save his cousin and uncle.

Solange held her tongue in the documentary video, just like she held her tongue that evening with Nana and me in her kitchen. It was one of those stories that she sometimes would not or could not finish. When Nana finished the story for me, later than evening in Paris, she said that this was the only thing that Solange ever held against her, but she doesn't judge. Then, thinking about her brother, Nana said to me that you can never judge another until you have been in their shoes, as you never know what you would have done.

---

33 Solange's testimony can be found at https://entretiens.ina.fr/-de-la-shoah/Najman/solange-najman/sommaire

CHAPTER 32

Solange in the Shoah, Part Two: From Radom to Auschwitz

The following morning after Solange's father and brother were taken, Solange and her mother heard shots. This was not an uncommon occurrence. The shots came from Wolanow, a village a short distance to the west of Radom. Today we would call it a suburb of Radom. Jews were taken there, shot and buried in mass graves there. Solange's brother, Adam was taken there, with several others. They were ordered to undress, and, naked, they were given shovels and told to dig. After they had dug their graves, they were shot.

The three women, Solange, her mother and Helène, heard the shots. Solange remembers her mother saying instantly "It's my son."

Solange replied "Maman, what are you saying? Why are you saying this?" When Solange described these events, years later, she understood, having lost her first born son.

"Maman had a feeling."

After her brother's murder was confirmed through contacts with the ghetto police, Solange and her mother were in bed for days. Her brother, Adam, was dead. Her father was taken with her brother. She learned that he was taken to Auschwitz, but at that time, she did not yet know what

Auschwitz was. She learned this from a woman who approached Solange one day around that time.

The woman said "Listen to me. I am a *kapo* and I know where your father is. I was in Auschwitz and your father is in Auschwitz."

The woman was not a kapo, as kapos were prisoners, and were not free to leave and re-enter the camp. Yet despite identifying herself as a **Kapo**, she did have access into the camp.

She continued "I know the guard at the entrance, who, what's the name, the one who opens prisons, eh? And you can give me a little letter if you want."

She said that she would not only deliver the letter but would bring back a return letter from Solange's father.

"But you have to pay for that," she concluded.

The money was not important. Solange's mother was relieved to hear that her husband Maurice was alive. Hearing that he was alive and that they could connect with him reawakened her will to live. The death of her son was a low point but hearing that her husband was alive revived her. She went to the black market and purchased eggs and other basic food supplies. Her son was gone, but she had to eat to be strong for her husband, as the next day the Kapo woman was coming to pick up the package for Maurice.

They sold some things to raise the money the woman demanded and gave it to her. It was a risk, but a risk they had to take. They were rewarded a few days later with a note from Maurice. He wrote that he was alive and he asked about Abram, his son. He concluded the note by telling the three women, Solange, Henya and his wife, Manya, that they must stay strong, because "for us, it is over", apparently referring to himself and his son, Abram.

Solange wrote a response that they sent back with the woman. Solange wrote that she and her mother and Henya were surviving and well. She did not say anything about her brother.

People were sent to Auschwitz to die. In 1943 in Radom, Solange did not yet realize what that meant, what her father meant when he wrote "for us, it is over." Solange had heard the shots that killed her brothers. She had witnessed hangings in Radom, but, she says that when she exchanged these short notes with her father, she had no idea about the ovens and the magnitude of the machinery of Auschwitz as a death camp. She and her mother sent a few more packages with cakes, but soon there were no more responses from her father.

Solange did not want to think that her father was dead. They tried always to maintain hope. After they lost communication with her father, Solange, Henya and Manya were taken from the ghetto in Radom to a labor camp in Pionki. The Nazis were clearing out the remaining Jews in Radom and closing the ghetto.

A labor camp was better than a death camp, but the work was hard. Solange and Henya worked in munitions factories there, making gunpowder in chemical plants. Solange and Henya were among the women whose job was, as Solange put it "to dry the ammunition to kill people". They had a terrible boss. They worked long, twelve-hour, even sixteen-hour days. The work was hard and the factory brutally hot in the heat of the summer. If something went wrong, the boss made them work even longer, until late into the night, or even all night.

Women would collapse at the job and be taken away, so Solange and Henya struggled to keep each other going. Solange would later say that they were being worked to death in order to help the Nazis kill other people. They slept in a barrack with twenty or thirty other women and had to be careful about what they did and said, as they didn't know who was an informant. Solange had a jewel that her father had given her that she kept in her shoe and her mother had some rings and other jewelry that they exchanged for food through the barbed wire. If you were caught trading for food through the barbed wire, both you and the Pole selling the food might be shot on the spot. Or you might just get 25 lashes with the whip if you were a good worker and they wanted to keep you alive longer.

The one thing the three of them—Solange, her mother, and Henya—had was each other. They committed to do whatever they could to stay together. Having each other gave the three of them strength.

In the summer of 1944, the three of them were transported to Auschwitz. The Germans were emptying Pionki, moving most of the prisoners who remained to Auschwitz. Solange, Henya, and Manya were packed onto hot and crowded cattle cars. People were piled upon each other. Within a couple of hours there were already corpses.

Compounding the heat was clothing. "We were told we were going to work, so we were dressed well", Solange related. Soon people began removing layers of clothing. Many stripped naked, men, women and children, all squeezed together, nowhere to urinate or defecate, except on each other. "We knew no shame", Solange lamented.

Two or three hours into the trip, many people had already died. The smell of death had become horrible. A young man, maybe seventeen, approached Solange. He pointed to the little windows and invited her to jump with him. Solange declined, explaining that she had her mother with her and would not leave her, but suggested that maybe her sister-in-law would go with him.

Henya also declined, preferring to stay with her sister-in-law and mother-in-law. This turned out to be a wise choice. As soon as the young man got out the window, he was shot.

By the time the train stopped, the three women were parched and thirsty. They were starting to go crazy. Manya turned to Solange and demanded Solange give her the diamond ring her father had given her and that Solange was keeping in her shoe. They inventoried the few pieces of jewelry they had. At the time Solange did not realize that her mother had swallowed the ring, taking a small piece of bread she had to help her get the ring down. Outside the window, Solange saw Poles and Ukrainians looking at the stopped cattle train packed so tightly with people, with Jews.

"Give me some water," Solange screamed out the little window. "I'll throw you a gold watch." She threw the watch out the window, but no one gave her any water.

CHAPTER 33

Solange in the Shoah, Part Three Auschwitz, Hindenburg and the Death March to Bergen-Belsen

The train arrived at Birkenau Auschwitz. There was an orchestra playing, to give them a good feeling, and the sign over the entry gates that said *Arbeit Macht Frei*, which means "Work Will Make You Free". But there were also the Nazi soldiers with whips shouting "*Schnell! Schnell! Schnell!*" which means "Quickly! Quickly! Quickly!"

Shortly after they arrived, they were given a tattoo, their number. Solange's number was A15037. Physically, it was not so painful, but Solange found it so humiliating that she could not stop crying. She cried so much that the young German soldier giving her the tattoo slapped her and shouted, "You shut up or I will make you a number from here until there, like that," threatening to tattoo a number all the way down her arm.

The woman that greeted them said "Here we are at Birkenau Auschwitz, we must listen, we must obey. Otherwise it is over there. You see what there is over there?"

She was pointing to the big oven, the crematoria. Solange, Henya, and Manya could see and smell the chimneys. They were now in the hands of the SS, the special soldiers in charge of eliminating the Jews and other so-called undesirables. As Solange explained, "we were no longer people. We were numbers." They were directed towards three German women with baskets, who told them to put everything they had— rings, watches—into the baskets. The three women looked carefully to see that everything was thrown into the baskets, even inspecting everyone's private parts, as Solange, her mother, Henya, and the other arrivals were told to take all their clothes off. Their hair on their heads and their bodies was shaved, and they were told, "now you will have a shower."

As they headed into the shower, they expected to be gassed. Solange, her mother and Henya were actually in the gas chamber. Then a man ran in and said, "Listen, this transport must be left because Goebbels has called. These are young women. They can still work."

The man operating the gas already had his hand on the throttle. Instead, it was what Solange rightfully called a miracle, just at the last minute. They were taken out and given long, oversized robes that did not fit. Solange and Henya started laughing and could not stop. Solange's mother yelled at them "Are you crazy?" but they could not stop laughing.

Then the guards threatened to shoot them if they did not stop, but Solange and Henya could not stop laughing. The more the guards threatened, the more they laughed.

The guards did not shoot them. The guards just took Solange, her mother and Henya back to the barracks with other women. They were given the striped dresses that were worn by the prisoners in the camps. The laughter turned to fear. That night, at the end of their first day in Auschwitz the selection started. Young German soldiers began herding the women into the transports, shooting at them to make them move, to the left, to the right. The German soldiers seemed to get pleasure from this.

Solange could no longer see her mother. Then she lost sight of Henya. The soldiers were commanding "to the right" and "to the left". Solange did not know which way to go, which way meant life and which way meant death. She began to feel like she was no longer a human being. Unsure what to do, she approached a young soldier. She knew a little German that her father had taught her, and with the Yiddish she knew, she was able to ask him in German which way to go.

She said "I don't know where to go. Do I have to go left or do I have to go right? I lost my mother. I lost my sister-in-law."

The soldier answered "Go to the back," and pushed her to the back. So she had life. As she moved back, Solange realized she was being pushed from behind. She tuned and realized it was Henya, who had come up and grabbed Solange from behind. Solange turned and was relieved to see her sister-in-law. But her mother, Manya, her Manya, was nowhere to be seen. Solange was sure she had gone into the gas chamber and was gone forever.

Solange and Henya had been sent to the right, which meant life, at least for the moment. They were in Birkenau, one of the more than forty camps that comprised the Auschwitz complex. The barracks where they were sent was surrounded by an electrified barbed wire fence. Many women, in their desperation, hurled themselves onto the fence, but Solange and Henya had each other for support. In the nights that followed, Solange looked at the crematorium, thinking that her mother had perished inside there, but Henya said, "We don't know," and encouraged Solange to have hope. Solange was lucky to have Henya.

They received a piece of bread each day, from which they took a bite in the morning and saved the rest for later. They were given a cup of soup, which Solange described as warm water, and a cup of coffee, which she also described as warm water. The women were also given pills so that they would not have their period, which Solange said was a good thing, because they had no way to wash or clean themselves. They looked at the smokestack of the crematorium and Solange thought that if only she were a cat or a mouse, she could sneak out under the door of the barracks.

Solange and Henya were in Auschwitz for only a few days longer before there was another "selection". The women, actually young girls in their teens and twenties, were again stripped naked and the Germans looked them over and made their selections with a singular cruelty. Solange recalled a German soldier pulling out one very attractive young girl, maybe fourteen or fifteen years old, whom he threw down on the ground. Then he stomped on her stomach with his boots until she was dead.

Solange and Henya were among the 350-500 young women sent to the newly opened Hindenberg work camp, a newly opened Auschwitz sub-camp at the Donnersmarck mill. The women prisoners were put to work there producing artillery ammunition and grenades, as well as welding bomb carts. When Solange and Henya arrived with this first group of young women, the new camp was already built, but the organization and the staffing all had to be put in order. The SS had to choose housekeepers for the chiefs and for the soldiers and they had to choose all the kapos. Henya was selected to be the housekeeper for the "Lagerführer", the commanding officer of the camp.

This put Henya in a position with enough sway that she was able to get Solange assigned to the kitchen staff for the kitchen that served the SS officers running the camp. Working in a kitchen was a much better than being worked to death in the factory. In addition, the woman the Germans had chosen as the head kapo of the kitchen was a German Jewess whom Solange had met and they had grown friendly during their time in Auschwitz.

The struggle for survival had become a little bit easier, now that Solange had become a cook's helper for the SS, but survival was still a daily struggle, with life and death balanced precariously on almost every daily choice. Things did not start well.

Her first morning, Solange arrived in the kitchen early and ready to start. The cook was already in an angry mood because he was being transferred to the Russian front, where the accommodations in the January winter were not as comfortable as the officers kitchen and where his life would be at risk. His first command to Solange was to start the fire, so they could make coffee and start breakfast.

Solange did not know how to start a fire, but she was too afraid to say anything. She started to take some wood. She piled it up. She fumbled around. She took a chance and she tried to light it. The wood started to burn. The fire got good and hot. When the embers turned red, red hot, the cook then ordered "now with your hands", ordering her to stir he fire with her bare hands

Solange started to move her hands toward the flame, but as her hands got closer, it was too hot and she pulled her hands back. So the cook began to beat her. He beat her until she was unconscious. Word of Solange's beating reached the commanding officers. Henya was informed and she was allowed to care for Solange. When Solange regained consciousness, the next day, she found the marks his hands had left on her face. The marks would be there for days.

Did he beat Solange because he was angry that he was being transferred to the front or because he was angry that Solange had done something wrong? Or did he just beat her for the fun of it, because he was cruel and he could act out his cruelty, as Solange would later speculate, "to act out his needs"?

Solange was reluctant to return to the kitchen, but when she went back the angry cook was gone. She was told that he had been sent to the front. In his place was a much younger cook, twenty-eight years old. The first thing he said was "I am not going to hurt you."

Solange looked at him. She felt comfortable from the look in his eyes. When he asked her to do this or to do that she felt comfortable enough to ask him questions. She explained that she did not know how to cook or anything about the kitchen, but whatever he told her to do, she would do. She thought at the time that maybe he was moved by her. He told her to take a little chair and use it as a stool. The pots were large, large enough to hold fifty or so servings, but Solange managed to stand on the chair and stir the rice pudding or the other dishes they prepared.

One Friday a short time later, this new young cook, called her over. "Pitula," he said. Solange never understood why he called her Pitula, but he began to tell her about his family.

"You know I have a young woman in Berlin with two children and my neighbors are Jews, and every Friday evening, they invited us for the gefilte fish. You know what that is, the stuffed fish?"

Of course Solange knew what gefilte fish was, but she did not answer. As she listened, she was nervous and a bit suspicious. She was afraid and her fear made her suspicious. She answered "Good, you ate gefilte fish at your neighbor's house."

The new young cook continued "Yes, they were very nice. We lived so well. I don't know what I am doing here." The cook finished by saying that he had no quarrel with Solange.

Solange was stunned. She did not know how to answer, so she said nothing. Nothing at all. She just did everything he asked of her. She had learned to make a fire, which she had ready for him every morning, and did whatever else he asked. Before long, he gave Solange the keys to the cabinets where the food for the SS officers was stored, saying "and when you need something in the kitchen, if I'm not there, you go, you open and you take."

It now was easier for Solange. As she was in the officers' kitchen, the food, even the leftovers on the plates, the bones and scraps from the regular mess hall, was much better than what was served to the Jewish prisoners. Now Solange was eating well. But she recognized that being trusted with the keys also carried a burden. As the days went by, she slowly gained a little confidence, but she still was afraid.

She knew that the guards in the watchtowers were watching her. They could see when she left the kitchen and if she was carrying anything. She did not know who knew that she had keys to the food cabinets. But Solange also had a little bit of a rebel spirit. Everyone does, she would say. When she cleared the plates, she would not only keep the food left on the plates for herself. She would gesture to the other girls, outside, to come share the table scraps.

Once she managed to take a large container of honey out of the kitchen. It was large, perhaps a kilo of honey, but she managed to hide the honey under her dress against her stomach. In the yard, she spotted the Lagerführer. He looked at her and she thought "I am not a good thief. He'll look at my eyes and he'll know. I am really in trouble!"

Solange quickly turned the other way. She spotted the wooden outhouse that the women prisoners used, and she went right in. There were three holes that the women could use and there were two other girls inside. She took the honey from under her dress, said "here", handing them the honey and telling them to enjoy. It was a close call.

One day, as Solange cleared the plates, the cook saw her take one bowl that still had some soup in it and put the bowl aside, underneath the sink, so that she could finish the soup later. Solange knew that he saw her put the bowl aside. The cook didn't say anything, and Solange also did not say anything. Solange continued to serve breakfast each morning, and other meals through the day. Among others, she regularly served the commander of the camp, an SS officer with a reputation for his cruelty. Solange would serve him coffee and check that he had butter for his bread, as she did the other officers.

A few days later, Solange noticed a piece of chocolate, a cigarette, a piece of bread and a piece of sausage on the kitchen table. These were not just table scraps. They posed a terrible, terrible temptation. The temptation had Solange pulling out her hair, as she knew the danger. But she resisted, telling herself that no she would not take any of these appealing treats, as she did not know why these things were there or what the consequences might be if she took them.

When the cook returned, he asked Solange why she didn't take the things. He said to her that they were there for her. Solange answered that she was scared to touch anything because he hadn't told her to take anything and so it was not hers to touch. The cook answered that every time that he left something, she should take it. What he then left was something special. She couldn't imagine: a cigarette!

Solange took the cigarette and put it in her pocket. That evening she returned to her room, which she shared it with the nine other girls, the cooks, the cleaning ladies, and the kapos. She arrived very happy, with a smile on her face, saying "The girls have a cigarette."

No one asked her how she got it. They each just took turns taking a puff of the cigarette. The cigarette came back around to Solange. As she was holding it in her hand, about to take a drag on the cigarette, the Lagerführer, the cruel commanding officer of the camp, came in and saw Solange with the cigarette in her hand.

He called Solange by her name, Zlata, saying "Come on my friend, let's go out my friend."

Solange thought that her death was assured. She went out with him. He started in with her.

"Who gave you that cigarette?"

All the girls were scared, for themselves and for each other, too.

"Who gave it to you?"

Solange answered "When I went out after cooking in the barracks, I found the cigarette ends in the dirt."

The Lagerführer looked at the burning cigarette. At that moment it was golden, still burning.

He repeated "Now, you have to tell me who it is who gave you."

Solange answered. "I cannot say who it is who gave me. I found the butt in the camp there."

The Lagerführer took out his gun, looked at her and said, "If you don't tell me you're going to heaven."

Solange went crazy with fear. She got down on her knees and kissed his shoes. She begged him. She said, "Do whatever you want with me, but give me my life."

Solange lifted her head and saw him looking at her with terrible contempt, as if he were thinking that she was going to die, not today, maybe tomorrow or maybe after tomorrow, good.

As he turned away, he said, "Tomorrow you don't go in the kitchen anymore, you go to work in the factory."

The next morning Solange did not know what to do. She was afraid to go to the kitchen, as she usually did, but equally afraid not to. She could not sleep that night, thinking about what she would do. She decided to go to her job as usual, despite knowing that the Lagerführer comes every day for breakfast. She thought "If he asks me, I will say why I came. I will say that I came to make you your breakfast."

At five in the morning, Solange was in the kitchen, to make the fire, the coffee, for the officers, for everyone. The Lagerführer came in with a cigarette in his mouth. He threw the cigarette on the ground.

He looked at Solange and said "You pick it up. Why don't you pick it up? "

"I'm afraid to pick it up now," Solange answered, very calmly. She was surprised at how docile she was.

The Lagerführer said "No, you take the cigarette, you take the cigarette."

He started to get angry. Solange took the cigarette but she didn't bring it to her lips or smoke it.

The Lagerführer said "Now you crush that cigarette with your fingers," and he sat down to watch her put the cigarette out with her fingers.

Solange tensed with pain as the embers burnt her fingers, as Lagerführer watched her extinguish the cigarette.

She said to him, "I came to make you breakfast, a good breakfast. See how I tremble?"

The Lagerführer got up and left, and Solange was able to stay in the kitchen, but her confrontation with the Lagerführer was not Solange's only test. There were others, for although she did not know it yet, the Germans were getting desperate. Allied forces led by the Americans and the British were approaching western Germany from France. The Soviets were rapidly crossing Poland and approaching Germany from the east.

Solange told of another time that a high-ranking officer came and demanded that she open the cabinets and give him some extra food "for his mother" or someone whom he claimed was starving. He knew that she had keys to the kitchen storage cabinets. Again, she did not know what to do, and again, as she got to this point in the story, she stopped. She did not say any more. Every time this happened, Solange had a hard choice to make. Her choices might not have been so hard if she had known how desperate the Germans were getting.

One day a transport arrived, and the chef said, calling Solange by his pet name for her, "Pitula, maybe your mother has arrived."

Solange went out, but she did not see her mother.

"It's a shame," the chef answered. Then he asked, quietly, "If the war is over, are you going to make me hari-kari?"

Solange said "No, I won't do anything to you at all. You're nice to me. I won't do anything to you."

Like the other Germans, the chef saw that the end was near, and was beginning to fear what would happen. In January 1945, Russians planes flew over the Hindenburg Camp, but instead of bombs they dropped flyers, pieces of paper that said "Hold on tight! We are coming, we are coming."

Clutching the leaflets, Solange, Henya and the other women cried and laughed and hugged each other with joy. They did not know what to expect next, but whatever it was, they were ready for it, even if it were death, "as long as it came quickly", as Solange explained in her testimony to the *Foundation pour la Memoire de la Shoah*. They just could not go on any longer as what they had become. "We couldn't. We couldn't [go on any longer]. We were really, we really were not people. We were . . . we are no longer people. We were, . . . we were there really . . . I can't tell you. There are no words. Slaves without names with numbers, with wild eyes, all wild."

The morning after the leaflets were dropped, or perhaps the morning after, the head of the camp had all the prisoners gather outside. At this point, the Russians were only ten kilometers, just over six miles, away from the camp. The women wrote with pencils in the barracks "save us, save us, save us, save us" before they were brought outside. Each of the prisoners was given a loaf of bread, some water and little else. Then the Germans counted the prisoners. Solange recalls "They counted us maybe a hundred times, thirty times. They counted us all the time, all the time, all the time."

As they were being counted Solange saw her cook. Before she looked away, she saw that he had shed his uniform and was running away in civilian clothes. Then the Hindenburg prisoners were forced to join the death march of January, 1945. The first to march were prisoners from Gleiwitz, another sub-camp of Auschwitz not far from Hindenburg. Gleiwitz, a men's camp, had political prisoners as well as Jews. The Germans evacuated the Hindenburg work camp next, the Hindenburg prisoners joining the Gleiwitz prisoners. The prisoners from Hindenburg were the first females these men had seen in years.

The Germans marched them a short distance to Dora, another men's camp. At Dora, one of the German political prisoners brought Solange and Henya hot potatoes and milk, a rare treat that Henya later spoke about in Charles's movie about Solange. Solange and Henya remembered that his name was Herber. This would be their last good meal until their liberation.

The Germans were retreating west to Germany with their prisoners. They had to travel quickly to stay ahead of the advancing Soviet forces, who were moving rapidly across Poland. The Germans could have abandoned the Jewish prisoners. Leaving them behind would have been the better tactical decision. But the Germans chose not to do so. Instead, the prisoners were evacuated on foot, in what became known as the Death March.

It was winter. It was cold. It was snowing. Solange and the other prisoners had no hats or coats or gloves. They only had their prison garb. Solange had makeshift shoes that she made from wood she scavenged from the prison barracks, using paper to hold them together. The commanders of the camp watched over them and marched with them on this hurried retreat.

There were several trucks. The prisoners were allowed to climb onto the trucks to relieve themselves. One woman, a companion of Solange's from the camp, was pregnant. She began contractions as they marched. Fortunately, there was a doctor among the male prisoners, and he assisted with the birth where they had stopped for the night. What happened to the baby? Solange does not know.

One morning Solange, Henya, and the other prisoners awoke to find that they had all been bitten. They scratched themselves and each other. Solange's description is that they had become like savages, unrecognizable as humans. In her words, "We scratched each other. We fought. It was horrible and that is this suffering, this pain, this lack of everything, this savagery. And we got to Bergen-Belsen."

CHAPTER 34

Bergen-Belsen and Liberation

Between 1935 and 1937, the Nazis constructed a large military complex close to the village of Belson, which is part of the town of Bergen in north central Germany. The training base became the largest military training base in Germany, primarily for armored units with barracks to house the workers who constructed the base. Since the end of the war it has been used as a NATO military base.

When they began the war in 1939, the Nazis started using the then empty barracks to house captured soldiers, and these barracks became a POW camp, a prisoner of war camp. It was intended to hold up to 20,000 Soviet POWs. In April 1943, a part of the Bergen-Belsen POW camp was taken for use by the SS as a concentration camp. Initially it was used as a "holding camp" or "exchange camp" for Jews who the Nazis intended to exchange for Germans interned in other countries, or for hard currency.

Between the summer of 1943 and December 1944 at least 14,600 Jews, including 2,750 children and minors were transported to the Bergen-Belsen "holding" or exchange camp, but only around 2,560 Jewish prisoners were ever actually released from Bergen-Belsen and allowed to leave Germany. In March 1944, part of the camp was redesignated as a "recovery" camp, for prisoners too sick to work. These prisoners were brought from other concentration camps. They were supposedly in Belsen to recover and then return to their original camps and resume work, but most of them died in Belsen of disease, starvation, exhaustion and lack of medical attention.

In July 1944 there were about 7,300 mostly Jewish prisoners in the Bergen-Belson concentration camp (as opposed to the POW camp). By December 1944 the number had increased to 15,000. When the Germans began closing Auschwitz and the other concentration camps, in the face of the Soviet advance, some 85,000 Jews were evacuated and transported to Bergen-Belson, some in cattle cars and others by foot, on the infamous death marches. Many did not make it.

Those who did make it grew the number of prisoners at Bergen-Belson to around 60,000 by April 15, 1945. They included Margot Frank, who died at Bergen-Belson in February 1945 and her more famous sister Anne Frank, who died a few days later in March 1945, about the time or shortly after Solange and Henya arrived at Bergen-Belson. When they arrived, their whole group was immediately quarantined, which seemed odd, as they were being thrown into a place rife with diseases, including typhus, tuberculosis, typhoid fever, dysentery and malnutrition. The overcrowding in a facility meant to house no more than 10,000 prisoners only increased the number of deaths from diseases. The special status of those brought there to be exchanged no longer applied. All inmates were equally subject to starvation and epidemics.

Solange described Bergen-Belson as a death camp without a crematorium, filling up with people from all over the world, not just Jews and Romany (then known as Gypsies) but also Czechs, Tunisians, and many other nationalities and races, piled on top of each other, without even room to urinate except onto each other. Even with what Solange had been through she had never seen anything like this. Corpses lay everywhere, so that one could not walk with stepping on them.

Solange contracted typhoid. She had a fever but did not want to go to the camp hospital, as there were "selections" in the hospital. The Germans would come to the hospital and select who to take out and shoot. Aside from the shootings, "selections" were also made for cruel and inhumane medical experiments. So the hospital was something to avoid. Solange's companions rubbed red and orange colored papers on Solange's face. This gave her face enough color that she avoided being sent to the hospital.

On April 15, 1945, British forces, which included American and Canadian troops assigned to them, entered the camp. The prisoners, including Solange, Helène, and their group of women were liberated. The British distributed cans of sardines and packages of chocolate. The prisoners were not used to such food and many of them, already sick with dysentery, died because their stomachs could not handle such rich food.

"There were a lot of deaths, many, many deaths from dysentery," Solange said, in her recorded testimony. "Enormous numbers of dead. This is what is terrible. Freed and dead."

Solange was too sick with typhoid even to think about eating. In her recorded testimony, Solange would later say "I was lucky that I was sick, that I probably had a lot of fever, and that I didn't feel like eating chocolate or anything at all."

The British gave the prisoners three days to do anything they liked with the Germans who ran the camps who had not already fled. Some of the prisoners took revenge but Solange was too sick and too scared to think of revenge. She was afraid the Nazis would come back. There was no spontaneous burst of singing in Bergen-Belsen as there had been when the Russians approached the Hindenburg Camp.

Once it was clear that the British were in control, Solange, Henya, and two other young women sang, just the four of them. What did they sing? Solange does not remember, only that it was a song of freedom. The hard things were over. Solange was still sick with typhoid. Henya was also sick. They still did not know if they would live or die. But it was over.

There were soon many comings and goings. People were coming and going. Others did not know where to go. Some wanted to go to the United States, others to Palestine. People were sending and receiving messages through the Red Cross and other relief agencies. Through the Red Cross Henya heard from her brother Avram, who was in France. He was working with the French Red Cross and was able to have the Red Cross bring his sister to France. Solange had four uncles in France, her mother's brothers, but first she had to find her mother, Manya.

Solange stayed in Bergen-Belsen until she spoke to someone who had recently seen her mother in Lodz. So Solange left Bergen-Belsen, for Lodz, to look for her mother. The trip to Lodz was a difficult trip. There were no trains, no public transit. She traveled by foot through the forests. It took her three weeks to get to Lodz.

In Lodz, as in much of eastern Europe, people were coming and going, looking for family, trying to return home. Most of the Jews who lived in Lodz before the war were dead or gone. They were replaced by Jews from surrounding towns, whom the Nazis had brought to the Lodz ghetto, as they killed off Jews or transported Jews to the death camps from the Lodz Ghetto. Some of these outside Jews returned to their villages after the liberation. Others stayed in Lodz, occupying Jewish homes that had been abandoned or were otherwise empty.

Slawomir Grinberg's 2019 film, *Still Life in Lodz* is about the transition and continuity of Jewish life in Lodz after the war. But when Solange got to Lodz in the spring of 1945, there was no continuity or stability, just people coming and going. People gathered to inquire about family or friends at a restaurant in the train station, but Solange did not linger there as she had no money to buy any food. Solange went to the apartment building where her family had lived. She asked around. After about a week in Lodz, Solange learned that her mother had been in Lodz, but was no longer there. Manya had gone to Bergen-Belsen looking for her daughter.

Solange turned around and returned to Bergen-Belsen, but her mother was no longer there, either. Her mother was in Czechoslovakia, in prison. Solange never really explained how her mother ended up in prison, or how she got out. Perhaps Solange never knew, herself. In any event, a week or more later, her mother, Manya, appeared in Bergen-Belsen. How did she get there? Solange answered the question simply: "*Je ne sais pas.*" (I don't know.)

Solange would later describe this period of comings and goings on the part of herself and her mother by saying, "After many adventures, we found each other."

When they finally rendezvoused, Manya said to her daughter "I have something for you"

Solange responded with surprise, "From Auschwitz? You brought me something from Auschwitz?"

Manya pulled out the diamond, the diamond from the ring that she had taken from Solange when they were on the train to Auschwitz and Solange had thrown down her watch for a morsel of food.

Solange looked at the ring and said "It's not possible! Since we were together, you remember when we were searched and everything."

Manya told her daughter how she managed to keep the ring. Manya explained that she would always save a little morsel of bread and keep it. Every time she heard that a search or a "selection" in the camp was "being prepared", she would take the diamond and put in it the middle of the morsel of bread and swallow it. In a couple of days, the ring would come out the other end. Manya took a piece of bread, demonstrating for Solange. She must have smiled as she added that every time she looked at the diamond, it made her think of her daughter.

Manya was skinny, weighing only thirty kilos, barely a hundred pounds. But she was alive. Solange kept the diamond. Years later, she had the diamond set into a horseshoe ring while on a trip to Israel. It became her good luck piece, and always would remind her of her mother, Manya, when she looked at it.

During their time in Lodz, liberated prisoners were seeking out family. Solange met a man who had known her father Maurice and who was with him in Auschwitz, when he died. The man told her that as Maurice lay sick and dying, he called, deliriously, for his children, Adamik and Solange, and for his wife, Miriam. As for other family members, Solange did not find any other survivors in Lodz. No one knew what happened to Henry, youngest of the ten Szylberstajn siblings, Henry, the uncle whom Nana and Zlata both adored. Slowly, some stories were uncovered, but others are left unknown.

CHAPTER 35
Zlata becomes Solange

Once they were reunited, Solange and her mother were not sure where to go or how. Henya, Solange's sister-in-law, her *belle soeur*, and her companion for the last two years, was on her way to France, where she became Helène and was reunited with her brother Avram, who had become Albert. Avram had left Poland in 1932 with his other sister, Rachel. They fled hastily to France to avoid being arrested for their activities in the Jewish Bund, a socialist workers movement. Avram became Albert Najman and spent the war in France, fighting the Nazis in the Resistance, the French underground. When the war ended, Albert learned that his sister Henya was in Bergen-Belsen, sent for her through the French Red Cross and arranged for her to join him in Lille, where he was then living.

From Lille, Henya, now Helène, sent Solange a letter, a letter of introduction, which Solange was to show to a certain French officer named Kalka who would be looking for Solange and Manya. Kalka found them, and this was how, with Helène's help, Solange and Manya made it to Lille, where they rejoined Helène. Manya was quite content to stay in Lille and she wanted her daughter to stay with her. Solange wanted to learn a trade so she could support herself and not depend on anyone. Additionally, Solange wanted to go to Paris. She had four uncles there, four of her mother's eight brothers and Paris. . . . well, Paris is Paris.

Solange's four uncles, who had the last name Luxembourg, had left Poland long before the Second World War, coming to Paris after some years in Belgium. They were well established in Paris. One owned a large department store and was quite wealthy. The other brothers owned businesses, as well. Another brother, Itzhik, was a soccer player in Poland, where he was well known as Itzhik Luxembourg. This is how we know that the Luxembourg name was from Poland, and not acquired during the time the brothers were in Belgium, before getting to Paris.

Solange and Manya took the train from Lille. Solange did not know anyone in Paris, but when they got off of the train at the Gare du Nord train station, one of her uncles was on the platform waiting for them. As soon as he found them, he whisked them away to his home. Her four uncles helped Solange and her mother, their sister Manya, establish themselves in Paris. In Paris, the Polish girl called Zlata, or Sonya, became Solange.

Solange was eager to start a new life. She had started learning French while still in the camp at Bergen-Belsen, telling their escort, Officer Kalka, "Speak to me in French and I will answer, even if my French is not good. I want to learn."

When she got to Paris, Solange knew only two places, la Gare du Nord, the train station where she arrived, and la Rue de Montorgueil, the street where her uncle who picked her up at the station lived. Undaunted, she was ready to start her new life, as Solange the Parisian. She quickly found a job, cutting leather for an artisan who made handbags, purses, and wallets on Rue de Lancry. She wasn't paid very much, but it was enough for her to buy some new clothes. She later remembered that the first thing she bought as soon as she had a bit of money was a fancy bra. With lacy French underwear, she began to feel like a woman.

One of her uncles, who owned a clothing factory, made a beige frock coat and a new navy blue-and-white dress for her. With new clothes, Solange began to look as well as to feel elegant. In Paris she reconnected with Helène, and through Helène, Solange met Helène's brother, Albert.

Albert instantly fell in love with Solange, who now was a beautiful young woman. Albert offered to show her Paris. He took her to the artists' neighborhood of Montmartre and to the gardens of the Trocadero and to other romantic sites. He showed her a world she could not have imagined, after what she had been through.

"Paris, it was a dream!" she told me, years later.

Solange was smitten with Paris, but Albert, who was then living on Rue de Montrueil, and working in a factory that made raincoats, was smitten with Solange. He did all he could to win Solange's heart, but Solange resisted. He proposed to her, but after Auschwitz and Bergen-Belsen, she was not yet able to give in to romance or love, notwithstanding her feelings for Albert. Despite Paris and its charms, she was not yet capable of *l'amour*. After what she had been through and what she had to do, emotionally, to survive, she was just not able to allow herself to trust or to feel and show her emotions. Albert persisted. He was *formidable*, to use one of Solange's favorite words, and which in French means wonderful or magnificent.

Solange would later say, "Albert healed my wounds from the war."

Solange continued to hesitate. Albert persisted. He continued courting Solange. He pursued her for almost a year. Then one day, when leaving the leather atelier where she worked, Solange decided she would say "yes". Albert and Solange were married shortly thereafter in an apartment in Rue Duroc. It was in 1946. In the apartment they had a veritable feast consisting of canned food rations. They did not marry in a synagogue as Albert, the leftist, did not believe in God, and Solange, after Auschwitz, had also lost her faith in God.

Solange and Albert

The newlywed Albert and Solange lived in an apartment on Rue Blanc, where Albert continued to make raincoats for a living on a simple sewing machine. Solange was still making leather goods, while learning to speak French at the Alliance Française. Solange's mother, Miriam, who was quite fond of Albert, was living with them, "busy being the 'elder'", as Solange put it.

This marriage made Solange and Helène "*belle soeurs*", or sisters-in-law, a second time. The first was when Helène, then Henya, married Solange's brother, Abram, in the Radom ghetto. This second time, when Solange married Helène's brother, was in much better circumstances. It was a civil and not a religious marriage. Solange, never a pious or religious woman, had lost her faith in God.

While she did not go to synagogue, Solange called Helène every Friday evening, before dinner. Solange said "That was my shabbat." Although she was not a religious woman, Solange remained avowedly Jewish, maintaining a bond with both the Jewish people and with Israel.

Albert and Solange enjoyed some very happy years together. They had two sons, Maurice, born in 1948, and Charles, born in 1956. Solange called the two boys her "two wonderful children". These two boys were two of eight French Najman cousins, two children each of four of the seven children of Yitzhak and Perla Najman of Radom, two brothers and two sisters, who ended up in France. In addition to Albert, Rachel and Helène, they were joined by their brother, Mordecai, who became Marcel. A fifth Najman sibling, Menashe, was greeted by his two brothers and two sisters in Marseilles, but he continued on to Israel, with his wife and two daughters, Shoshana, or "Shosh", and Zipporah, or "Zipi". This made a total of ten Najman cousins that included our cousins, Maurice and Charlie.

Rachel, who had come to France with Albert in 1932, had married Baruch Flank and they lived in an apartment in a Paris neighborhood during the German occupation. Paris streets were dangerous. They were never certain who was a "nationalist" or collaborator, but Rachel and Baruch survived. Their first son, Maurice, was born while they were in hiding. They sent him to the countryside about 125 miles outside of Paris, where he was hidden until the end of the occupation. Maurice is a retired professor of German who lives in Paris. Maurice has one son, Sami. Sami lives with his mother, Habiba, in Brest, in Bretagne.

Rachel and Baruch's second son, Yves, was born in Paris in 1949. Yves lives in southern France, in Montpelier, where he teaches theatre, writes and produces plays, and does some other writing. With his first wife, Anne Marie, Yves has two daughters: Nadja, born in 1970, and Maud, born in 1977. With his second wife, Martine, he has two sons: Leo, born in 1990, and Mathias, born in 1991.

Yves's daughter Nadja has a son, Joey, born in 1993 and a daughter, Cyanna, born in 2000. Yves's daughter Maud has a child named Luz, born in 2007. Yves's son Leo has a daughter Alya, born in 2020.

After joining Albert and Rachel in France, Helène married Serge Alembic, also a survivor of the Shoah. He came from a very rich family in Poland, an industrial family that owned factories before the war. Upon arriving in Paris, he worked in the leather business, like Albert and Solange. Helène and Serge had two sons, Pierre and Yves Michel (sometimes just called Yves and sometimes just Michel).

Pierre, the elder of Helène and Serge's sons, died of cancer at the age of 61. He worked in a bank, but his true passion was playing guitar, especially Bob Dylan songs. Pierre spoke Yiddish and a little Hebrew.

He was married twice and has two children, a son and a daughter. His son, Sebastien, married an Asian woman, Ling Jin and they have one son. Pierre's daughter, Camille, is married and has a daughter. Pierre visited Israel often, and developed a close relationship with his Israeli cousins Shoshana and Zipporah. He spoke often on the phone with Zipi, close to once a week.

Yves, Helène's and Serge's younger son, is a doctor. He married Lucien Toledano, a Moroccan Sephardi woman, and the two of them live in Strasbourg. Yves Michel has two daughters, Lena, who lives in Paris, and Claire, and a son, Victor. One of these daughters accompanied Helène at Solange's funeral. She pushed her grandmother Helène with one hand on Helène's wheelchair, and held her daughter, Helène's great granddaughter, with the other. Helène was still healthy enough to speak at the funeral, saying a few words about Solange, but Helène has since passed away.

The fourth French Najman was Marcel, or Mordecai. Marcel and his wife Betty had two daughters, Paulette and Jocelyne. Paulette died young, in her thirties. Jocelyne, is married to Jean Michel. They have a daughter, Judith, who lives in Toulouse.

Menashe passed through France on his way to making *aliyah*. He had met his wife Miriam Glicklich in Warsaw, where they married in 1938. After their wedding, Menashe returned to Radom with his wife. Miriam was pregnant when the ghetto was set up in Radom, and they fled east, with Miriam's two sisters, across the frontier into Soviet territory. They kept moving east, as the Nazis advanced. At some point the Soviets drafted Menashe into the military. Fortunately, Miriam was with her two sisters when she gave birth to their first daughter, Shoshana, in a town called Krasnodar in the Caucasus, as they were moving east. They were still in Russia when Miriam gave birth to a second daughter, Zipporah, in 1947, in Stalinsk in Siberia.

After Zipporah was born, Menashe and Miriam returned to Poland, hoping to go home to Radom with their two baby girls. On the way to Radom, or in Radom, where there was a pogrom, they were greeted at a train station by jeering antisemitic Poles, unhappy at seeing Jews returning to reclaim their homes.

"They killed so many Jews, and look how many came back!" one Pole shouted.

Not feeling very welcomed, Miriam said "we are not staying here."

Menashe and Miriam left Poland. They found shelter in Germany, in Bergen Belsen, which had become a DP camp, at that time operated by a Jewish settlement agency. From there they made it to France, where Menashe's four surviving siblings had settled. Menashe's siblings met their brother, his wife and two daughters, when they arrived in Marseilles. Menashe would have stayed in France, with his siblings, but Miriam wanted to go to Israel.

Miriam said that after all the hardships they went through, this is her place to go, now that the Jews finally have a country. In addition she did not want to say goodbye to her sister who went through the whole war with her. Shoshana and Zipi both grew up in Israel, where they remained close as sisters, until Shoshana's death in 2008. Shoshana had a son, Yaron Yair, who is married with two sons of his own, Dor Yair and Amit Yair.

Zipi Naiman lives in Giva'taim, between Tel Aviv and Ramat Aviv. After school and the army, Zipi visited Paris where she met her cousins and became friendly with Charlie. She also was close with her cousin, Pierre, Helène's older son, until he died. Zipi has a daughter, Roni Naiman, who is the director of a city theatre company in Netanya. Roni also runs psychodrama workshops, included a workshop for holocaust, survivors. Roni has a daughter, Lyri Fadlon, and a son, Ori Fadlon.

Of the two other Najman siblings, the youngest, David, died as a young boy before the Shoah. The oldest, Moishe, followed in the footsteps of their father Yitzhak's brother, Yachiel, who was a proud member of the Jewish Bund. Moishe joined the **Dabrowski Battalion**, Polish volunteers who fought with the International Brigade against the fascist Nationalists of Francisco Franco in the Spanish Civil War. Moshe died in 1936, in the first months of the Spanish Civil War defending Madrid from the fascists. He was a hero to his brothers and sisters and all his nieces and nephews. Yves remembers his Aunt Helène taking him to Spain to see the monument in memory of her brother and Yves's uncle's brigade.

After Albert and Solange married, Albert continued to make raincoats in their apartment. He also remained active in socialist politics. He would remain a tradesman, always politically active, speaking as a voice of the working class. He passed this on to both his sons. However, Albert was much more than just a worker of the working class. He was an intellectual, a writer, self-educated, and sophisticated. With money from her Luxembourg uncles, Solange was able to buy a half interest in a leather goods store on Boulevard de Sébastopol. She eventually made the store her own. She was able to move from cutting leather to successfully operating the leather goods store, but she could not have done it without Albert's help. Indeed, as Solange's partner he proved as capable a businessman as he was a voice of the working class.

Together they stocked the store with a range of leather goods, from handbags, wallets and briefcases, to belts, gloves and luggage. They also sold scarves and other accessories. The store slowly evolved into an elegant shop, as Solange learned new skills such as how to create attractive window displays. In fact, in the 1960s, Solange received a commendation from the Mayor of Paris for having the most attractive window displays on the Boulevard.

The store did well and became a steady source of income. Solange and Albert bought the third-floor flat at 36 Rue d'Hauteville where Solange would live until her death in 2018. The flat was in the heart of what was then the leather district, across the street from a leather *atelier* with a large neon sign that you could see from Solange's windows announcing *Cuir et Peaux* (Leather and Skins). Whenever I walked down Rue d'Hauteville on my way to visit Solange, I always knew I had arrived when I saw that neon sign that seemed to depict a Native American with the words *Cuir et Peaux*.

Solange and Albert set up workshop space for Albert's sewing machine in their flat. He would work there and they would raise their two sons together there. These were good years for Solange, who enjoyed raising her two boys with Albert. There were evenings out together, when the two of them went dancing. There were summer vacations to the country or to the beach with the boys, and there was a yearly trip to Evian, where Solange and Helène joined their fellow Holocaust survivors in a yearly retreat paid for by German reparation money.

These good years lasted until 1970, when Albert died. When Albert died, Maurice was 22, a confident and self-assured young man. Charles, on the other hand, was barely a teenager, just 14 years old, still a student in school. After his father died, Charles took his mother aside and told her he would take care of her.

"Look, I'm going to offer you something," It was always Charles' dream to be a director. "I would like to make a film of you".

Charles knew about his mother's nightmares, the nightmares that still tormented her and would torment her for the rest of her life. He knew about these nightmares and about many of his mother's secrets because Solange talked with her son, Charles, as she did with no one else.

Solange in Paris

"I would like to make a film of you," Charles told his mother. It was always Charles's dream to be a director.

Solange was taken aback. "But you're too young." And then, because Charles was a diabetic, she added, "And you are not well! How are you going to do it? It will be a failure!"

"It will be very good," he answered.

Solange was hesitant. "Yes, but I can't guarantee what it will be. Your first film, if it will be a fiasco, I would be very sorry."

Charles was confident. "You won't be sorry because it won't be a fiasco."

Solange still hesitated. "Oh, I don't know if I could relate all that to myself . . . to remember all of these things. It's terrible! I don't know, I will give you the answer in three days."

As Solange considered Charles's offer, she thought to herself, "Since I am still alive, I must do something for the youth, and especially for my son."

Solange finally agreed to let Charles make a film about her experiences in the Shoah, but it would be years before Charles would write the screenplay. He would first finish school, begin his career and establish himself as a director. The film was finished and released some twenty-five years after Albert's death, in 1995, with its American debut at the Boston Jewish Festival in 1996. It was entitled *La Mémoire est-elle soluble dans l'eau?* (*Memory, Can it be Dissolved in Water?*), but it was known simply as *Memoire*.

CHAPTER 36

Solange's First Visit to America and Nana's Last Trip to Paris

Solange came to Boston for the 1996 American debut of *Mémoire*. That was not her first trip to America. That first trip, when she came to visit her long-lost cousin, Nana, in Cherry Hill, New Jersey, was in 1970 or 1971. After Solange and Nana reconnected in Paris in 1965, Nana was eager to host her new-found cousin, Solange. It took a few years. International travel and transatlantic flights were still expensive and unusual events then.

Nonetheless, Nana was eager to show Solange her home in America, proud of the successful life she had built. The pleasure Nana took from the visit lasted long after Solange returned home to Paris. For years after the visit, Nana would joke with Vivian and me about how Solange pronounced the name of our street, Nature Drive, as "Na-too-ra Dree-va". Nana would mimic Solange's unique Yiddish French accent and we would laugh. Nana laughed a lot when talking about Solange and about the times when she was with Solange.

Although Solange had lost her husband, Albert, she had a traveling companion, Henri Dymant, to accompany her on this first trip to the United States. Also a Holocaust survivor, Henri and Solange had known each other for years. He was one of the French survivors, along with Solange and her *belle-soeur*, Helène, whose annual summer gathering at

Evian was the basis for Charles's film tribute to his mother. Henri and Solange had become closer after Solange lost Albert. Henri was also alone, as his wife, long suffering from debilitating mental illness, had been in a sanitorium for many years. She spent the rest of her life institutionalized. As long as she was alive but not mentally competent, she could not agree to a divorce, leaving Henri unable to remarry.

Marriage was not an issue for Solange and Henri, who were happy to have each other's companionship. It was not an issue in France, where affairs of love and marriage had always been treated much more openly. It shouldn't have been a problem in Litka's house, either, but the house was Jan's house as well, and Solange and Henri's relationship was a serious problem for Jan. The practical sleeping arrangement would have been to offer Solange and Henri Vivian's room, which had a double bed, and have Vivian sleep in my room, as I was away at college. Jan would not allow this, refusing to permit Solange and Henri to set what he thought was a bad example for his teenage daughter.

Instead of offering the double bed in Vivian's room to Solange and Henri, Jan offered Solange the single bed in my bedroom and insisted that Henri sleep downstairs on the fold-out couch in the den. Solange would have none of this. She and Henri took their bags and slept in a nearby motel. Nana, caught in the middle, never spoke about how embarrassed she must have been.

Solange was not upset with her dear older cousin, Litka, but she never forgave Jan. Solange, an open-minded French woman, took Jan's behavior personally and she never understood how he could treat his wife with such disrespect.

Years later, when I first visited Solange in Paris, I unwittingly gave Solange further fodder to support her dislike for my father. We were sitting at her kitchen table, discussing family, life, the world situation and affairs of love. Asking about the family and recalling her visit to her cousin, she asked me how I liked the belt.

I did not know what she was talking about, and asked, quite innocently, "What belt?"

Then I remembered the gifts that Solange had brought for Nana and Vivian and my father. Solange, of course, had brought me a gift as well, a belt from her leather goods store. As I was not there, she had left my gift with my father, expecting he would give it to me. Little did she realize that at the time Jan and I did not speak. Unhappy with me over my opposition to the war in Vietnam and my harsh criticism of then-President Richard Nixon, which he considered unpatriotic, Jan had said to me, "No one in my house will speak this way about the president."

"Then I am out of this house," I said and I walked out the front door, slamming it behind me. I did not return for years. Nor did I speak to my father for a long time after that. I spoke to Nana, who called me from time to time, but from that point on, I was on my own. I was a sophomore at Penn at the time, the spring of 1969. I paid my own way for the remainder of my college career, earning my tuition and the cost of my room and board from scholarships, loans, and from student work-study jobs and summer jobs.

I never knew about the belt, nor did I ever learn what happened to the belt. Maybe it was put aside for me, and lost, or just forgotten over time. For Solange, it was one more measure of Jan's selfishness, reaffirming her dislike for Jan. The belt was not so important to me as other wrongs. The biggest was not allowing me to meet Maurice and Charles in 1965, when I was 15, when we were all still teenagers. This hurt me much more, as it would be many years before I got to meet Maurice and Charles. I would only know Maurice for ten years before he died.

In January 1990, I returned to Paris with Nana. At this time, I called Nana every Friday, sometimes more often, and on one of those calls, Nana mentioned that she was getting old, and that Uncle Adolphe was over 90. She said that she wanted to see Adolphe one more time and she wanted to visit Solange again while she could still travel. She asked if I would be her escort.

"Of course!" I said.

That would be a very different trip from the visit a year and a half earlier with Linda and our children. Nana and I stayed with Solange for a week or maybe ten days. We also visited with Adolphe and Maggie. It was on this trip that Adolphe discussed his views about truth and fidelity in a marriage. It was also on this trip that I first spent time with Maurice and Charles, the first time that I got to know them each a little.

I was traveling with a guitar, as I often do. The guitar and two copies of Neil Young's then-new CD "Rocking in the Free World", which I had brought as gifts for Maurice and Charles, were on the bed in the bedroom where I was staying. When Maurice and Charles arrived to see me, they saw the guitar and two identical CDs. They asked about the guitar and the CDs and I said that I often traveled with a guitar and gave an explanation why. Then I said that the two CDs were gifts for them. The two brothers looked at each other as they thanked me for the gift. I sensed that the guitar and the Neil Young CDs, gave me some credibility in their eyes.

Over the week I got to know them. Maurice was busy preparing for a large event he was organizing. The Berlin Wall had recently come down, on November 9, 1989, just two months earlier. Maurice was organizing an exhibition of art by artists from East Germany. It was the first opportunity for East German artists to show their work in the western world. The exhibition was entitled "*Est ou Est*", a clever play on the French words for east (*est*), or (*ou*) and west (*ouest*), so you can read the poster as "East or West" or as "East West". It was a subtle suggestion of the two extremes coming together.

Maurice took me with him to the exhibition hall, La Grande Halle. The "Grande Halle" was a former slaughterhouse that was part of La Villette, a large new park built in the 1980s on the northern outskirts of Paris. It was built for Parisians, off the tourist path and not exactly a tourist attraction.

When we arrived at the hall, preparations for the exhibition were underway. The exhibit had been scheduled only a few months before, as opposed to the usual scheduling of an exhibit a year or two in advance. We arrived mere days before it was scheduled to open. The scene was chaotic as there was little time before the opening and much still to do. No sooner did we enter the hall than various people started approaching Maurice with this question or that problem.

Maurice addressed each of them in a calm and collected manner, despite the seeming chaos of activity around him. He addressed each person's problems while we proceeded through the exhibition hall, managing to balance telling me about the exhibition and attending to the business of getting the exhibit set up and ready to open. I only regretted that I never saw the finished exhibition as Nana and I left a day or two before it opened.

Charlie also found time to take me out for a drink. We went to the bar at the Grand Rex Cinema. Over the years, after I began visiting Solange regularly, Charlie always found time to meet me for drinks or dinner, if he was in Paris. Along with the Brasserie Flo, where Charles took his mother for dinner every Sunday, the Grand Rex was one of Charlie's favorite venues. It was on Blvd. Poissionnièrre, the grand boulevard at the end of Rue d'Hauteville, a short walk from Solange's apartment, where Charlie had grown up. The Grand Rex was a classic movie house that showed not just French films but popular and classic American films. It was where Charlie learned to love film, but it was also the venue for rock and roll shows and where Charlie saw Bob Dylan, Neil Young, Van Morrison and many other American and British rock stars.

I was taken by how much better Charlie spoke English than I spoke French. He may have studied English in the lycée, but I had studied French in college at Penn as well as in high school and during my summer in France. I asked Charlie how he was able to learn to speak English so much better than I spoke French.

Charlie replied, without hesitation, "Bob Dylan, the Rolling Stones, and American movies."

CHAPTER 37

Charlie, Solange's Shomer

Over the years, especially after Nana died and I began visiting Paris regularly to see Solange, Charlie always made time to meet me if he was in Paris when I came. Perhaps it was because he recognized the affection I had for his mother, for I was not only visiting Solange regularly, but calling her, if not weekly, close to that often. If she did not answer after I called several times, I would begin to worry. It was not just that I was concerned about Solange: it was also that I got so much from these phone calls myself.

I don't think Solange realized the wisdom she had acquired from her experiences and relationships, but the more we communicated, the more I appreciated her humble wisdom. She had seen a lot and suffered the loss of home, family, and friends. As the bonds between us grew, she asked me probing questions about my children, about my sister and her children, about our relationship, and about my marriage and my sister's marriage. She always had wise advice to give.

Maybe Charlie saw the strength of the relationship between his mother and me, and maybe that was why he always found time for me. After Maurice died and as Solange was getting older, Charlie appreciated the love and respect I had for his mother, whom he guarded so carefully. But I think there was something more that Charlie sought. Something that had to do not just with Charlie's family past, but with his Jewish past.

Charlie always had an interest in his Jewish past. His film *"Memoire"* was a film about his mother's grace and strength but it was about more than that. In the film Solange symbolized the strength of the Jewish people, their ability to survive. Charlie was not religious or observant in any way, but as the child of a survivor, he was intrigued by the impact of the holocaust and by the abilities of the Jewish people to survive such assaults on our existence. This fascination with the Jewish people and our survival became something he would share with me after the debut of "*Memoire*", often and in different ways, as he explored Jewish-themed projects and the after effects of the holocaust that not only intrigued him but haunted him as well.

My first insight into Charlie's fascination with Judaism came on a Friday night in Paris in the summer of 1996. After my daughter Shira's graduation from Brookline High School, I took her on a bicycle trip to tour the chateaus in the Loire Valley as a graduation present. When we arrived in Paris, Solange's companion, Henri, picked us up at the airport and brought us, our luggage, and our bicycles, to Solange's apartment in his car. (Solange did not drive or have a car.) Little did Solange realize that I would be unpacking and reassembling the bikes in the entryway of her apartment.

We stayed with Solange for several days before beginning our cycling trip to the Loire Valley. In those few days in Paris we saw Adolphe and Maggie, Jean Claude, and Lilian, ascended the Eiffel Tower, and had dessert at the Café de la Paix, the setting of many films and works of literature. Without question, however, the highlight of our stay in Paris was dinner Friday night at Solange's house. Maurice and Charlie came and each of them had brought a surprise. Maurice brought his daughter Esther, whom Shira and I were meeting for the first time. Esther was a bright, precocious young redhead, just like Shira. It would seem that the two would easily find something they had in common and they sat next to each other. But Esther chain-smoked through the meal, and Shira had a hard time trying to avoid the cigarette smoke. An inauspicious first meeting.

After we ate, Charlie pulled out his surprise. It was a videocassette. He got up, went over to the TV and without much ado put the cassette into the VCR. He said that it was his most recent film, *La Memoire, est-elle soluble dans l'eau?*, and that it was about Solange. He also said that he and Solange would be showing the film at film festivals in Krakow and Berlin.

Shabbat Dinner June 1996

The film was in French with English sub-titles. It was *incroyable* (incredible), to use one of Solange's favorite words. We sat with our eyes glued to the screen from the opening scene, Solange bringing out a cake for a celebration, the celebration of the 50th anniversary of the liberation from Auschwitz, until the last scene of Solange dancing. Both these scenes were filmed in Solange's dining room, where we were sitting.

In between these scenes, we saw an amazing film about an amazing woman. The film was about the Holocaust, but it was unlike any Holocaust film I have ever seen. It was about the annual vacation Solange and her fellow survivors, this group of friends, took to the healing waters at

Evian, paid for by the German government. The German government paid reparations to each of these survivors and covered the cost of the week at Evian as part of their psychological treatment.

Every summer, each survivor had to get a letter from their therapist, saying that they were still affected by their concentration camp experience and that their treatment required the quiet of a week with the healing waters of Evian. Both the French title and its English translation of the title of Charlie's film, *Can Healing Waters Wash Away the Memories?*, in posing this question, offer a taste of Charlie's irony, but his droll sense of humor fully emerges in the scene where Solange meets with her therapist to get her letter, after perfunctorily recounting the symptoms she still suffered: nightmares, depression, her fears and other symptoms. Indeed, what she went through never left her.

Solange, Helène, and Henri all played themselves in the film. There was only one professional actor in the cast. He circulated among the group of survivors asking questions to keep the story moving. While the film did not mask the horror of what Solange and her fellow survivors went through, it was not about the horrors of the past. The film did not show what happened the camps, the torture, the deaths or the physical suffering.

Charlie was interested in life after Auschwitz. The film is about the mother he knew as he was growing up and what she carried with her from what she went through. It is about how she still suffered, years, decades, later, indeed for the rest of her life, but how she lived in spite of the damage to her that she carried inside her. It was about how she carried on. The film is a positive film, about how Solange triumphed over what had been inflicted on her, although it did not hide how she continued to suffer. The film was about how those who survived the horrors were able to live life again. The colors of the film were bright, not the somber grays and browns, the dark colors we expect in films of the Shoah. Throughout the film, Charlie's droll sense of humor helped establish the tone, serious but uplifting, and often tongue-in-cheek.

My favorite scene is during a portion of the film showing the trip some of the group took back to Auschwitz as part of the 50th anniversary. Solange and Helène are walking down a now tree lined path inside what was the camp. It is a gorgeous sunny day and the trees are lush and green.

As Solange and Helène walk, Solange smiles as she says to Helène "If only the capo could see us now." Her words were a declaration of victory.

I was so taken by the film that I immediately asked Charlie when the film would be shown in the United States. Despite no experience or knowledge of the film industry or distribution of international films, I convinced Charlie to let me help him get the film shown in the United States. I knew it was the perfect film for the Boston Jewish Film Festival, and I was eager to follow up on getting the film shown in the States once Shira and I completed our bike trip and returned home.

That Friday night was a very special evening. There was only one thing wrong with that evening, something that, in my excitement about the film, I did not realize until years later, when I innocently mentioned that evening to Jean Claude. The thing that was wrong with the evening was that Jean Claude and Lilian had not been invited, and Jean Claude was very hurt by his exclusion.

I don't think that Solange deliberately excluded Jean Claude or Lilian from that Friday night dinner. I suspect she never thought about inviting them. For her it was a family shabbat dinner she was putting together for Litka's son and granddaughter. Her two sons and one granddaughter were also invited, as well as Henri. It just never would have occurred to her to invite Jean Claude or Lilian. They weren't Jewish. They went to church, not synagogue and they didn't know about shabbat or a shabbat meal. A Friday night shabbat dinner was not something that involved them.

Solange had an extended Jewish family, but Jean Claude or Lilian had never been part of it. Solange was close to her mother and their experience during the Shoah just brought them closer. Miriam, or Chacha Manya, was a presence in Solange's house until she died. Manya also was close to her brothers, Solange's uncles, who had brought them to Paris, provided for them, helped them settle in, and helped Solange get started in a business. Vivian and I both remember Chacha Manya, dressed in black, looking like an old Jewish grandmother, in Solange's kitchen

Adolphe, Jean Claude's father, had married a Catholic woman and their children were raised as Catholics. I don't think that Solange was judgmental about this. She just did not think to invite Jean Claude or Lilian to her shabbat dinner, just as she would not invite them to go to shul to say kaddish. Solange probably never even noticed that she did not invite Jean Claude or Lilian to that Friday night dinner. Yet Jean Claude remembered, just as he remembered the confirmation suit.

On a later visit to Paris, years later, when I mentioned that Friday night, Jean Claude opened up to me about how hurt he was that he and Lilian were not invited that evening. I then realized that, aside from Lilian's surprise visits to Solange's flat when I was visiting, in my years visiting Paris, I rarely saw Lilian or Jean Claude together with Solange. Lilian would show up at Solange's, with very short notice, when I was visiting. She would bring some chocolates, a bag of pastries or some other delights, smile her effervescent smile and joke and laugh until she had Solange joining her in song. Lilian's exuberant manner, always on display during these visits, hid emotions that only revealed themselves in the paintings that were so prolific late in her life.

It was rare for Jean Claude to appear at Solange's, although occasionally, especially in Solange's last years, the three of us would meet at a restaurant, usually one near Solange's flat. Jean Claude was much more reserved than his sister about his inner feelings, but over time I became aware of the depth of the hurt that began when he was a boy.

Jean Claude carried the hurt over Solange's uncles refusing to help his family with his confirmation suit for the rest of his life. The refusal had nothing to do with Solange, who may not have been present or even known about the confirmation suit incident.

Adolphe did not really know Solange before he came to Paris. When Adolphe left Lodz for Vienna as a teenager, Solange had not been born. Adolphe met Solange during her mother's "seal you lip" trip to Vienna, but Solange was still a little child then, a Polish girl named Zlata. The grown woman, Solange, who lived in Paris after the war, as an adult, was living with her mother, but Solange had nothing to do with Adolphe's request to her mother and her uncle. Nor did her two sons, Maurice and Charles, who probably never knew about the incident.

Yet the aftereffects of the confirmation suit refusal nonetheless continued into the next generations. Jean Claude carried the slight for the rest of his life. It complicated the relationship between Jean Claude and Lilian with their first cousin, Solange. While my visits to Paris may not have been the only times Jean Claude or Lilian saw Solange, their contact with Solange were rare. I also suspected that Jean Claude and Lilian were hurt that I had such a close relationship with Solange even though I had known Anna, the former Lilian, and Jean Claude much longer.

Over these years, Solange and I grew closer, especially after she lost her firstborn son, Maurice, and I lost my mother. Solange was a Jewish mother, a role she would come to play almost as though she had been typecast, while Lilian and Jean Claude were more French, more aloof, not always available the way Solange was whenever I visited, although I must confess that my trips to Paris were planned around Solange's schedule, and not theirs. Not until years after that wonderful shabbat dinner in 1996 did I realize how this slight over the confirmation suit affected my visits to Paris. Nor did I realize that my visits to Paris, to Solange, added to the hurt caused by the confirmation suit.

Jean Claude and Lilian never really knew Maurice or Charlie, either. I am not sure that they ever even met Maurice or Charlie as adults. If I had known that at the time, I would have seen that they were invited to the 1996 shabbat dinner. By the time I realized that I could have been the link to connecting Jean Claude to Solange's sons, it was too late. That realization did not come until after Maurice had died, when Jean Claude asked me to introduce him to Esther and her son, Simon.

Was this pain all because of the slight over the confirmation suit, or was it because of what Adolphe had done for his brother in Vienna, many years earlier? Jean Claude remembers the Luxembourg brothers as men in black suits sitting in Solange's house when he went there with his father when he asked for help with the suit. The Luxembourgs were religious enough that they might have refused Adolphe's request for a suit for Jean Claude because it was for a confirmation, not a bar mitzvah. They were also loyal brothers, supporting their sister.

By the time I learned about the confirmation suit incident, it was already old history. It had festered with Jean Claude for a long time. Yet it had little to do with Solange, and after his father's passing, Jean Claude felt an obligation of respect to Solange, whom he felt had become the matriarch of the family after his father's death. It became clear to me that it was difficult for Jean Claude to put his hurt behind him, but he did so with the dignity that he always presented outwardly, to mask his innermost feelings.

After Solange died, Jean Claude became, in my eyes, the patriarch of the family. He stayed in touch and always asked about my children and grandchildren. Jean Claude and Nana always had a warm and close relationship and before Nana died, Jean Claude promised her he would stay in touch with her children. He took this promise seriously, as an obligation perhaps to his father as well as to Nana. He was very helpful to me in gathering his father's story, years later, after I took on the task of documenting our family history.

Charlie had begun that task with his film *Memoire*. I was so taken by the film that Friday night that I wanted the world to see it. It took some doing, but I managed to convince Charlie to let me help him get the film shown in United States. When Shira and I returned to Boston that summer, I had a videocassette of the film, with English subtitles and I called the director of the Boston Jewish Film Festival.

Most of the films for that November's festival had already been selected, but I convinced the director to look at my videocassette copy of *Memoire*. She was impressed enough to ask me about the logistics of getting permission and a celluloid copy of the film. The next step was to put her in touch with Jean-Marc Rouget, the producer, who owned the rights to the film.

When the film was accepted by the festival, I took on a second project: raising money to bring Charlie and Solange to Boston for the screening. I arranged for a private showing of the film that would be a fundraiser for the travel costs. I asked Hillel Levine to host the event. A professor at Boston University, he was then still riding the acclaim of his book, co-authored with Larry Harmon, *The Death of an American Jewish Community*, their 1992 study of redlining of Jewish neighborhoods in Dorchester, Roxbury, and Mattapan and the Jewish flight from these communities to Brookline, Newton, and elsewhere.

With support from friends, especially from the Brookline Havurah Minyan, I raised the airfare for Charlie and Solange. They came, staying with us in Brookline. Charlie was introduced at the debut of the film at the Coolidge Corner Cinema and spoke and answered questions after the screening. Solange also was introduced and also answered some questions. It was quite an event and I was quite proud of my cousin and his mother.

After the film debut, Charlie and Solange stayed for a couple of days. I was happy to be their tour guide. Charlie wanted to go to the Museum of Fine Arts. The MFA is not quite the Louvre or the Musée D'Orsay, and I was curious what he wanted to see there. He was interested in an exhibit of the photographs of **Man Ray**. It was the one thing he wanted to see in Boston. I knew Man Ray as an experimental twentieth century artist and photographer, part of the **Dada** and **Surrealist** "scene" in Paris in the twenties. From Charlie, I learned that Man Ray's real name was Emmanuel Radnitzky and that he was Jewish and American.

I gave them the full tour. We went to downtown and Beacon Hill. We went to Cambridge and walked through Harvard Square and saw Harvard University, walking past the entrance to the Kennedy School, with the inspirational quotes from John F. Kennedy engraved on the gates. On their last night in Boston, I took them to the revolving rooftop restaurant on the top floor of the Hyatt Hotel on Memorial Drive, with the great views of Boston. Not quite the Eiffel Tower, but the best Boston had to offer.

I was proud to show off my home city of Boston, proud of getting Charlie's film shown at the Boston Jewish Film Festival, proud of the film and proud of my cousins. I was proud that I was able to bring them to Boston and proud that they had come to Boston. A year or two later, Solange returned to Boston. She and Henri attended the wedding of the daughter of a friend or relative of Henri in New Jersey. Solange came to Boston with Henri, to visit me for a few days after the wedding.

That night in November 1996, the night after *Memoire* was screened at the Boston Jewish Film Festival, I was proud to walk the red brick sidewalks of Harvard Square with Solange and Charles. I wanted to show them more, to walk with Solange and Charles all night. Charlie would not have it. When he sensed that his mother was tiring, he suggested that we take a cab back to my home. Speaking in English, so she would not understand, Charlie reminded me that his mother was 74 years old, it was getting late for her. He acknowledged that she, like me, would have liked the evening to continue, but he said that she had already walked too much.

This was the first time I had seen Charlie act as his mother's guardian, her *shomer*, to use the Hebrew word, which means "guard" as well as "guardian". *Shomer* is a better word to describe the way Charlie watched over, cared for and protected his mother. Over the years to come, I would see what a *shomer* was, as I saw how Charlie cared for his mother as she aged, especially after Maurice died in 1999. It was a small step for Charlie to assume this role, as Solange had always had a trusting relationship with her younger son. She talked with Charlie as with no one else. She had always opened up to Charlie and confided in him as with no one else.

I don't know when Charlie started to take his mother to dinner every Sunday afternoon. In our phone conversations, Solange would tell me about her dinner with Charlie, as if I knew he took her to dinner every Sunday, and at some point, I did. Unless he was away working on a film, they would walk to the Brasserie Floderer, more commonly known to Charlie, Solange, and others as Brasserie Flo. It was a short two block walk from Solange's Rue D'Hauteville flat. I had the pleasure of several meals there with Charlie and Solange, sometimes with others. My last meal at Brasserie Flo was after Charlie died, with Solange, Esther, Simon, and Esther's partner, Kristoff.

The success of *Memoire* marked a change not only for Charles, but also for Solange. In her mid-seventies, she found a new career in cinema. The trip to Boston was only one of several she and Charlie made to promote the film at festivals and other venues in various European cities. Charlie never felt it was a burden to bring his mother when she went to events with him. To the contrary, many of Charlie's friends, professional and otherwise, became Solange's friends as well. and when she did not come to events with Charlie they would ask after her.

After the success of *Memoire*, Solange was asked to play the character of a Jewish grandmother in bit parts in various films and productions. She became an actress, which is how she is identified by Wikidata.org, as a "French actress". For example, she had a role in the 2007 film *Deux Vies Plus Une*, which starred French actress Emmanuelle Devos. Solange played the mother of Devos's lead character. In an interview in Le Figaro,[34] Devos was asked to name the person who inspired her the most and she answered "*Solange Najman, une femme juivé polonaise qui, malgré un passé terrible, a une force de vie incroyable.*" (Solange Najman, a Jewish woman who, in spite of a terrible past, has an incredible passion for life.)

Now in her seventies, Solange had a new role, as an actress. She was just a character actress and not a film star, but she was recognized on **Wikidata. org** as a "French actress". More important she was an inspiration to those with whom she worked in the film industry. When she went to events with her son, the director, Charlie never felt it was a burden to bring his mother. To the contrary, many of Charlie's friends, professional and otherwise, were her friends, as well. and when she did not come with Charlie to events, they would ask after her. Solange had become not just the star of a film, an actress, but a celebrity. Solange traveled with Charlie to major cities and locations throughout Europe where the film was shown, at film festivals and Jewish cultural events in places like Krakow.

When they were in Berlin, the festival provided them with an escort, named Suzanne.[35] In the few days of the festival, Suzanne accompanied Charles and Solange everywhere and Suzanne and Solange fast became friends. Before returning to Paris when the festival ended, Solange invited Suzanne to visit her in Paris. Suzanne accepted and stayed with Solange for the first time not long after the festival. Suzanne's visits became frequent and regular. She stayed at Solange's Rue d'Hauteville flat for a few days to a week, or longer, continuing perhaps a couple of times a year for the rest of Solange' life.

I first met Suzanne during one of my visits to Paris to visit Solange. By this time I was visiting Paris at least once a year. Occasionally Suzanne would also be there. The three of us had many interesting conversations, about the Holocaust, about Germans and Jews and Israel, about world politics, about art, and about life, but mostly about Germans and Jews, during the Shoah and today. Sometimes these conversations took place in Solange's kitchen, and sometimes Suzanne and I took Solange for a walk to the café at the corner of Rue d'Hauteville and the Grand Boulevard, where we talked over coffee or tea and a pastry or a croissant. I have fond memories of sitting in that café with Solange and Suzanne.

---

34 The August 15, 2007 edition.
35 Her name may have been Susan, but when spoken in French, it sounded like Suzanne.

The last time I saw Suzanne was in June, 2018. I had been to Paris just a few months earlier. Solange was 96 years old by this time and she had a regular home caretaker, a Polish woman named Lucina. Lucina knew who I was, as she usually answered the phone when I called Solange. That spring, Lucina told me that I should come visit soon, if I wanted to see Solange again. I was not so surprised.

Solange had lost her second son, her shomer, Charlie, two years earlier, and I feared she would not last long after Charles died. I flew to Paris in early June and saw Solange for the last time. The one time we left her apartment was to go to Charlie's grave. He was buried, with his brother, father and grandmother in a family plot at the Cimetière Parisien de Bagneaux, in Bagneaux, a city bordering Paris to the south. The cemetery is one of three large public cemeteries owned by the city government of Paris that sit outside the city limits. It has a large Jewish section. Indeed, it is commonly known as the "Jewish" cemetery. Many of the "divisions", or portions, of the cemetery have exclusively Jewish graves. These "divisions", with Jewish graves, are all close together, comprising the "Jewish" section of the larger cemetery.

Lucina's husband Adam, a burly construction worker who was used to driving in Paris traffic, drove us to the cemetery and dropped us off at the entrance. Solange was in a wheelchair, and I pushed her to the gravesite, a family plot in the Jewish section, with room for four coffins, one stacked on top of the other. Originally one of the spaces was intended for Solange, but Charlie had taken the last of the four spaces, joining his brother, father, and grandmother Miriam in the plot. I held Solange's hand and wiped a tear from her eye. The next day I said good-bye and left. For years, each time we parted and said good-bye, I feared it would be the last time, but this time we both knew she was saying good-bye for good as she took my hand, smiled, and said good-bye. I left Paris very sadly, to return in three months for her funeral.

Just three months later, Esther called me to tell me Solange had died. I asked about the funeral, and said I wanted to come, and Esther arranged for me to stay at Solange's now empty apartment at 36 Rue d'Hauteville. I arranged a flight quickly. When I landed, early in the morning, Jean Claude was there, at Charles de Gaulle Airport waiting for me. He took me to the hospital where Solange's body was lying in a small morgue. Jean Claude wanted to see Solange before she was buried. He insisted, over my protest, that he would not come to the funeral. After viewing Solange's body, we parted, and I took the Metro back to Solange's apartment.

I had the code to unlock the front gate to the courtyard with Solange's address in my phone, but I could not get the code to work. The code had been changed. I was standing there with my overnight bag wondering what to do when a man and woman came up from behind and offered to let me in. I didn't recognize them but the man knew me and reminded me who he was. It was Charlie's much younger cousin, Leo, Leo Flank, a cousin on Charlie's father's side, and Leo's girlfriend, Camille. I had met Leo through Charlie on earlier trips to Paris. Leo was a drummer and was comfortable with Charlie's circle of friends, musicians and artists. Leo and I had gotten to know each other in my earlier visits. We had found common ground talking about music and about playing music.

Leo punched in the combination to open the gate and as we went in, Leo explained that others would be gathering at Solange's for lunch before the funeral. There was already a woman sitting at the kitchen table who recognized me and greeted me, although I had not recognized her. It was Suzanne, Solange's friend and former escort from the Berlin film festival. Soon others arrived and we had lunch together, French bread and cheese and Vietnamese spring rolls that Leo's father, Yves, had brought.

We walked to the hospital where Solange's body lay, where people were gathering to see Solange for the last time. As we walked, Yves explained that he lived in Montpelier, where he worked with a theatre company, doing productions. He also wrote novels. His daughter, Maude, an elementary school teacher, walked with us. When we got to the hospital where Solange's body lay, perhaps a dozen people were already there, including Esther, Kristoff, Simon, and Esther's mother Corinne. Others were still arriving. Lucina, Solange's home caretaker, arrived with her husband, Adam, then Malka, the other caretaker, arrived.

We waited there and talked quietly until it was time to leave for the cemetery. I rode with Esther, Simon, Corinne, and Kristoff who was driving his father's car. It was a long drive, and we had a chance to talk.

Some years before, on an earlier trip to Paris, I had helped assure that Solange's apartment would go to Esther upon Solange's passing. This was my first venture into French law of inheritance and intestacy. I knew little about French law and less about inheritance and intestacy but I was successful in this venture and was pleased to preserve Esther's inheritance. This is another story for another time, although what I did for Esther then may explain Corinne's kindness to me on the day of the funeral.

On the drive to the cemetery, Esther answered that she did not expect to be able to afford to keep the apartment, because of the high property values and real estate taxes. Its sale, however, would allow her to purchase a home in an apartment building in a more modest neighborhood of Paris near where her mother lived.

It was a long drive to the cemetery. It took much longer than it had taken when Adam, who was comfortable driving in Paris traffic and knew where he was going, drove Solange and me there to visit Charlie's grave. The hospital was somewhat further north than Solange's apartment, and Kristoff, who was not used to driving at all, much less in heavy Paris traffic, had to get us from the north side of Paris across the city to the cemetery in Bagneux, which was south of the city. Mid-day traffic jams magnified by multiple construction detours slowed us further. Esther began to get nervous about getting to the cemetery on time and soon everyone but me was consulting the Waze apps on their cell phones.

Despite the delays we arrived in ample time. In all, there was a large crowd, more than fifty people gathered, comprising a wide range. Solange's double *belle-soeur*, Helène, was there, in a wheelchair pushed by one of her granddaughters. She was accompanied by her children and grandchildren. There was also a range of Bohemian types, including one man whom I recognized as the avant-garde singer, Cyrius, whom I recognized from a publicity photo of him on the bulletin board in Solange's kitchen. There were others, some who recognized me, some well-dressed and stylish, including one woman whose poise and air of confidence made clear that she recognized how attractive a woman she was. It was Charlie's wife, Emmanuelle Honorin. I had a chance to introduce myself as the broad assortment of people gathered.

When the hearse with Solange's body arrived, the rabbi had us all walk behind it, as it proceeded slowly through the divisions of the cemetery to the section where Solange was to be buried.

There are about ten burials a day in the cemetery in Bagneaux, many of them Jewish. Solange's burial was a traditional Jewish burial, but it was also a celebration of a remarkable life. Esther, Solange's only grandchild, made this possible.

There was no room for Solange in the Najman family plot. Solange would be laid to rest in a group grave of survivors of the Radom ghetto, one or two rows away from her own loved ones. When the hearse arrived at the entrance to that row, the casket was removed and set on a pedestal sitting on the paved way next to the grave site. The procession to the gravesite took a few minutes. We proceeded slowly. We passed the aisle where the Najman family plot was.

The rabbi, a reform rabbi, stood behind the casket and began by explaining that it is a part of Jewish tradition to walk behind the casket. The rabbi then read some psalms, in both French and Hebrew, made a number of blessings, also in French and Hebrew, then spoke eloquently about Solange. The rabbi had never met and never knew Solange, and it was quite apparent that Esther had spent time with the rabbi talking about her grandmother. Esther later confirmed this to me.

The rabbi started by saying that Solange had many stages in her life, beginning as the Polish girl Zlata, or the diminutive Zoshia, and continuing to talk about her father and mother and how Solange lost her father to the Nazis, and her brother, and how she survived. By this time, I recognized Helène in her wheelchair, perhaps from meeting her before, or perhaps from the pictures in Solange's kitchen, or from seeing her in *Memoire*. The rabbi continued to talk about how Solange came to Paris with her mother and became a Parisian lady, about how she met Albert, only to lose him too soon, and how she rebuilt her life again, around her two sons.

The rabbi then talked how Solange educated herself, becoming an "intellectual" in order to fit into her sons' world. This was something both Esther and Corinne later emphasized when we spoke later that evening. Then the rabbi talked about the film, *Memoire*, and how that led to Solange's final role in life, as an actress, playing bit roles, typecast as a Jewish grandmother, and moving about comfortably in the Bohemian and arts world of her sons' friends.

Indeed these were the people at Solange's funeral, playing tribute to a remarkable survivor. It was a fitting tribute. After the Rabbi's eulogy, Esther spoke, and then others. A friend of Charlie and Maurice named Helen spoke, and then, after few others spoke, Helène approached, in her wheelchair pushed by her grand-daughter, and spoke briefly.

In the midst of the speeches, Solange's grandson Simon, a tall teenager, swooned and began to faint. Someone provided a chair, and he sat down with his head between his knees, perhaps a bit overwhelmed, as we all were.

As the others left, Emmanuelle stopped before Charlie's grave and stood there silently for some moments, perhaps unaware that anyone was watching her. Clearly Solange was not the only person who missed Charlie. But of all those who missed Charlie, only Solange was not able to live without him. Solange suffered unimaginably in the Shoah. She lost her father, her brother, her home, and her family. Solange built a new life in Paris, with a husband who adored her. She lost that dear husband, Albert, in 1970. He was only 57 years old. Then she lost her first-born son, Maurice, in 1999. He was only 51 years old. Solange was a survivor, strong despite all the wounds and hurt she endured, but she could not survive the loss of Charlie.

When his father Albert died, Charlie, who was then just 14, promised his mother he would make a film about her and what she went through in the Shoah. As confident as Charlie was that he would succeed in this gift for his mother, he could not have imagined the success he would have. *Memoire* changed Solange's life. It gave her self-pride and a new life in her old age. The success of the movie was the greatest gift her son Charles had given her.

The movie was not all that Charlie did for his mother. He cared for her until the day he died. Yet he could not take away her pain. Solange had nightmares until she died. She took medications for her memories. The play on words in the full title of the film, *La Memoire, est-elle soluble dans l'Eau*, (*Can Memories be Dissolved in Water?*) reveals a horrible truth. Nothing could ever undo what Solange went through, nothing could make the painful memories go away.

Solange ends her testimony to the Foundation pour la Memoire de la Shoah with the words "I did not pass on a Jewish heritage to my sons . . . [I] had moved away from God. I was too revolted. I was too outraged after this war. When we could do sadistic things like that, when we could, children who are innocent, who have not even touched the earth, burn them alive, and screw them up like that! If there was God, he would have arrested the Nazis! Well, there are a lot of versions but I really don't feel . . . Yes! I am a practitioner. That is to say, I am like my mother: when there is Rosh Hashanah, when there is Yom Kippur, I go to the synagogue, because there is a prayer for the dead. This is not the same.

"I don't forget my dead. I cherish them. So I go to the synagogue. I like this atmosphere because it brings me peace when I go to a synagogue. And prayer, you see, but for the dead, I go . . . Yizkor, have you heard of Yizkor? This is the prayer for the dead. So I always go. Kol Nidré, I go, and there is one more time. I like the Jewish tradition, I like it a lot. Because among the Jews, it's like that, like the movies: atrocities told, and tears, and laughter, at the same time. I really like this tradition. I am a Jew. I don't believe, I may be wrong, because when you believe, you hold on, you hold on to something, and life is easier.

"Me, now, I lost my son, I say: 'But how? So, do you have to be bad to stay alive? When we are too good, do we go to God? And we die?' I am looking for the explanation and I cannot find it."

CHAPTER 38

Then There's Maurice

Trying to explain Maurice to me, Uncle Adolphe took me aside and said "There's the left, the far left, and the radical left. Then there's Maurice." Uncle Adolphe was right. But Maurice was much more than that.

Maurice was named after his grandfather, Solange's father, but he took more after his socialist worker father, Albert. With his father's guidance, Maurice became a political activist and organizer early in his life. Maurice had a radical left heritage on his mother Solange's side, as well. **Rosa Luxemburg** was an aunt or cousin of Maurice's grandmother Miriam, Solange's mother. But it was his father who was his model and his mentor. At the age of seven he joined his father selling the Sunday edition of the leftist daily newspaper, *l'Humanité Dimanche* on the streets of Paris.

Maurice attended high school at the Collège-lycée Jacques-Decour on 12 Avenue Trudaine, not a long walk from 36 d'Hauteville. The lycée Jacques-Decour is a prestigious secondary school that prepared top Parisian students for the top universities. Maurice was a member of the Young Communists while a student at the lycée, but he and his father, together, moved away from the communist movement. He was still a student at the lycée when he joined the heretical Trotskyists: for Maurice the French Communist Party, which supported dictator Stalin and the Soviet dictatorship which followed, was no longer revolutionary and he reproached the Soviet Union for having renounced the World Revolution.

In 1968, when anti-war protests were spreading across the United States, Maurice was actively organizing students at the Lycée. The 1968 protest movement led by a young generation opposed to the Vietnam War was not limited to opposition to the Vietnam War or the United States. The **1968 protests** were worldwide. Perhaps the most spectacular manifestation of these was the **May 1968 protests** in France, in which students linked up with wildcat strikes of up to ten million French workers. There was a time, for a few days, that it appeared the movement would overthrow the government.

As a young communist at the lycée Jacques-Decour, Maurice had become a leading member of the Marxist-Revolutionary Alliance, and a protégé of French Trotskyist leader **Michel Pablo Raptis**, who was known as Pablo. Raptis was one of the leaders of the Parti Communiste Internationaliste, or PCI, a French Trotskyist political party separate from the Communist Party.

Through Pablo, Maurice, while still a high school student, met Ahmed Ben Bella. Ben Bella was the leader of the National Liberation Front (FLN), the guerilla group that had fought for independence in the French colony of Algeria. He then became the first president of newly independent Algeria in 1963. Ben Bella was the first of many leftist revolutionary leaders Maurice came to know. Maurice's relationship with the Algerian separatists was the logical consequence of his positions and Maurice openly took a stand in support of the Algerian revolution.

However, by the late 1960s, it was hard to organize French students around the Algerian cause. The Algerian War had ended, but not before many French families had lost fathers, sons, brothers and uncles in the Algerian struggles. The antiwar movement moved to organizing students around opposition to the American war in Vietnam. This is what Maurice did.

In the fall of 1966, Maurice and fellow lycée Jacques-Decour student Michel Recanati established the first *Comité Vietnam Lyceé* (CVL), or High School Vietnam Committee. It was the first of many such secondary school anti-Vietnam war committees in secondary schools, as well as universities, across Paris and France. Like Maurice, **Michel Recanati** was also a son of leftist

Holocaust survivors, but it was Maurice, two years older than Recanati, who instigated and led this first "committee", as others formed and the protests spread.

By the spring of 1968, student groups had set up barricades of cobblestones, bricks, abandoned vehicles, and construction materials to block Paris streets. The student barricades were literally just several hundred yards away from the Najman home on Rue d'Hauteville. Maurice lead the protests with **Danny Cohn Bendit**, who became the public face of the student protests,[36] and with **Jacques Sauvageot**, **Alain Geismar**, and **Alain Krivine**, all college students older than Maurice. Perhaps not surprisingly, many of these Parisian student protest leaders were not only Jewish but were also the children of Holocaust survivors. Their Judaism did not go unnoticed.

Maurice on the barricades

Daniel Cohn-Bendit was attacked, in a manner reminiscent of the Dreyfus Affair by opponents of the student movement who impugned

---

36 Cohn-Bendit became known as "Danny the Red", for both the color of his hair and for his left politics, but despite his media notoriety as the face of the 1968 barricades, he actually had participated little in the May 1968 Paris events. He was later able to use his notoriety to launch a successful political career, no longer as "Danny the Red", but as a more mainstream politician. In 1984 he joined the German Green Party. He returned to France, where he was involved with the French Green party. In 2004 he led the foundation of the European Green Party https://en.wikipedia.org/wiki/European_Green_Party in Rome. He was elected to the European Union Parliament, where he served for many years.

his loyalty to France because of his "foreign," meaning his Jewish, origins. Like Maurice and his high school classmate Michel Recanati, Cohn-Bendit was born to Jews who had survived the Nazis. Cohn-Bendit's parents were German Jews, and in response to the anti-Semitic accusations against Cohn-Bendit, student protestors took up the chant, "*Nous sommes tous des juifs allemands.*" (We are all German Jews.)

As for Maurice, Jacques Bleibtreu, who, with Maurice, was one of the founders and leaders of the AMR, the *Alliance Marxiste Revolutionaire*, wrote "Maurice was a Jew, unavoidably, resolutely, definitively Jewish, and atheist, without the slightest trouble." [37]

Maurice was often in the front row of the large demonstrations, and he was often arrested. It was only natural for Maurice to be there. He was his father's son. Growing up, Maurice had two heroes: his father Albert and his uncle Moishe Najman. Maurice had been impressed that Moishe, Albert's older brother, died fighting the fascists as a member of the Dabrowski Brigade, Polish volunteers who fought in the Spanish Civil War. Moshe died defending Madrid from the Fascists. He was a hero not just to his brother Albert and the other Najman siblings, but also to their children, Moishe's nieces and nephews. This included Maurice and Charles, and their cousin, Yves Flank, the son of Albert's sister Rachel Najman and Baruch Flank, who remembers his Aunt Helène taking him to Madrid to see the memorial for the Dabrowski Brigade volunteers.

Maurice was among the high school students who arrived in the *Quartier Latin* on May 6, 1968 and provoked an uprising that resulted in left-wing students barricading themselves in the Sorbonne against the police. A few days later, Maurice was among the demonstrators in front of the American Express on March 20, 1968, when its windows were smashed. Maurice established himself as the representative of the high school groups within the protests. He became a fiery speaker, later to be described as a "brilliant orator, cigarette in hand, hoarse voice, fighting for his ideas".

Among the other protestors from the secondary schools was Romain Goupil, who like Maurice, was also a militant Marxist and Trotskyite.

---

37 In Portrait de Maurice Najman [archive], L'École émancipée, February 23, 1999. [https://chsprod.hypotheses.org/4703]

Goupil would become a prominent French filmmaker. In 1982, Goupil released his documentary about the 1968 student protests, *Die at Thirty*. The film featured two young people from the protests. One was Maurice. The other was Veronique Kantor. In the course of making the film, Maurice got to know Kantor. She would later become the wife of Michel Colucci, another student protestor who would go on to other successes.

Adopting the stage name **Coluche**, Colucci went on to become a comedian and actor of notoriety, with a style and persona akin to Lennie Bruce in his off color language and irreverent political commentary. Coluche would later, in 1980, run for president. His campaign foreshadowed the humor of Stephen Colbert, with slogans such as "before me, France was divided in two; now it will be folded in four" (a pun in French, as more idiomatically *"être plié en quatre"* could be translated as "doubled over laughing"), and "Coluche - the only candidate who has no reason to lie."

Initially, Coluche's campaign was not taken seriously, despite having Maurice Najman, then 32, as a campaign advisor. When Coluche reached 16% in the pre-election polls, candidates who took themselves more seriously went to some lengths to persuade Coluche to withdraw. Even the eventual winner, **Francois Mitterand** feared Coluche might be a spoiler and joined this effort to get him to drop out of the race.

The 1968 student organizing was not just where Maurice began to make the many political and other connections that would shape his life: it was also when Maurice began to write as well. With Jacques Bleibtrau, he co-founded a newspaper which they called *Barricades*. This was the beginning of a career as a journalist which brought him front stage of most every left political movement of the next thirty years. Maurice soon acquired a reputation for being at the forefront of every political struggle. The reputation was earned and well deserved.

The French political journal *L'Evénement*, to which Maurice would become a regular contributor, wrote, "Others had the eloquence, he had the insolent grace. The fear of missing the next revolution, too often made us miss the last metro. When a new idea was evoked — from self management to Ecology — Maurice Najman was always there. Whenever anywhere in the world a movement appeared, he knew its objectives, trends and leaders."

In 1969, Maurice, along with Jacques Bleibtreu was among the founders of the *Alliance Marxiste Révolutionnaire* (**AMR**), a Trotskyite[38] party inspired by the thinking of Maurice's mentor, Michel Pablo Raptis. It was in AMR that Maurice first met Corinne Welger, and Pierre Barboza, who would become Corinne's husband. Maurice would eventually separate from the Trotskyist organization, but he remained in contact with these two of his companions.

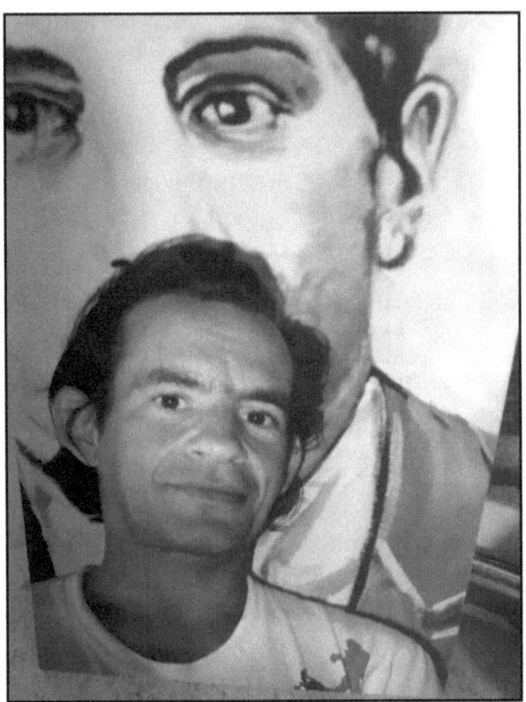

Maurice Najman

---

38 A Trotskyite Marxist revolutionary party sounds much more extreme to an American reader than to a European. Trotsky, born Lev (Leon) Bronstein, [https://en.wikipedia.org/wiki/Leon_Trotsky], a Jew like Karl Marx, was active in the Russian revolution. In fact he led the Red Army and played a vital role in the Bolshevik victory in the Russian Civil War of 1917–1922 [https://en.wikipedia.org/wiki/Russian_Civil_War], and became one of the members of the first Bolshevik Politburo in 1919. After the death of Lenin and the ascension of Stalin, Trotsky opposed Stalinism and was forced into exile after being accused of plotting to kill Stalin. While in exile, Trotsky wrote several key works, including his *History of the Russian Revolution* (1930) and *The Revolution Betrayed* (1936), a critique of the Soviet Union under Stalinism. He argued that the Soviet state had become a "degenerate workers' state" controlled by an undemocratic bureaucracy, which would eventually either be overthrown via a political revolution establishing a workers' democracy, or degenerate into a capitalist class. Being a Trotskyite was a way to be a Marxist without supporting Stalin, the Soviet Union, or the Eastern European dictatorships.

By this time, Maurice had become a committed political journalist, champion of leftist revolutions. This had become his way of doing politics. He went to Chile to report on the Popular Unity government of Salvador Allende, the first Marxist elected president of a democracy in Latin America. He was in Chile through the summer of 1972, writing about the **Allende revolution**. Maurice also reported from El Salvador, meeting with and reporting about the FMLN, the Farabundo Martí National Liberation Front, a coalition of left-wing groups that fought a guerilla war against the Salvadoran military dictatorship supported by the Reagan administration. From Chiapas, Mexico, he reported on the Zapatista insurgency of indigenous people led by **Subcomandante Marcos**, also a prolific writer, intellectual, and political thinker.

Press credentials from Chiapas and Cuba hung in Solange's kitchen. Maurice made multiple trips to Cuba, where he met Fidel Castro and wrote and reported on the Cuban revolution. Solange proudly displayed Maurice's Cuban press credentials on her kitchen bulletin board. Maurice returned to Cuba more than once, at some point with filmmaker Wim Wenders. Through his friend Wenders, Maurice met Maggie Bohringer, the one-time wife of French actor Richard Bohringer. Maggie, known in French as Maguy, became the great love of Maurice's life. Born to a French Corsican father and a Vietnamese mother, she was a stunningly beautiful woman, but for Maurice, she would prove to be a true *femme fatale*.

Maurice was involved in the popular uprisings in communist Eastern Europe in the 1980s, writing about and providing support for the Workers Defense Committees, or KOR (the Polish acronym), that supported families of striking workers in the Polish shipyards, in the strikes led by **Lech Walesa** and **Solidarity**, the independent Polish trade union and the first independent trade union in any Warsaw Pact country to be recognized by the state. Through a colleague at the French leftist journal *Liberation* (the French journal founded by Jean Paul Sartre, as opposed to the American journal *Liberation*, both left journals), Maurice was connected with Plastic People of the Universe, a Czech rock band. This would lead to Maurice meeting

Vaclav Havel, years later.

In the 1970s, Plastic People of the Universe was little more than a cover band playing songs by American counterculture bands like the Velvet Underground and Frank Zappa and the Mothers of Invention. The band's name comes from the title of a Frank Zappa song on the first Mothers of Invention album. Plastic People of the Universe would have remained just another European rock cover band had the Czech Communist government not targeted the band, revoking Plastic People's license to perform as musicians in 1970. The band continued to play at private occasions, such as weddings and private parties, and at what the Czech government called "subversive" counter-cultural events. By 1973, the clampdown had become a permanent way of life for the band.

Being forced underground gave the otherwise apolitical rock musicians a reason to become political and no longer just a cover band. They publicized their performances through the **samizdat** world of underground literature and journalism. The band incorporated Czech philosopher and poet Egon Bondy's texts into their lyrics after the Czech government banned his writing.

A rock music afficionado like so many of us who grew up in the sixties, Maurice was one of a trio of young Trotskyites often found together in Paris clubs like the Palace. When Maurice learned of the Plastic People's situation, it was only natural that he would respond to their plight. He brought the band to Paris in the late 1970s where he organized a recording session, and the band's first album was released in 1978. The album was entitled *Egon Bondy's Happy Hearts Club Banned*, a clever play on The Beatles' *Sgt. Pepper's Lonely Hearts Club Band*.

Maurice did not expect any reward for his efforts in bringing the band to Paris and making the connections and arrangements for them to record their first studio album. He just did what he thought was the right thing. Years later, after the Berlin Wall fell, the Czechoslovak Socialist Republic was overthrown in a nonviolent revolution known as the Velvet Revolution. Some say it was called the Velvet Revolution because of the role in the uprising of the Plastic People, who covered the music of The

Velvet Underground. Playwright and dissident Vaclev Havel was elected the first president of the Czech Republic. Havel called upon Maurice, whom he knew through members of the Plastic People, to help organize the Czech Citizen's Assembly.

In the days and years following the turmoil of 1968, it was hard for Maurice to live a stable or settled life. He was too busy on the front lines of the revolution. It was out of the question for him to lead an orderly life, let alone think of starting a family. This was not on his agenda in September 1971when Corinne Welger joined the Revolutionary Marxist Alliance, the radical collective Maurice had helped to found. Nonetheless, Corinne would become an integral part of Maurice's life.

Corinne fell in love with Maurice, but Maurice was never in love with Corinne. Maurice was too enthralled with the beauty and charms of Maguy. The exotic Maguy was said to be as gifted intellectually as she was physically beautiful. As a couple, Maurice and Maguy were extraordinary. Their relationship was not just sexual. It was also of great intellectual refinement. Maurice and Maguy shared the same passion for reading. Their small apartment was full of books. When visiting, friends felt as though they had disturbed the couple in their reading and that as soon as the visit ended, Maurice and Maguy would return to their books.

The relationship was not without its difficulties. They had resolved not to be dependent on each other. Both Maurice and Maguy had other relationships from time to time, but they always returned to each other. Maurice could not be without Maguy. When he had not seen Maguy for too long, he would weep in the arms of a friend. Most damaging, Maguy had long been a user of hard drugs, which came to play a critical role in their relationship. They shared everything in their lives together, and sharing hard drugs was something Maurice may have felt he needed to share to be close to her. This would, in the end, prove fatal to Maurice. Although he did not become HIV positive from his relationship with Maguy, who had HIV and knew it, he acquired the hepatitis from which he would die in 1999 from sharing needles with Maguy.

Maguy and Maurice would sometimes lock themselves away for days, even a whole week at a time. Their friends interpreted this as a good sign, because Maurice seemed to emerge transformed and rejuvenated for a while. His usual energy would seem "of another nature". Wim Wenders claims that Maurice knew how to manage what he was doing and was never out of the loop. This may well have been true. On the other hand, Maurice appeared to ignore the mortal danger to which he was exposed because Maguy was HIV-positive. For Maurice she was an angel. Was she perhaps a dark angel?

Maguy's sudden death, in 1986, long before that of Maurice, was not the consequence of her HIV status but due to a cerebral hemorrhage. That day a world collapsed for Maurice. Friends, mostly Wenders, took care of him. After Maguy was cremated, Maurice's friends took the ashes to Maurice's one time residence in the south of France, where they scattered her ashes to the four winds. Maurice was never the same. Wenders, who still spent much time with Maurice, said his friend's wild playfulness was over, his flame had burned out.

Maurice would never marry. His life did remain entwined with Corinne, however. In 1975 Corinne became pregnant with Maurice's child, Esther, who was born on January 15, 1976. At the time, Maurice had no interest in becoming a father, but Corinne wanted the child and they came to an understanding. Corinne would raise the child on her own, and Maurice would not be involved at all. In fact, Corinne's husband, Pierre Barboza, adopted Esther as his own daughter and became her legal father.

Once she grew old enough, Esther wanted to know who her real father was. When she became old enough to ask, she insisted on meeting him. As he got to know her, Maurice grew fond of her, and then proud of her. Over time, they grew close, as a daughter and father should. As Esther matured, her relationship with Maurice evolved, and she was blessed to have two fathers.

I did not get to meet Maurice until 1989, when Linda and I traveled to Paris with our three children, one a not yet four-year-old boy who chased pigeons in the parks of Paris. Maurice graciously hosted us all on that visit at his home at 3 Impasse St. Pierre, a charming apartment on a small cul-de-sac with a tiny but lovely little courtyard. He had wine for Linda and me and an afternoon meal with small plates of smoked fish, cheeses, and fruit, but no French pastries, croissants, or eclairs that might have appealed to a nine-year-old Shira, a seven-year-old Miriam, or their almost four-year-old little brother, Teddy. Nonetheless, it was a very nice afternoon. Maurice was a gracious host, but it was clear that he was not used to having children around. He never mentioned Esther.

When I returned to Paris with Nana a few months later, I met Esther. She was then 14. I also met her mother, Corinne, although it was a cursory meeting. At the time and in the circumstances in which we met, I did not know that Corinne was Esther's mother or who she was. We met at La Grande Halle, the large exhibition hall on the edge of Paris, where Maurice was preparing his *Est ou Est* exhibit of West German artists.

At the time Corinne was working for La Villette, the park in the north of Paris where La Grande Halle was located. Corinne was one of a number of people who approached Maurice with a question or concern while he and I walked through the chaotic exhibit hall.

It was through Corinne that Maurice was able to obtain the use of La Grande Halle as the exhibition space. He had asked Corinne about using the hall and Corinne had persuaded her boss to organize something. Soon after, Corinne and her boss, François Barré, were on a plane to Berlin with Maurice to meet the artists. They put together an exhibit and program in just a few days, as opposed to the usual lead time of a year to two years for an exhibit.

The *Est ou Est* exhibit was a significant accomplishment for Maurice. Maurice received a greater reward, something much more valuable and long lasting, from his reporting of the fall of the Berlin Wall. This was the friendship and mentorship of Markus Wolf, notorious as the longtime head of the foreign branch of the Stasi,[39] East Germany's foreign intelligence service.

Wolf was the son of a prominent German Jewish author, physician, and communist activist, Friedrich Wolf. Wolf lived in exile with his family in the Soviet Union during the Nazi era. After the war, Wolf returned to Germany and began his career with the East German Stasi, or security police, where, during the Cold War, he was known as "the man without a face" due to his success in avoiding being photographed. In fact, _Man Without a Face_, published in 1997, is the title of one of the English translations of his autobiography. Wolf would emerge from the shadows

---

39 The Stasi was the East German intelligence agency, akin to the KGB, the FBI or the CIA, much hated and feared, one of the "most effective and repressive intelligence and secret police agencies to have ever existed".

with speculation that he was the model for the character of Karla, the shadowy spymaster in John le Carré's popular Cold War spy thrillers. Le Carré felt obliged to go out of his way to publicly deny that any of his characters was based on Markus Wolf.

Maurice stood out to Wolf from the gaggle of journalists in the multiple interviews Wolf gave in the tumultuous days of 1989 surrounding the fall of the Wall and unification of Germany. As Wolf would later write to Solange in a lengthy letter that was intended to substitute for a eulogy at Maurice's funeral ten years later, Maurice caught Wolf's attention as an aggressive and smart journalist:

> Amid countless journalists thronging Berlin's Alexanderplatz behind the podium, a short, nimble black-haired Frenchman came up to me asking for an interview. As with most people in his position, it would have been pointless if there hadn't been that indefinable spark between us. . . . Among hundreds of conversations with journalists in this dramatic fall of '89, the interview for *L'Autre Journal* stands out clearly in my memory. Neither Maurice nor the Editor-in-Chief asked superficial questions and the conscientious restitution of several hours of exchanges testifies to the high level of these journalists.
>
> Maurice proved to be tough: he pursued me in 1990-1991 until I fled to Moscow. He was one of the few to whom I gave not only short interviews, but long conversations and even photo shoots, despite quasi-conspiratorial conditions. Maurice had prepared himself: he asked well-directed questions and showed himself to be an attentive listener. His interest went above all to the hidden ins and outs of the complex developments in the East, to the reasons for the collapse of the socialist experiment.

In the same seven-page eulogy that he wrote to Solange, Wolf wrote "At the beginning, nothing suggested that, in this turbulent decade, an exceptional relationship would come out of an interview." Wolf continued "[f]rom there was born our relationship so close, incomprehensible for some. In addition to interviews and the book, he designed television programs and a document on the fall of the wall which won an award at the Premier Plans Film Festival in Angers."[40]

Wolf would become not just a friend and mentor, but a father figure for Maurice, a replacement for his father, Albert, whose loss Maurice still felt, some twenty years later. The relationship was such that Wolf would write with surprising warmth about Friday night dinners at Solange's table, not unlike the momentous one Shira and I enjoyed in the summer of 1996. He wrote of "flowers on the long round table, the long series of Jewish dishes and, despite her duties as mistress of the house, Solange remained the quicksilver center around which our evening gravitated."

The relationship would be mutually beneficial. After the fall of the Berlin Wall, and the reunification of Germany, Marcus Wolf, the spy "without a face", soon became a man without a country. When the wall came down, in 1989, and secrets were exposed, Wolf's years with the Stasi unfolded as a time where there were double and triple agents, defectors, kidnappings and so many betrayals that neither side, not the Russians, for whom Wolf ostensibly served, nor the CIA and Britain's MI5, on the other side, could determine with any certainty for which side any German agent was working.

Wolf fled Germany in September 1990, shortly before he was charged with treason by the government of the new unified Germany. After both Russia and Austria denied his requests for asylum, Wolf returned to Germany, where he was tried for treason in 1993. The initial guilty finding was overturned on the grounds that he didn't betray his country, the Federal Republic of Germany, because he was not a traitor to the Republic of Germany, but worked in the service of a different country, the German Democratic Republic (GDR), commonly known as East Germany, a country which no longer existed.

Wolf's troubles did not end, however, with the reversal of this conviction. No longer neither the man without a face nor the man without a country, he had become the man who knew too much. Among the things he knew was what happened to former Russian agents. This concerned him.

Perhaps he would have been safer with the protection of the United States, which had proved more than willing to take in Wernher von

---

40 The Premier Plans Film Festival in Angers has been a major French film festival since 1989, focusing on European films.

Braun, and other scientists who had worked for the Nazis. Such choices were accepted as necessary in the United States, in light of the Cold War battle with the communist Soviet Union. On the other hand Wolf was not treated favorably in the American press. Wolf claimed to have refused an offer of a large amount of money, a new identity with plastic surgery to change his features, and a home in California from the CIA to defect to the United States[41], but could he trust the CIA? Where would it be safe for him to go?

Maurice became Wolf's advocate. He remained so until his death in 1999. Maurice turned his interviews with Wolf into a book, *Markus Wolf, the Eye of Berlin*, and shared the royalties with Wolf. This gave Wolf an income stream after the collapse of East Germany, as he was being pursued by both the Soviets and the West, when, in Wolf's words his "situation had become precarious".

Maurice had contacts not just in Cuba but throughout Latin America, from Allende's Chile to Commandante Zero in Chiapas. Wolf would say that Maurice "rubbed shoulders with a number of the most unexpected people. . . . [H]is passion was for Third World liberation activists and he followed with curiosity the upheavals in the GDR and Eastern Europe. From there was born our relationship so close, incomprehensible for some."

In his eulogy for Maurice, Wolf would say "Maurice was a faithful friend like there are few. We felt him close to us like our own son."

As Maurice's health deteriorated, he suffered considerably, complaining about "the torture of medical examinations" but remained stoical about his pain. In his last days he took refuge in the countryside. In his eulogy to his surrogate son, Wolf would say "Unlike many of those at the front of the 1968 barricades, who, like Cohn-Bendit moderated their views to 'work within the system', Maurice retained his idealism, his left-wing beliefs and his alternative lifestyle to the end."

Wolf concluded "Maurice was an insurgent who knew how to dream without pathos, a sympathetic and modest rebel. Is this perhaps the modesty of those who leave their signature on the good pages of history? Such men disappear, like other men, but they are the grains of salt of the earth."

---

41 Wise, David (13 July 1997). "Spy vs. Spy". The New York Times. November 7, 2019.

Wolf understood Maurice's passion for a just world, but he also understood that Maurice's sense of social justice came not just from his father, the socialist worker, but from his mother. Solange was a Jewish mother in the most positive way. All their lives, both Maurice and Charles had a special relationship with their mother. They shared not just their accomplishments but their lives with their mother, Solange.

For Maurice, that was summed up best by Wolf: "after the fact [Maurice] was very proud that his mother had lived up to her role as a Jewish mother in a particularly remarkable way."

CHAPTER 39

The Enigma that was Charlie

Charlie, like Maurice, was named after one of his grandfathers. Maurice was named after Solange's father, Maurice, and Charlie was named after his father Albert's father. Like Maurice, perhaps even more so, Charlie was shaped by their Jewish mother. Solange and Albert may not have given their boys much formal religious education, but the boys grew up in a Jewish home. The Friday night dinners were just the most visible pieces of their Jewish home and Jewish upbringing. It came from Solange, and also Albert and also their grandmother, Miriam, Chacha Manya, as the boys called her in Yiddish. But there was a special bond with their mother, their Jewish mother, with Charles, even more than Maurice.

Charles was too young to join Maurice and Yves on the barricades in 1968. Charles was just fourteen, just starting secondary school at Collège-lycée Jacques-Decour when his father died in 1970. That was when he first promised his mother that he would make a film about her. At the time, he was following in the footsteps of his father and older brother, Maurice, serving first as high school student representative then as student representative within the Alliance Revolutionary Marxist (AMR), which his older brother had led earlier.

The footsteps of his charismatic and dynamic older brother were hard footsteps to follow, but Charlie, as he was known as an adult, had his own vision of his future. He would make films, be a director, a *realisateur*. Perhaps this was so he could keep his promise to his mother to make a film about her. After finishing secondary school at the Collège-lycée Jacques-Decour, Charlie studied philosophy at the Sorbonne, and was soon writing for various journals. His writings started as movie reviews but soon expanded to a wide and eccentric range of style and subject.

While still in his early twenties, Charlie co-authored a book with Nicolas Tourlière entitled *La Police des Images*. Although the book bears a 1980 copyright, it was probably completed in 1978. It is a 150-page history of police photography, an oversized coffee table type book, with many photographs of police booking photos, crime scenes and evidence photos and dead bodies. The photographs were interesting, unusual and often shocking.

Tourlière, who collected the photographs, is a photographer with a long career that includes portrait work, photos on rock music album covers and several other books, published in the 1990s, for which he collected the photographs in collaboration with an author who wrote the text. Charlie wrote the text for this history of crime photography, an impressive work for a young man of twenty-two. It was a first clue not just to Charlie's creativity, but to his interest in the unusual and the bizarre and his attraction to a darker side of "civilization" that would later be evident in his work about his two passions, his mother and the Shoah, and Haiti.

Charlie the quintessential Parisian.

Charlie's film reviews and articles about cinema would be his entry into what would become his principal genre. By the late 1970s he was making short films and documentaries, mostly for French public television. Charlie's reviews and other pieces on film were published in *Cinématographe, Libération, Les Nouvelles Littéraires, Le Matin, Le Monde, L'Autre Journal, Politis, L'Etudiant* and other journals. Charlie had always gone to a lot of films, not just at the Rex, but as a film critic, he began attending film festivals, regularly, and writing about them, not just the major French film festivals, like those in **Cannes** and **Angers**, but other festivals across Europe, and even **Telluride** in Colorado. At Telluride Charles met a young American woman whom he may have married.

My sister Vivian and her husband Rich remember Charlie telling them about this possible marriage some years later. They were in Paris, for a medical conference Rich was attending, and Charlie dropped by their hotel to see them. When Vivian and Rich told him they were living in New Mexico, Charlie mentioned that he had lived with his American wife in Colorado for a few years.

Charlie returned to Paris with this woman, whose name no one recalls, and the couple lived together there for a while, but the marriage, if there was one, did not last. This relationship does account, however, for something else. Perhaps Charlie's good English was not due just to American movies, Bob Dylan and the Rolling Stones, as he had proclaimed to me.

It is not clear when Charlie got involved in Haiti, which became the other passion in his life besides his mother and the Holocaust. It was before Charlie met Emmanuelle Honorin, the Haitian ex-patriot, who would become the love of his life and, eventually, his wife. It seems he met Emmanuelle as a result of his new passion for Haiti. Most likely, Charlie's passion for Haiti grew from meeting Emmanuelle. Or was she attracted to him because of his involvement in her native culture? Like many details of Charlie's life, the facts are not always so clear. As his cousin, Yves, would say to me, in trying to answer my questions about him, "Charlie was an enigma."

Charlie met Emmanuelle at the screening of his 1992 film *Le Serment du Bois Caiman* (*The Oath of the Cayman Woods*), Charlie's 33 minute short about the myth of the revolution that led to the founding of Haiti. This was Charlie's second film about Haiti. The first was a seventeen minute short entitled *Rock Vaudou Boukman Eksperyans*, which was about two Haitian rock bands. The name of the band Boukman Eksperyans was taken in part from that of Dutty Boukman, a voodoo priest who was one of the leaders of the 1791 rebellion of enslaved people that led to Haiti's independence. *Ekxperyans* was in tribute to Jimi Hendrix, the great guitarist of the late 1960s whose band was called the Jimi Hendrix Experience.

Le Serment du Bois Caiman was about the beginning of the Haitian slave revolution. On August 14, 1791, representatives of all the ethnic groups of enslaved Africans in Haiti gathered in the *Bois Caiman*, the Caiman Woods (in English, alligator woods), in the northern region of the island under the leadership of voodoo priest Dutty Boukman and priestess Cécile Fatiman. The conspirators all signed a blood pact in which they bound themselves to each other in their fight for freedom and independence. According to the film, the conspirators sealed their agreement by drinking a mystical beverage and invoking the voodoo, more properly known as vodou in Haiti. Vodou, originally an African religion brought to the western hemisphere by slaves from West Africa, evolved uniquely in Haiti and then New Orleans, from the mix of the different West African traditions of the workers forced into slavery.

According to the Institute Francais webpage, of the film, the pact and the date of the pact, August 14, 1791, is considered in the Black world to be the equivalent of July 14th, Bastille Day, in France, or to the Fourth of July in the United States. The Institute Francais webpage lists Charles Najman as the director of the film, and, strangely, lists the director's nationality as Haitian. Thus, by the time Charlie met Emmanuelle he was already immersed enough in Haitian culture that the Institute Francais identified this Jewish son of a concentration camp survivor as Haitian.

Charlie and Emmanuelle were soon working together on projects about Haiti and about other native cultures. They were also in love with each other. Charlie soon moved in with Emmanuelle, who was then living in the Chateau Rentier. The Chateau Rentier was the home of Jean Rouch, the esteemed French new wave filmmaker and anthropologist, one of the founders of *cinéma vérité* in France. His house was a gathering place of artists, writers and filmmakers, some of whom lived there. These included both Emmanuelle and Cyrius Martinez, a Spanish born *chanteur* or singer, who had been romantically involved with Emmanuelle before she met Charlie and would be again.

Rouch's practice as a filmmaker, for over sixty years in Africa, was characterized by the idea of "shared anthropology" but also influenced by surrealism. Many of his films blurred the line between fiction and documentary, creating a new style: ethnofiction. He was an influence on many younger artists and filmmakers, as he would be on Charlie, as is evident in Charlie's films. It was while he was living in the Chateau Rentier that Charlie began writing *Memoire*, the film he promised his mother he would make about her.

Charlie met Cyrius Martinez when he moved into the Chateau de Rentier. Cyrius would become not just his roommate but his closest friend for the rest of his life. The two of them and Emmanuelle would live together until Charlie's death in 2016.

Cyrius appreciated Charlie's breadth of knowledge of the arts and culture, both high and low, and respected and valued Charlie's taste. Cyrius described Charlie as the ultimate Parisian intellect, with not just an opinion, but an accurate, probing, and often witty observation about music, the arts, good food, and politics. He was adept at finding the beauty and meaning and humor in all forms of art, even in trashy art. The two quickly became close friends, with Emmanuelle becoming the third part of who the three of them became together.

"I wanted to make him my brother, my everyday friend. We had this triangular life, with me as a safeguard for the couple that both of us rejected," Cyrius explained.

"It was a privilege to be at his side, both for his intelligence and his humor", said Cyrius. "We felt Jewish even if we were not. He made us love his world that he invented before our eyes with humor and free speech. He had a strong taste for art. He quickly knew how to spot the good culture in the bad. In cinema he was unbeatable, most often going to the big names. His references were numerous but in the first place, he adored Pasolini, Fassbinder, Cassavetes . . ."

Charlie's bedroom contained an impressive library and video library that Charlie had assembled. Cyrius recalled that the books and videos took up all Charles' living space, saying that this was Charlie's own decor, his way of life. It was also Charlie's refuge, where he could retreat from the storms that would increasingly torment him.

Charlie went to all the art exhibitions and to many concerts. He was "curious and generous, always thirsty to know and transmit", explained Cyrius, "the king of Parisian dinners". Cyrius described Charlie's as "daring" to wear clothes that were, while both stylish and neat, also provocative. According to Cyrius, Charlie expressed himself and his attitude through his dress and his manner, Cyrius explained, adopting a peculiarity of body poise that could be both tense and dancing, in a manner of self-expression that Cyrius likened to the cult of self that Baudelaire expressed.

Charlie was a quintessential Parisian, like Jean Claude, or Anna or even like his mother, Solange, had become, but Charlie was a Parisian of a different generation. Like his brother, Maurice, Charles was a child of the sixties. As much as he was a Parisian, he traveled frequently to the Caribbean, and not just to Haiti. He was in Cuba with Emmanuelle, in the early 1990s, a place where he would frequently return. Upon returning from Cuba, Emmanuelle, with Charlie's involvement, organized a French tour for two Cuban singers she or they had met in Cuba.

Emmanuelle was a promoter of music and the arts, not just of Haitian music and arts, but of the music and arts of various third world cultures. I first met Emmanuelle on one of my trips to Paris to visit Solange. Charlie took me to an "event" to celebrate Haitian arts. We entered an unassuming entryway that opened into a large space filled with colored lights and Haitian music. There were Haitian crafts and art and many people. Charlie introduced me to a number of people as we circulated, including a woman he identified as the organizer of the event. Not until much later, did I realize that this woman was Emmanuelle, who played such an important role in Charlie's life.

This event was typical of the cultural events and musical events that Emmanuelle organized, produced, and promoted. She produced not just events in Paris, but French and European tours for Haitian and other third world performers. She was a woman of many connections. When Charlie's cousin, Leo, was struggling to start his career as a drummer, Emmanuelle found work in Paris for him. Leo then came to

Paris, staying with Solange until he established himself as a drummer. He has since settled in Lyons, with his partner and daughter. Lyons is much more affordable for a working musician.

In 1995, Charlie published a second book, *Haïti, Dieu Seul Me Voit*. (In English, *Haiti, God Alone Sees Me*.) The title, in keeping with Charlie's ever-present sense of humor, mixing the profound with the profane, is based on the Haitian expression "*Dieu seul me voit*" a Haitian sexual euphemism that is another inside joke. Like much of Charlie's work, both on paper and on the screen, the book mixes accurate and perceptive observations of Haiti with imaginative fantasy, in a gonzo journalism imagery a la Hunter Thompson and the illustrations of Ralph Steadman that accompany works like *Fear and Loathing in Las Vegas*. The book reflects Charlie's fascination with Haiti, on the one hand, and on the other, the grey areas where the line between reality and imagination become unclear. This blurring of reality and an imagined world was always apparent in Charlie's creative work.

This was true of his film *Memoire*. The film was a documentary featuring actual Holocaust survivors, but it included an actor asking questions as a device to elicit key dialogue. Charlie did not hesitate to break rules and insert an actor into what was otherwise a documentary.

Charles life reached a high point in 1996, the year after *Memoire* came out with much critical acclaim His creativity and self-confidence were united. He was invited to appear on television TV shows. He was writing for but also being written about in newspapers. He had around him his beloved mother Solange, his brother Maurice, and his lover Emmanuelle. It was a productive and happy time for Charlie.

There were constant house parties at the Chateau, with what seemed like a never-ending array of musicians and artists. Musicians ranged from the Moroccan Gnawas of Casablanca, led by **Malem Boussou** to the Haitian group **Ti Coca** that Charlie adored. Visitors to the house included Cuban musicians such as Compay Segundo and Eliades Ochoa from the Buena Vista Social Club, and the Faez Sisters of Casa de la Trova, also from Cuba. They also included the Black Eyes, a band that played Klezmer and other Yiddish music, a band that both Solange and her *belle-soeur*, Helène, adored. Other guests might include radio

DJ and journalist **Rémy Kolpa Kopoul**, who had a huge impact on the spread of what is now known as world music. Cyrius recalls that there were many others, as well.

Charlie at the Café Flo

At the end of 1996, while Cyrius was in Cuba, Charlie and Emmanuelle went to Haiti, where they collaborated to film *Les illuminations de Mme. Nerval*, a full length (78 minutes) film about Mme. Nerval, a Haitian *Manbo*, or priestess. Released in 1999, the film was directed by Charlie and co-written by Charlie and Emmanuelle. He and Emmanuelle received the Prix Jean Rouch for the film, with the prize awarded by Rouch himself, who must have been proud of his protégés.

A *manbo*, sometimes also written in Creole as *mambo*, is a priestess in traditional **Haitian Vodou**. Charlie developed a relationship with Mme. Nerval, either in the course of making the film or as the reason for making the film. Charlie's story isn't always so clear. This is the enigma that was Charlie. What is clear is that Charlie had an interest in the idea of spirit possession, the altered state of consciousness supposedly caused by the control of a human body by spirits and studied with Mme. Nerval. Charlie saw Haitian voodoo as a serious religion, decrying in *Haïti, Dieu Seul Me Voit*, his book on Haiti, how Hollywood prejudice treated vodou, or voodoo, as something primitive, to be looked down at, rather than as a serious religion.[42]

Cyrius said that "*Les Illuminations* marked a turning point for Charlie", who had what Cyrius called "a blinding passion for a territory, a language, an adoption of a living and demanding literature" in the course of making it.

Cyrius explained that "Charlie was at home in Haiti. The inhabitants gave him back something. It was all he had wanted to experience between poetry and baroque madness, with poetic beings and actors of their own madness." That becomes evident reading even a few pages of *Haïti, Dieu Seul Me Voit*.

Charlie and Emmanuelle traveled frequently to Haiti. One trip was a musical project, the production of the CD *Fonds des Nègres, Fonds des Blancs*, a compilation of peasant music from Haiti with Ti Coca and others. The CD was released on Buda, a French record label specializing in world music. Charlie and Emmanuelle, but mostly Emmanuelle, produced concerts with Ti Coca in France, and Charlie and Emmanuelle also produced a tour with Mme. Nerval. Madame Nerval became Charlie's *mambo*, his "second spirit mother".

Charlie continued to make films about Haiti, including his 2003 *Royal Bonbon*, his 2004 *Les Fins de Chimères* (*The End of Chimeras*), and *Une Étrange Cathédrale dans la Graisse des Ténèbres* (*A Strange Cathedral in the Thick Darkness*), which came out in 2010.

Charlie's 2003 *Royal Bonbon* was rooted in the themes of freedom and liberation that connected Charlie's two obsessions, Haiti and the Holocaust. It was Charlie's first full-length feature film, as opposed to a documentary, and it won the **Prix Jean Vigo**. *Royal Bonbon* is about a modern-day Haitian, Christophe Henry, a man who would be king. Christophe, a destitute wandering the streets of Gonaïves, Haiti's second largest city, believes himself to be Henri Christophe, one of the leaders

---

42 Charlie bases his argument on the theories regarding suppression of Black culture made by poet and political activist Aimé Césaire in his theory of Negritude and the philosophy of Frantz Fanon, another post-colonial Martinican writer known for his books *Black Skin, White Masks* and *The Wretched of the Earth*.

in Haiti's 1791 battle for independence from France. In the early 1800s, Christophe Henri declared himself King Christophe and established a kingdom in the northern part of independent Haiti with Gonaïves as its capital. This "kingdom" actually lasted for a few years.

The modern-day Christophe takes refuge in the ruins of Sans-Souci Palace, one of many public buildings the original Christophe had built with enslaved workers during his reign. Along with the Citadelle LaFerrière, the Royal Chapel of Milot, and a number of other buildings, Sans-Souci Palace is still standing, though the Royal Chapel was severely damaged by fire in 2020.

In Charlie's film, the modern-day Christophe declares himself the ruler of his imaginary kingdom. He takes the name King Chacha, perhaps a reference to Charlie's grandmother, Chacha Manya. This would be in keeping with Charlie's ever-present sense of humor. King Chacha lives with his lover and a young street urchin, Timothèe, whom he has taken under his wing. The local community, which has been waiting for the return of their mythic sovereign, initially welcomes King Chacha. The populace turns against Chacha after he becomes a tyrant, and Timothèe plots his patron's overthrow.

I have wanted to see *Royal Bonbon* since I first saw the colorful handbill for the film in Solange's kitchen, with the smiling King Chacha wrapped in a crimson robe, crown on his head, being paraded through the streets on his throne in a public celebration. This was just one of the mementos of her sons that Solange had displayed in her kitchen. In addition to Maurice's press credentials from Cuba and elsewhere in Latin America, there were photos of Maurice that I often looked at during my visits after his death in 1999. When I was in Solange's kitchen in 2018, during my trip to Paris for her funeral, I noticed a new item, a publicity photo of Cyrius's recording of his song "Yokahama," issued after Charlie's death and which he dedicated to Charlie.

Charlie's next film, *Haiti, la Fin des Chimères*, arose out of Charlie's February 2004 trip to Haiti to make what he thought would be a celebratory film about the restoration of people's rule to Haiti, the first African democracy. The film was to be about the success of **Jean Bertrand Aristide**, a former leftist priest, in restoring real democracy to Haiti after decades of dictatorships under Francois "Papa Doc" Duvalier and his son Jean-Claude "Baby Doc" Duvalier. Aristide was immensely popular among the Haitian people but his demands for restitution of the 90 million gold francs France demanded of Haiti following its claim of independence were unacceptable to the American and French powers.

Shortly after Charlie and his film crew arrived in Haiti that February, American-backed rebels began the fighting that lead to the coup that resulted to Aristide's resignation on February 29, 2004, under controversial circumstances. U.S. forces then kidnapped Aristide and flew him to Africa where he was exiled and prevented from completing his second term as president. So ended the chimera of democracy in Haiti.

Charlie bore witness to all of this, documenting it in a film that was not what it was originally supposed to be. Instead of a celebration of freedom, he saw the people and land he loved unravel from the hope that Aristide had brought. Charlie persisted, producing a film that shed light on the last days of Aristide's presidency. But those weeks spent watching the toppling of Aristide and the fall of Haitian democracy were a blow to Charlie, a hard blow.

How hard a blow this was to Charlie can be heard in his voice on an EP which he and Cyrius put together after the release of *Haiti, la Fin des Chimères*. Charlie sang his original lyrics, played to the music of Dylan, Patty Smith and others. Cyrius arranged the music and played piano. He was joined by Jean François Pauvros on guitar, and a bass player, John. Cyrius described Charlie's voice on the EP as "slow and deep like a tribute to the dead".

Charlie made one more film in Haiti, a few months after the deadly earthquake of January 2010. In *Une Étrange Cathédrale dans la Graisse des Ténèbres* (*A Strange Cathedral in the Viscous Darkness*), Haitian poet Frankétienne, considered by some to be Haiti's greatest poet, recites his visionary verses amid the ruins of Port-au-Prince. It also features the vodou singer Érol Josué. This film is, according to Cyrius, "a testimony to the love [Charles] had for this country and these common people whom he loved as a brother".

Cyrius's words capture Charlie's two true passions: "For many years, Charlie had been a familiar figure in Port-au-Prince and in the provinces where he toured regularly. His cinematographic work was indeed focused on the two major themes that marked his life: the genocide of the Jews and the Haitian universe. Few non-Haitians knew the country, its history, its people, its uniqueness, its spirituality and its imagination as well as he did." Cyrius's words capture Charlie's two true passions.

In his last years, Charlie's focus turned from Haiti back to the Shoah. When we spoke, Charlie often asked me about different American Jewish authors. He was always interested in a Holocaust or Israel connection.

Early on, in 1990, when I was in Paris with Nana, Charlie asked me if I knew Ben Hecht's novel, perhaps his only novel, _A Jew in Love_. I took note of the title and not until after Charlie died did I track down a copy and read it. I couldn't finish it. It was woefully dated. Its story of a Jewish man's multiple affairs was no longer politically correct, to say the least. I did not understand why Charlie was so enamored with Hecht, until I uncovered Hecht's Zionist background.

Charlie would have been familiar with Hecht from Charlie's background in American film history. Hecht was renowned as the face of Hollywood for the seventy or so screenplays for which he received the credits or co-credits from the 1920s to the 1940s and especially in the 1930s. Nominated for nine Oscars and winning seven, he was called "_the_ Hollywood screenwriter", and someone who "personified Hollywood itself".

What attracted Charlie to Hecht was not the now dated novel, about which Charlie must have been curious. It was Hecht's ardent and public Zionism. Hecht was a member of the Bergson Group, an Irgun front group in the United States run by Peter Bergson, which was active in raising money for the Irgun's activities and disseminating Irgun propaganda. As a result, Hecht was boycotted by the British and was writing his screenplays anonymously in the late 1940s and early 1950s to avoid the British boycott.

As part of his contribution to the Zionist cause, Hecht wrote the script for the Bergson Group's production of **A Flag is Born**, which opened on September 5, 1946, at the Alvin Playhouse in New York City. The play, which compared the Zionist underground's campaign in Palestine to the American Revolution, was intended to increase public support for the Zionist cause in the United States. The play's opening run starred Marlon Brando and Paul Muni. The proceeds from the play were used to purchase a ship that was renamed the **MS *Ben Hecht*** a ship that, like *The Exodus*, brought refugees to Palestine, carrying 900 Holocaust survivors to Palestine in March 1947. *The Ben Hecht* was later commissioned as a ship in the fledgling Israeli navy as *The INS Ma'oz* from 1948 to 1956. Charlie had a nose for anything Holocaust related.

Charlie also got me to read Phillip Roth's novel *Operation Shylock*. I have been a big fan of Phillip Roth since my undergraduate days at Penn, where I had the privilege of taking a seminar with him when I was an English major there. Roth was a visiting scholar my junior year and I was selected to take a small seminar with him. However, I had never read *Operation Shylock*, until Charlie asked me about the work.

Charlie wanted to talk to me about making a film based on Roth's thesis. The novel is about another Phillip Roth, either impersonating the author or just someone else named Phillip Roth. Roth the author travels to Israel looking for this imposter, who is promoting the idea that the Jews in Israel should all go back to Europe and the real Phillip Roth is getting blamed for this reverse Zionism theory that is not his. This is the kind of twist that both Roth and Charlie loved.

Charlie did not get to make that film, but he did make one more film, in 2015, before he died, also a holocaust themed film. Just as I learned about Ben Hecht's *A Jew in Love* and Phillip Roth's *Operation Shylock* from Charlie, I also learned about Pitchipoi from Charlie.

I first heard the term when Solange and Anna Sibert, Shira and I went to a kosher Jewish restaurant named Pitchipoi in the Marais, the Paris neighborhood which had become the Jewish neighborhood, replacing the area between Solange's house and the Grande Synagogue on the Rue de la Victoire. There are photos of us there. At the time, Solange had a hard time explaining to me what Pitchipoi exactly was. It was not until Charlie started telling me about the film that I began to understand. I was always learning from Charlie. From what Cyrius and others have told me, I wasn't the only one.

Pitchipoi was an imaginary place somewhere far to the east. It was an answer French Jews, interned by the Nazis in Drancy and waiting to be transported, gave their children who asked, "Where is that train going with our father?" or "Where is that train taking Uncle Mordecai?" or "Where is that train taking my parents?" Pitchipoi was the answer people gave their children instead of "Auschwitz". Pitchipoi was an imaginary place where one could dream they were going instead of to a death camp.

Julien Schulmann, the protagonist in Charlie's film *Pitchipoi*, is a bitter, obnoxious comedian who jokes cynically about his Jewish heritage and the current situation in Israel. He has just lost his father, a Polish Jew and concentration camp survivor. Before he died, Julien's father left a "will" in which he requested that his other son, Pierre, spread his ashes in Poland. His father's preference comes as a rude shock for Julien, as his brother hasn't been heard from for two years. Nonetheless, Julien feels obliged to take on the task his missing brother is not able to perform. Thus the plot unfolds, "slowly bringing to light an unspeakable secret", with the plot focusing "on the anxieties of cultural heritage and Jewish memory", as David Pountain writes in his review of the film on the filmdoo.com website.

Pountain continues, "With its sombre colour scheme and historically loaded subject matter, Charles Najman's *Pitchipoï* is hardly a film that screams 'absurdist comedy' at first glance. But as the film ventures into increasingly unpredictable, odd, challenging and sometimes downright confounding territory, it starts to resemble a trippier version of the Coen Brothers at their most cruelly strange and rambling, . . . or even one of Bob Dylan's socially aware tall tales from the mid-'60s", such as "Bob Dylan's 115th Dream".

The more I read Charlie's writings, as well as about his writing and his films, the more I discover about his creations, the more I find him to be like Bob Dylan. Charlie's fantastic nightmare images, fraught with Jewish and biblical imagery are stylistically akin to Dylan, another Jew whose work reflects a struggle with his Jewish identity and with Jewish beliefs. Both are artists who work in different media. Both mix the real with the surreal. Both exhibit a subtle but ever-present sense of humor. Both continually evolved and surprised. Both grapple with their Jewishness. And like Bob Dylan, Charlie was an enigma.

As I am writing this last chapter, Dylan latest book has been released.

<u>*The Philosophy of Modern Song*</u> contains essays on a broad assortment of American songs. In the essay on Little Richard's "Long Tall Sally" Dylan writes "Long Tall Sally was 12 feet tall. . . . She was part of the old biblical days in Samaria from the tribe called the Nephilim. They were giants that lived back before the cataclysm of the flood." Has anyone other than Charles Najman and Bob Dylan combined such surreal nightmare fantasies with a fascination with Jewish roots?

Once again, Charlie managed, in his creative work to combine reality with the fantastic. As Pountain's review concludes, "It's a darkly comic free jazz solo of a film where the past and present of the Jewish identity collapse into one."

CHAPTER 40

The Last Days

The darkness of "Pitchipoi" was a reflection of a darkness overcoming Charlie in his last years. The Haiti he loved was in ruins. His brother was gone. His mother, whom he adored and continued to care for, was in her nineties. A lifelong diabetic, his own health, physical and mental, was declining. He kept this hidden from his public persona, but he increasingly relied for support on his close friends and housemates, Emmanuelle and Cyrius, who would be there for him until the end.

In 2000, Emmanuelle had joined Cyrius in Cuba, and returned pregnant. Charlie moved out of the Chateau Rentier. He went to live by himself in the 20th district of Paris at the top of Rue Ménilmontant. After the baby, a son Emmanuelle named Areski, was born, she and Cyrius would visit Charlie often with the baby, Areski, and Charlie quickly became attached to this little boy who could have been his son.

Charlie and Areski soon developed their own independent relationship. When it was time for an outing, Areski wanted to go with Charlie. Charlie took the young Areski on special outings, to the Cinema, or to visit his mother, Solange. The regular outing to the cinema might also include Solange. She also grew attached to and fond of the young boy whom Solange called "Prince Areski", and they both laughed a lot together.

Neither Charlie nor Solange ever told me about Areski. Solange also did not tell me that Charlie was married to Emmanuelle. Although I suspected they were married, Solange never gave me a straight answer to this question, until after Charlie died. Then she revealed the marriage in order to explain to me that Emmanuelle had inherited Charlie's house in Bagnolet. Solange was very candid with me about her life, but I don't think she ever breached her son's trust in her.

The trust between them was mutual. There is only one thing about which Charlie did not tell his mother the truth. In my phone calls with Solange, I always asked about Charlie. He was often traveling, but Solange would often say he was filming. I would ask where and she would say Guadeloupe. Sometimes I knew from Charlie that he was in Haiti, but I never challenged Solange. I knew Charlie had told her he was "flying to Guadeloupe" because Haiti was dangerous, and he did not want his mother to worry about him.

Technically, what Charlie told his mother was true. The way one flies from Paris to Haiti is through Guadeloupe, still part of France, changing there to a smaller "puddle jumper" aircraft for the connecting short flight to Port-au-Prince. Sometimes I think Solange knew when Charlie was in Haiti but was content to maintain the fiction. She worried about him less that way.

In fact, Charlie did have reason to travel to Guadeloupe, as he had developed a relationship with **André Schwarz-Bart**, the French born son of Polish Jews who won the Goncourt prize, the 1967 Jerusalem Prize, and much other acclaim for his book *The Last of the Just*. Schwarz-Bart lived in Guadeloupe with his wife, the playwright and novelist **Simone Schwarz-Bart**. Charlie's relationship with the Schwarz-Barts may have been a little like his older brother Maurice's relationship with Marcus Wolf.

After André Schwarz-Bart passed away in 2006, Charlie's relationship with Simone continued. Charlie was intrigued by her book *The Mulatto Solitude*, a book whose subject haunted him until he started writing a screenplay of it and shared it with Simone. Charlie grew closer to Simone, close enough that he would say that she was his second mother. This displeased Solange terribly. Initially, Solange also did not get along well with Emmanuelle, either, but that is hardly uncommon between mothers and their daughters-in-law. There is an inherent conflict in the notion of two women competing for the attention of the same man. However, Solange's attitude changed as she saw the role Emmanuelle was playing in their lives as Charlie's health deteriorated.

I did not learn about Areski until 2020, four years after Charles had died. I had flown to Paris from Israel for a few days to meet with Jean Claude. It was the last time I saw Jean Claude. While in Paris, I contacted Emmanuelle and asked to visit her. I was seeking her help not just for information about Charles but also to help me obtain a copy of *Memoire*, hopefully a copy with English subtitles. Emmanuelle was very gracious and agreed to my request to meet with her. I visited her briefly and in the middle of the visit a tall young black male, maybe twenty years old, came in the front door. Emmanuelle introduced him as her son, Areski. He politely greeted me and excused himself.

Not until much later, after Yves Flank connected me to Cyrius, would I learn anything more about Areski. Cyrius told me that Charlie "loved Areski like no one else . . . he wanted to pass on his love of the cinema, of literature, of humor to him."

Cyrius preceded these words with what seemed at the time an odd turn of phrase: "In those moments of madness". This did not make sense to me in the context or at the time: "In those moments of madness, he loved Areski like no one else."

I would learn from Cyrius that, as Solange saw Charlie treat Areski like a son, she begin to view Areski as a grandson. Perhaps she realized that this very dark-skinned little boy could have been her grandson. Emmanuelle and Solange became closer, with the help of Areski. Solange began to appreciate the short visits. Sometimes Charlie came just with Areski, just the two of them, but other times Areski came with Charlie and Emmanuelle, or with the full trio, Charlie, Cyrius, and Emmanuelle. This led to short, then longer excursions, as Areski grew older. Eventually, Solange was pleased to have Areski join her and Charlie on a winter vacation to Morocco.

The bond between Solange and Emmanuelle solidified as Charlie's health deteriorated and Solange saw how Emmanuelle had become Charlie's guardian angel in his dying days. It was Emmanuelle who accompanied Charlie in his first hospitalization, at Centre Hospitalier Sainte-Anne, the main psychiatric hospital of Paris. It was an evening of great delirium. Charlie had not slept for nights and was ranting about his father, and how he died, and about his grandmother who every time she heard a knock on the door she thought of the Gestapo. At the hospital,

Charlie hid under the bed, as he saw butterflies flying from his body as the hospital room door closed.

Emmanuelle and Cyrius stayed there with Charlie until he was discharged. From Sainte-Anne, Charlie went home to the house in Bagnolet. He locked himself in his room and his bed then became his raft, from where he faced his demons, as Cyrius saw it. He spent a lot of time reading and writing screenplays that didn't always see the light of day. The books surrounding his bed became his buoys and beacons.

Two women joined him in Bagnolet, a friend who was the wife of an American slam poet and a Haitian woman, Lyline. Other people began passing through. It grew out of control and Emmanuelle and Cyrius moved in with Charlie, so they could be with him, care for him, and watch out for him.

As Cyrius recalls, that first hospitalization was a huge blow to Charlie. He never really recovered. He just weakened more and more. He was no longer able to take his mother to dinner at the Brasserie Flo, as he had done every Sunday for many years. He began to worry about who would care for her, if he couldn't, and about what he would do when she was no longer alive. He had crazy anxieties.

Emmanuelle and Cyrius urged him to see a psychoanalyst, but he refused, claiming to be more insightful and intelligent than them. As Cyrius explained, "Charlie was linked like a leitmotif to the memory of his mother's Holocaust experience. From his father who left too soon, the lack of his brother Maurice. All this was pain too heavy for Charlie to bear."

Charlie tried to spend his time reviewing and writing screenplays but when his work didn't always see the light of day, that depressed him a lot. He would lock himself in his room, and his bed again became a raft facing his demons.

Emmanuelle and Cyrius decided that Charlie needed a more normal everyday family life, with the rhythms of a child: school, regular schedules, weekends and holidays, set lunches and dinners, evening movies, card games and quiet discussions. With Areski, Emmanuelle and Cyrius derived an unusual pleasure living with and caring for Charlie in Bagnolet but his worsening condition continued to worry them.

They were still able to bring Charlie some moments of joy, such as the evening that brought the Slabiak brothers, the core of the Yiddish revival band *Les Yeux Noir* (The Black Eyes), to the house in Bagnolet. Charlie had wanted to surprise Solange for her birthday, and they had a small party, inviting some friends of Charlie and of Solange. Solange's *belle-soeur*, Helène, who also enjoyed the Yiddish music was there and both Solange and Helène enjoyed the music and the evening was a success, but it was clear to Cyrius and Emmanuelle that the end was near.

During this time Emmanuelle even more became Charlie's guardian angel. There were others who also provided support. Once Charlie began work on *Pitchipoi*, Marie Doler, an assistant on the film, and others involved in the making of this final film were part of his life, there to support him. They included its main actor Xavier Gallais, and actors Serge Merlin and Denis Lavant, Jackie Berroyer, Sabrina Seyvecou, Sarah Grappin and Jean Louis Coulloch.

Making that film had Charlie thinking and talking about things other than his father, his brother and his family. Working on the film breathed a bit of life into Charlie, but only momentarily, as memories of his father, his brother and his grandmother, Chacha Manya, continued to torment him in his nightmares and visions.

After the work on the film was finished and Marie was gone, Charlie returned to his bed, again alone with his books. He rarely went out. Cyrius described it as another descent into hell for him, again isolated in his ivory tower. Emmanuelle and Cyrius did what they could, but, as Cyrius would say "something was broken." Charlie returned to the hospital. Emmanuelle and Cyrius made regular and continual visits, sometimes with Solange, or with Areski, or both.

When Charlie was discharged from the hospital, he had regained some strength. This unusual family, consisting of Charlie, Emmanuelle, Cyrius and Areski, drove to Crans-Montana, a resort in the Swiss Alps, "to breathe the mountains". Charlie was debilitated by his diabetes and what it was doing to his mental state, but he was clinging to this life and eager to keep fighting.

Charlie increasingly found Emmanuelle to be his ally, an angel whose wings he could count on to be there for whatever he needed. He was grateful for her. Some years earlier, in 2012, they had gotten married at the

Paris town hall for the 20th Arrondisement. Was it for Areski? Was it for Emmanuelle? Was it so Emmanuelle would inherit the house in Bagnolet?

By then, Charlie knew, from the medical analysis results and the repetition of his comas that left him increasingly fragile, that his days were numbered. His dearest friend Cyrius found Charlie's dead body on the morning of July 18, 2016. He had passed quietly in his sleep.

Cyrius wrote that "Charlie was loved as a friend. We could count on his discernment and good artistic advice. Until the end of his life he had faithful friends such as the writer Claude Arnaud, Simone Schwarz-Bart, the composer Jean François Pauvros. He also had friendly relations with the directors Olivier Assayas and Bertrand Bonello, the actors Mathieu Amalric, Fabrice Luchini, Denis Lavant, Jackie Berroyer, Yvonne Ker the friend of the two brothers, Claude Santiago and the Haitian poets Frankétienne and James Noel, the singer Saul Wiliams and his wife Anisia, the Haitian singer James Germain, Sonia Feltesse, Maria Totaro, Lyline Charles, Germain Moulin, Dominique Abel."

Among his many works, written and on film, the most impressive was *Memoire*, his tribute to his mother, a true Holocaust survivor. The film is about both his mother and her Holocaust experience. One cannot separate Solange from that experience, not ever. Thus Charles' love for his mother led inevitably to his own preoccupation with the Holocaust. For many years, Solange did not talk about her Holocaust experience. When she did talk about it, she spoke first to Charles.

"To my son Charles, I spoke very easily. To my son Charles, we talked like that every day, a little bit, but really I was talking." She said in testimony to the Foundation pour la Memoire de la Shoah, continuing "Because there are cures, you see. That's why this film is also on two levels, because everything reminds of the deportation. It's past, but it hasn't happened yet. Yes, that doesn't hurt. There is still the greenery, there is the air which is very good, and they took enough, the health, the life, the money, everything, they took, the Nazis."

Solange outlasted both of her sons. What is left in Europe of the Fischers, the Glantzes, or the Szylberstajns? There are no Fischers and no Glantzes. What is left in Europe from our family is just the Szylberstajns. What is now left of the Szylberstajns are Solange's granddaughter Esther and Esther's son, Simon.

There was a photo of Simon in Solange's living room. It was on the end table to the right of the living room couch, next to where Solange would sit when she watched television. The photo was still there when I was in the apartment for Solange's funeral in June of 2018. In the photo, Simon was a cute little boy with a kippah.

The picture reminded me of the photos of Teddy when he was a little boy. I saw Simon again at his great-grandmother Solange's funeral. In 2018 he was tall, good looking, teenager, wearing a wide grin on his face. Two years later, he was planning to join his grandmother, Corinne, on a trip she was making to the United States to do research for a book she was writing. Simon was exploring colleges and wanted to visit a friend of his who was attending Amherst. Simon was thinking of leaving France to attend college in North America, but covid interrupted those plans. If Simon leaves, there will be no Szylberstajns left in Europe, either.

Epilogue

Solange always enjoyed the winter vacations with Charlie to Morocco. It was an opportunity to get away from the winter. At some point, Charlie made them an annual trip. They would go to the beach at Casablanca to warm up from the winter cold, ice and snow. Solange was sitting on the beach during one of these winter vacations, either with Suzanne, or Charlie or with both of them, when a tall blond man approached them.

He excused himself for intruding, and explained that he had seen Solange's tattoo, the number used to identify prisoners at Auschwitz, and he wanted to apologize. Solange looked back at him, somewhat perplexed. The man then explained that he was the grandson of **Hermann Göring**. Göring was one of the most powerful figures in the Nazi party and an architect of the Holocaust. The blond man then said that he was ashamed and wanted to convey his shame. That's the word he used: his shame.

When Solange told me this story, I thought about Katharina Maartens, whom for a while we thought of as our "fourth" child. In the late summer of 2005, Katharina came to America through Action Reconciliation Service for Peace, a German organization founded to confront the legacy of its Nazi past. She had just arrived to do a service year, the way many Americans do in the Peace Corp, or AmeriCorps, but Action Reconciliation Service consisted of young Germans seeking to make reparations for Nazi Germany's crimes.

Rabbi Sara Paasche-Orlow, the rabbi at Hebrew Rehabilitation Center had called Nona and me. Amy Schectman, our friend from the Brookline

Havurah Minyan, was then working at Hebrew Rehab and had given her our phone number. Rabbi Paasche-Orlow was looking for someone who could put up a young German girl who had arrived as a Reconciliation volunteer. She had didn't have a place to stay, and the rabbi wondered whether we could we put up the young woman for a few days until Hebrew Rehab located a home for the year for the young woman.

Nona and I agreed to put Katharina up for a few days, and then we talked about it further. With Teddy gone, we had just become empty nesters. We had three empty bedrooms. Why not take in Katharina? Once we met her, the deal was sealed. We learned a little about Katharina from the rabbi. From Katharina herself we would learn that her father was a minister and that her grandfather was an SS officer, but it was something her family did not talk about. We learned some other things about her but mostly she learned about us and about Jewish life.

Katharina wanted to work in a Jewish old age home so that she could meet Holocaust survivors. That is why she came to the United States. A placement in Eastern Europe would have involved providing social services, but there weren't many Jews left in eastern Europe. Reconciliation had recently expanded to the United States, where there were not only Jews, but Holocaust survivors.

Living with us proved an added bonus to her, and to us. In order to eat from our kitchen, she learned about keeping kosher. Every dinner conversation became an education for all three of us. She had endless questions. There were shabbat meals, then Rosh Hashana, Yom Kippur, and Sukkot. Every holiday prompted further questions from Katharina, some easy and some provocative. Dinner conversations proved enlightening to all three of us as Katharina posed questions about not just the reason behind rituals, but about faith and beliefs and our histories and the questions led to engaging discussions.

It was a difficult year for Katharina. In the middle of her placement, Katharina's father had a stroke, and she was torn between keeping her commitment to Reconciliation and going back to be with her father, not knowing if he would survive the stroke. She returned to Germany for a month or so, to be at her father's side, and then came back to finish her year at Hebrew Rehab. In the course of this crisis, we became Katharina's parents away from home, and she became like a fourth child to us.

Katharina knew a little about Israel from her father, who had spent time in Syria and Israel as a minister. A few years after she returned home to Germany, Nona and I invited her to join us in Israel. She came and stayed with us in Jerusalem for a week. I took her to Bethlehem, my first adventure into the West Bank, and she went to Christian sites in Galilee. We also went to Masada and the Dead Sea and other Jewish sites. We remained in touch and Katharina returned to Israel for Teddy's wedding.

I also think of Suzanne, who met Solange when she was the host and escort for Solange and Charlie at the Berlin film festival showing of *Memoire*. There are other Germans, as well. Many Jews, mostly Israelis and Russians have returned to live in Berlin. Does all this mean there has been reconciliation?

There has been reconciliation. Nonetheless, antisemitism has never gone away. The response to the Hamas massacre of October 7, 2023 has proven the resilience and strength of antisemitism. It has never been easy to be Jewish. This has always been true. Yet in my father's darkest days, it was his ability to answer the man muttering the *shema* under his breathe with the words "*Boruch shem k'vod malchuso l'olam vo'ed*" that kept my father fed and alive.

I once read, I no longer remember where, that being Jewish is not an accident of birth. It is the result of a deliberate choice, repeated generation after generation. It was my father's choice, and his father and grandfather before him. It is now my deliberate choice in writing this book, so that I can pass the stories of your Jewish forebearers on to you, my children and grandchildren. I make the choice not just for me but for you and the next generations, *Midor l'dor*.

Some Things My Father Used To Say

1. There is a reason God gave you two ears and only one mouth.
2. Finding the right woman is like catching a bus. You don't take the first one that comes along. It may not be going your way. You need to wait for the one that's going in your direction. [Uncle Herman used to say this, too]
3. A wise man knows what he doesn't know.
4. Sophomore in Latin means half smart
5. There are three kinds of liars: liars, damn liars and statistics
6. Statistics don't lie but you can lie with statistics.
7. Christmas is the best day of the year for Jews. It's the one day every anti-Semite is celebrating the birthday of a Jew. (left unsaid "and therefore the one day Jews don't have to worry about a pogrom.")
8. Father would say "He's not Chinese" or "It's not a Chinese name" to indicate subtly whether a person was Jewish.
9. When a student in first period or an early morning class did not know the answer to question, Father would ask the student if he had eaten breakfast and the student would invariably answer no, saying he was

running late, didn't have time or something like that. Father would then say "you wouldn't drive the car without putting gas in first."

10. Father predicted that the Dick Tracy two-way radio watch in the comics would become a reality, anticipating cell phones and apple watches.

11. Father wasn't a big shopper and he didn't believe in "sales". Nana would come in and say "We should buy this suit. It's on sale for half price. We can save $50." Father would answer "If we don't buy it at all, you can save $100." He would say that for any sale, just changing the item and the cost, or he would say, "If you don't buy it at all, it won't cost you anything."

12. Despite his proficiency in English, his complaints about how difficult it was to become proficient in English were often punctuated with his indignant response "I am not pulling your leg. I never even touched you", when told "you're pulling my leg" by a woman at a social event.

13. When Father told people the stories about the Shema saving his life or about the soldier who lost his eye, they would ask Father why he never wrote them down and he would answer "No one would believe them."

14. Father and Uncle Herman both used to tell a story about the farmer in Poland who was training his horse to live without eating. That way he could save a lot of money on hay and oats. The farmer said first I reduced the daily cup of oats to a half cup, then to a quarter cup, then to just a spoonful of oats a day. The farmer said "I was almost there, but then the horse died."

15. When a Jew gets in a car accident and breaks his leg, he says "It could have been worse. I could have broken both legs."

AND TWO THINGS NANA WOULD SAY

1. Nana would reply, when you complained the food was too hot, "I didn't cook it on ice."
2. If you complained about having to go out in the rain, Nana would answer "You aren't made of sugar. You won't melt."

Appendix

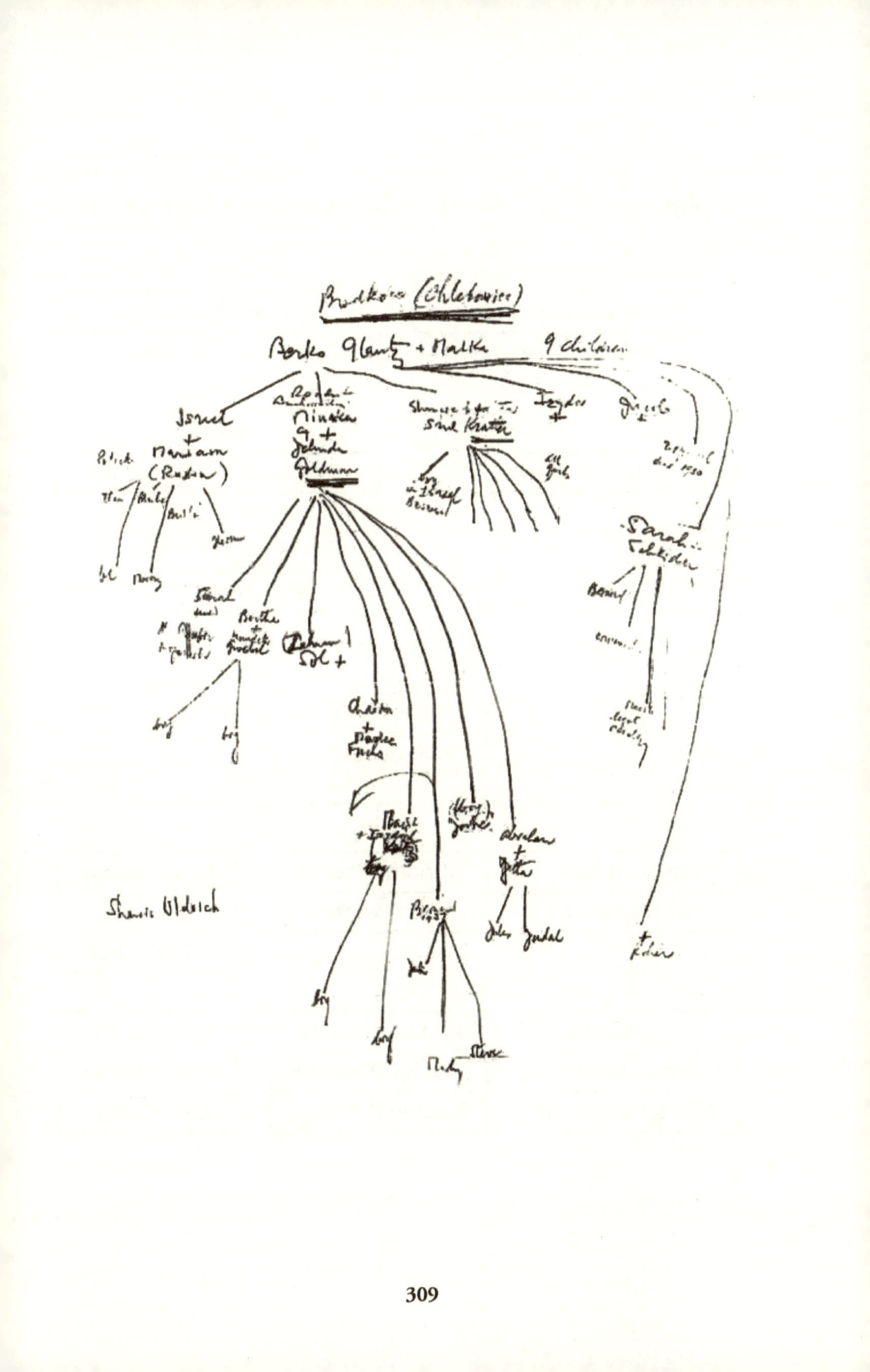

Appendix 2A: Fischer Szylberstajn Family Tree

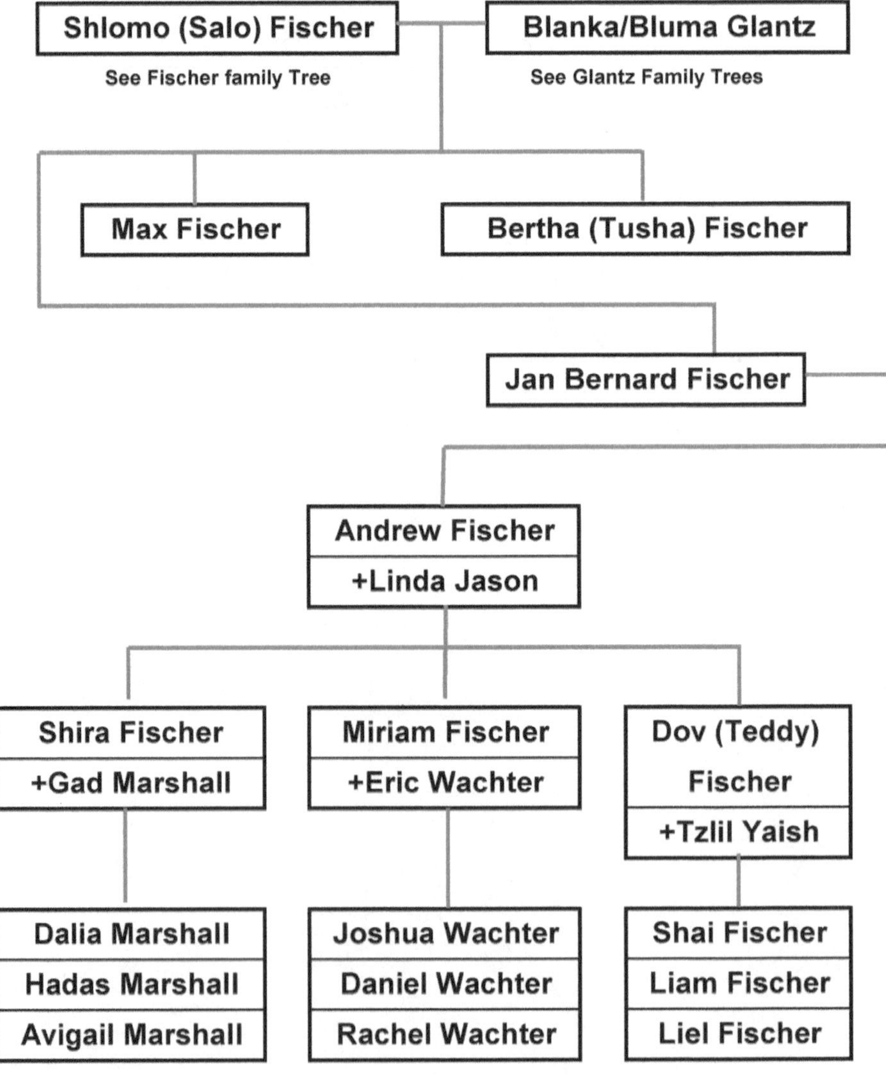

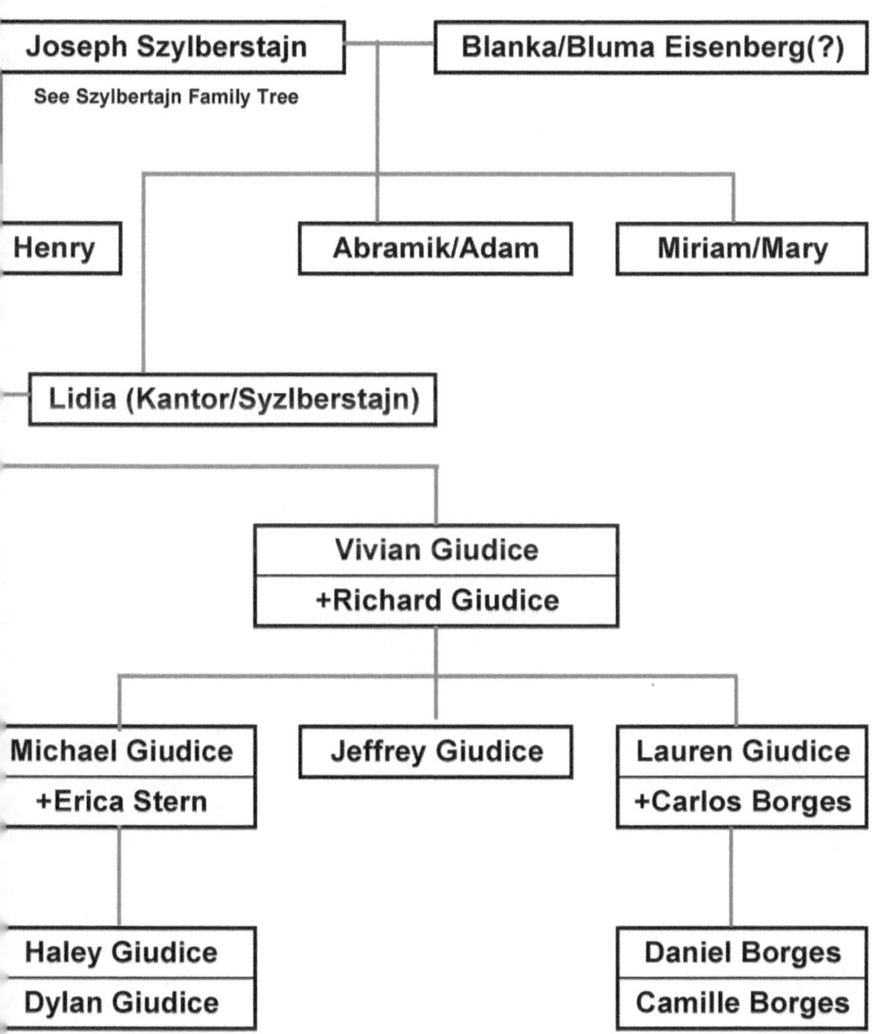

Joseph Szylberstajn
See Szylbertajn Family Tree
Blanka/Bluma Eisenberg(?)
Henry
Abramik/Adam
Miriam/Mary
Lidia (Kantor/Syzlberstajn)
Vivian Giudice
+Richard Giudice
Michael Giudice
+Erica Stern
Jeffrey Giudice
Lauren Giudice
+Carlos Borges
Haley Giudice
Dylan Giudice
Daniel Borges
Camille Borges

Appendix 2B: Fischer Family Tree

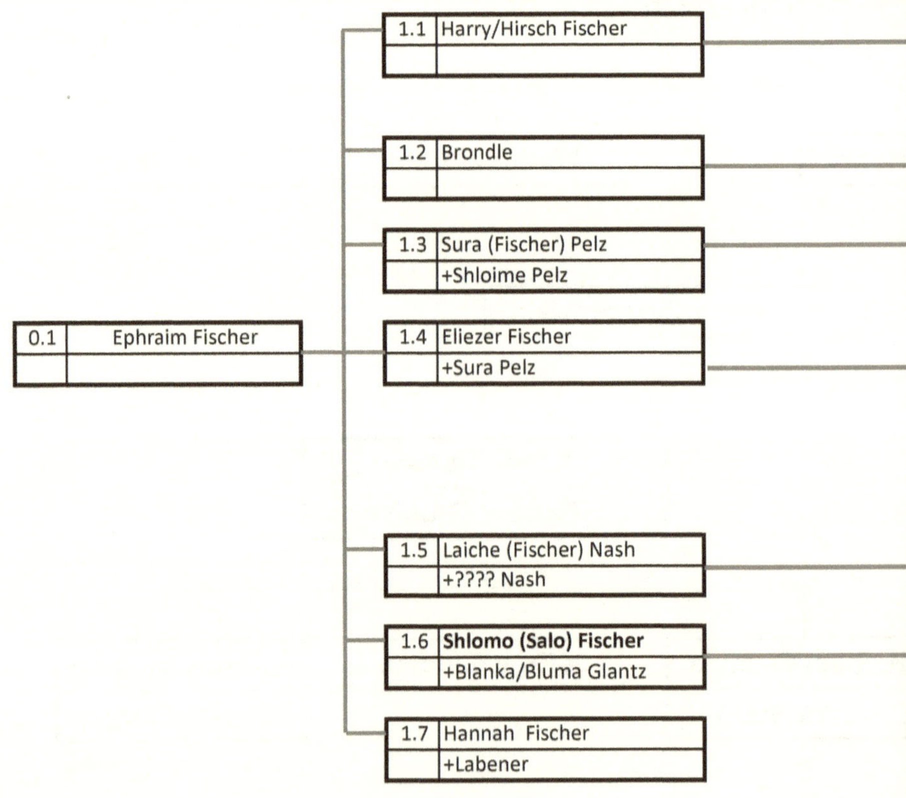

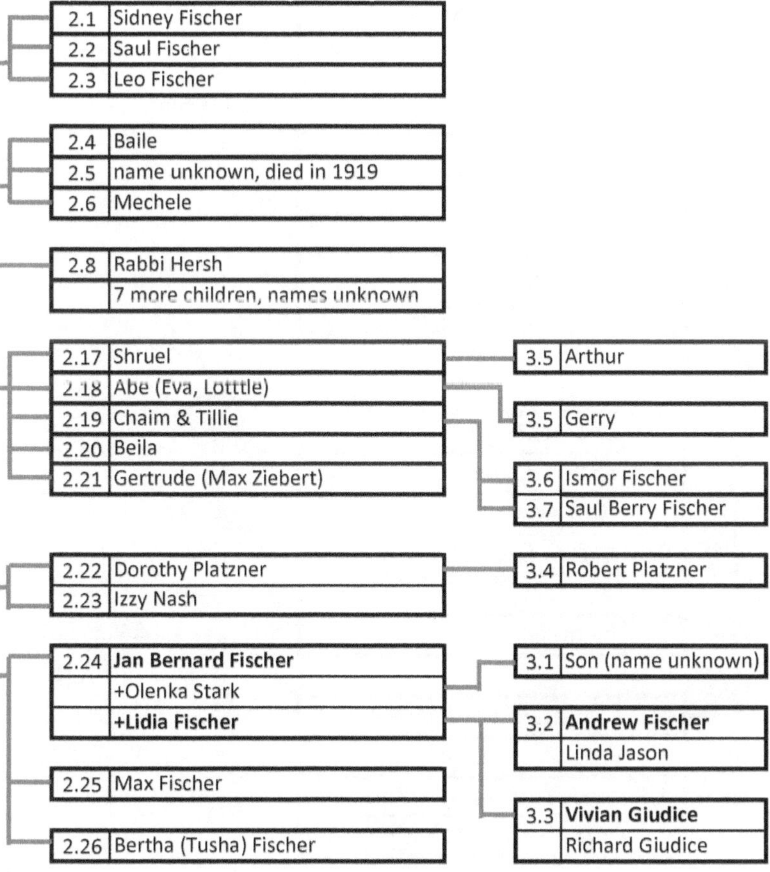

2.1 | Sidney Fischer
2.2 | Saul Fischer
2.3 | Leo Fischer
2.4 | Baile
2.5 | name unknown, died in 1919
2.6 | Mechele
2.8 | Rabbi Hersh
7 more children, names unknown
2.17 | Shruel
2.18 | Abe (Eva, Lotttle)
2.19 | Chaim & Tillie
2.20 | Beila
2.21 | Gertrude (Max Ziebert)
3.5 | Arthur
3.5 | Gerry
3.6 | Ismor Fischer
3.7 | Saul Berry Fischer
2.22 | Dorothy Platzner
2.23 | Izzy Nash
3.4 | Robert Platzner
2.24 | Jan Bernard Fischer
+Olenka Stark
+Lidia Fischer
2.25 | Max Fischer
2.26 | Bertha (Tusha) Fischer
3.1 | Son (name unknown)
3.2 | Andrew Fischer
Linda Jason
3.3 | Vivian Giudice
Richard Giudice

Appendix 2C: Berko Dov Glantz Family Tree

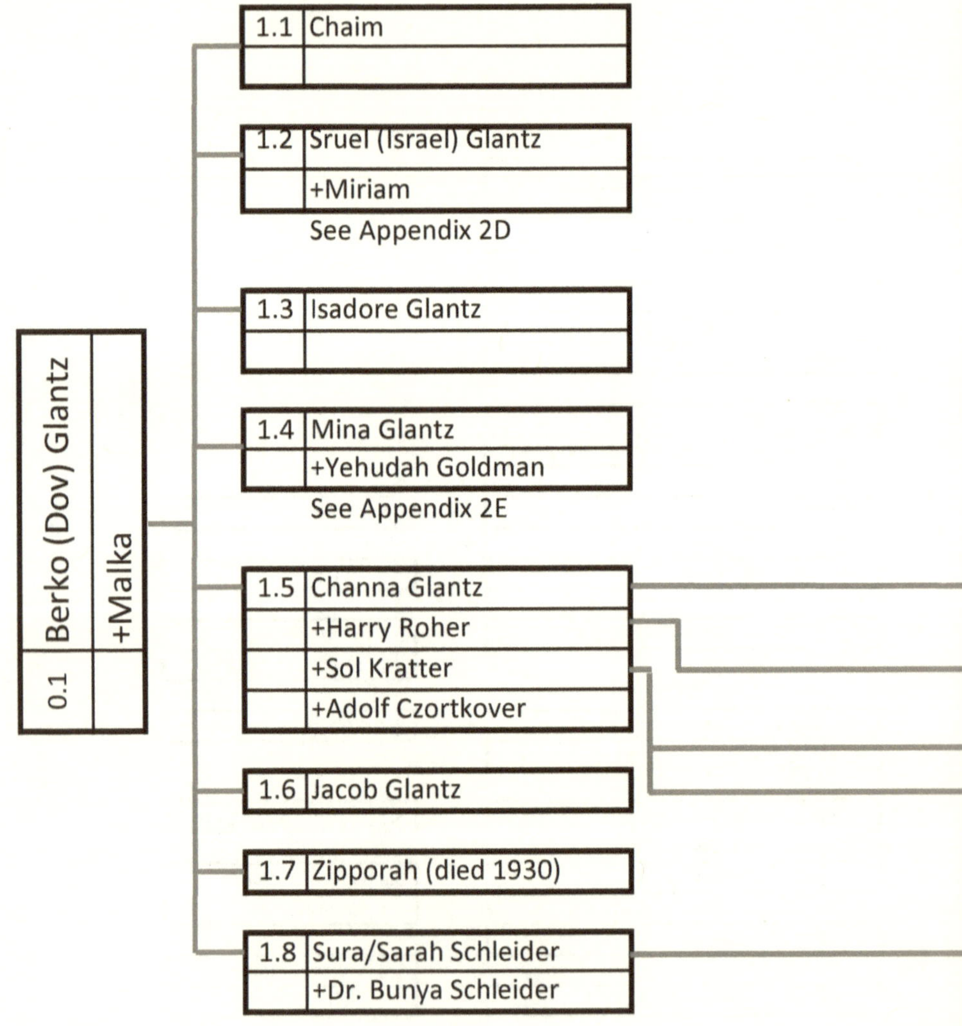

2.16	Sally Widrich (Roher/Kratter)		3.25	Arnold
			3.26	Henry

2.15	Murray Glantz

2.17	Bernard Kratter
	4 Daughters

2.22	Bernard
2.23	2 Additional children

Appendix 2D: Israel Sruel Glantz Family Tree

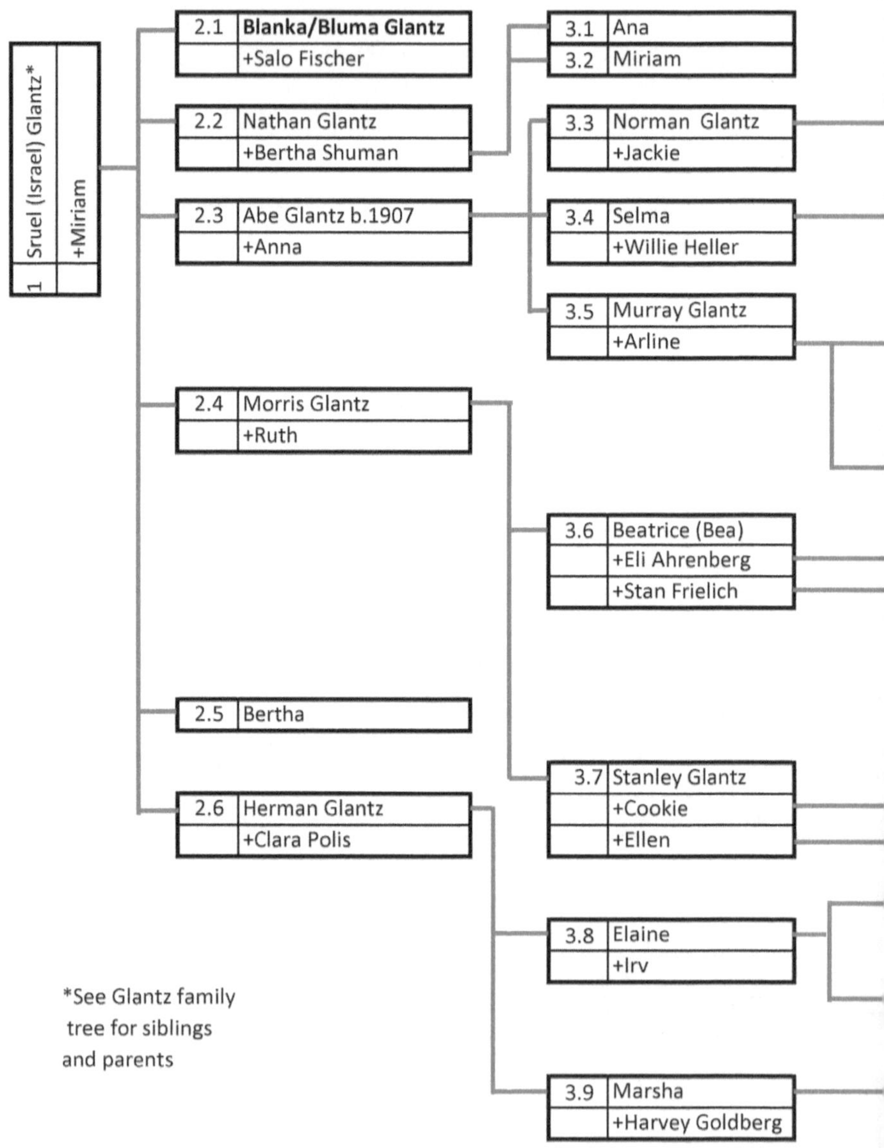

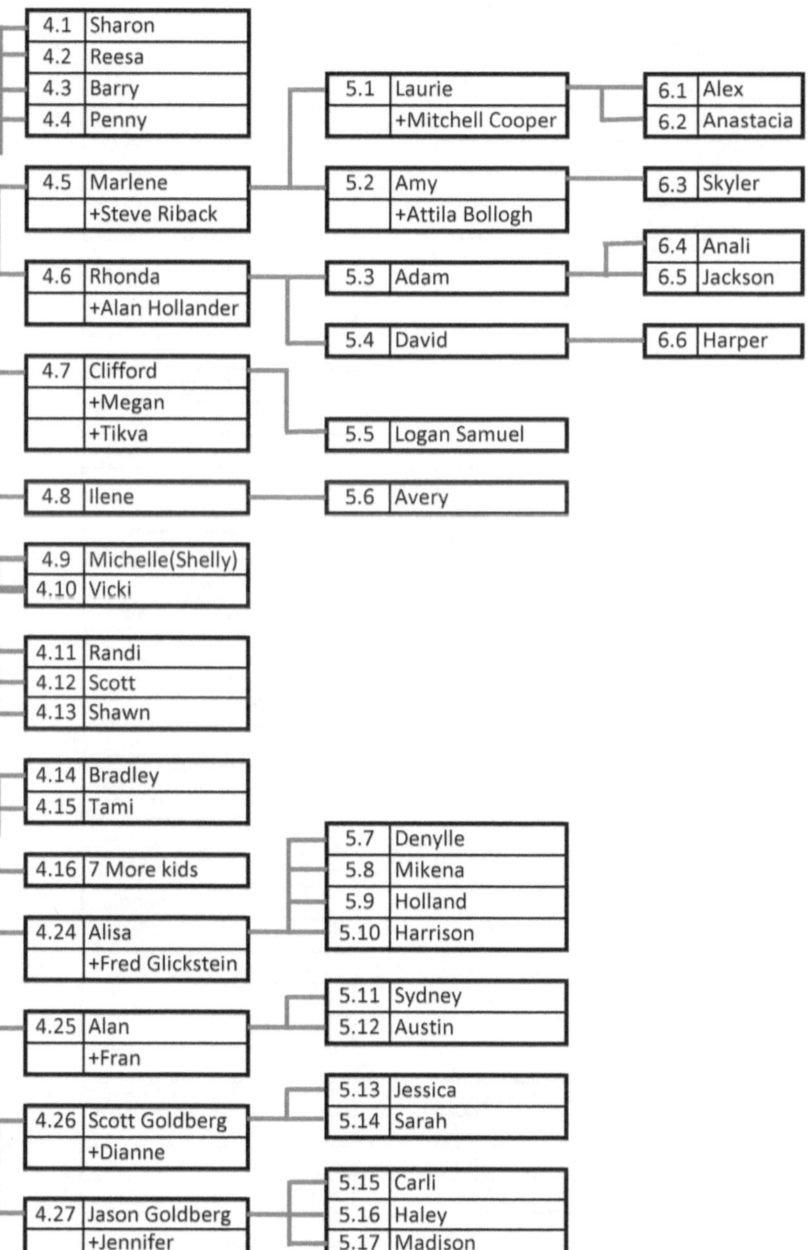

4.1 Sharon
4.2 Reesa
4.3 Barry
4.4 Penny
4.5 Marlene
+Steve Riback
4.6 Rhonda
+Alan Hollander
4.7 Clifford
+Megan
+Tikva
4.8 Ilene
4.9 Michelle(Shelly)
4.10 Vicki
4.11 Randi
4.12 Scott
4.13 Shawn
4.14 Bradley
4.15 Tami
4.16 7 More kids
4.24 Alisa
+Fred Glickstein
4.25 Alan
+Fran
4.26 Scott Goldberg
+Dianne
4.27 Jason Goldberg
+Jennifer
5.1 Laurie
+Mitchell Cooper
5.2 Amy
+Attila Bollogh
5.3 Adam
5.4 David
5.5 Logan Samuel
5.6 Avery
5.7 Denylle
5.8 Mikena
5.9 Holland
5.10 Harrison
5.11 Sydney
5.12 Austin
5.13 Jessica
5.14 Sarah
5.15 Carli
5.16 Haley
5.17 Madison
6.1 Alex
6.2 Anastacia
6.3 Skyler
6.4 Anali
6.5 Jackson
6.6 Harper

Appendix 2E: Glantz Goldman in America Family Tree

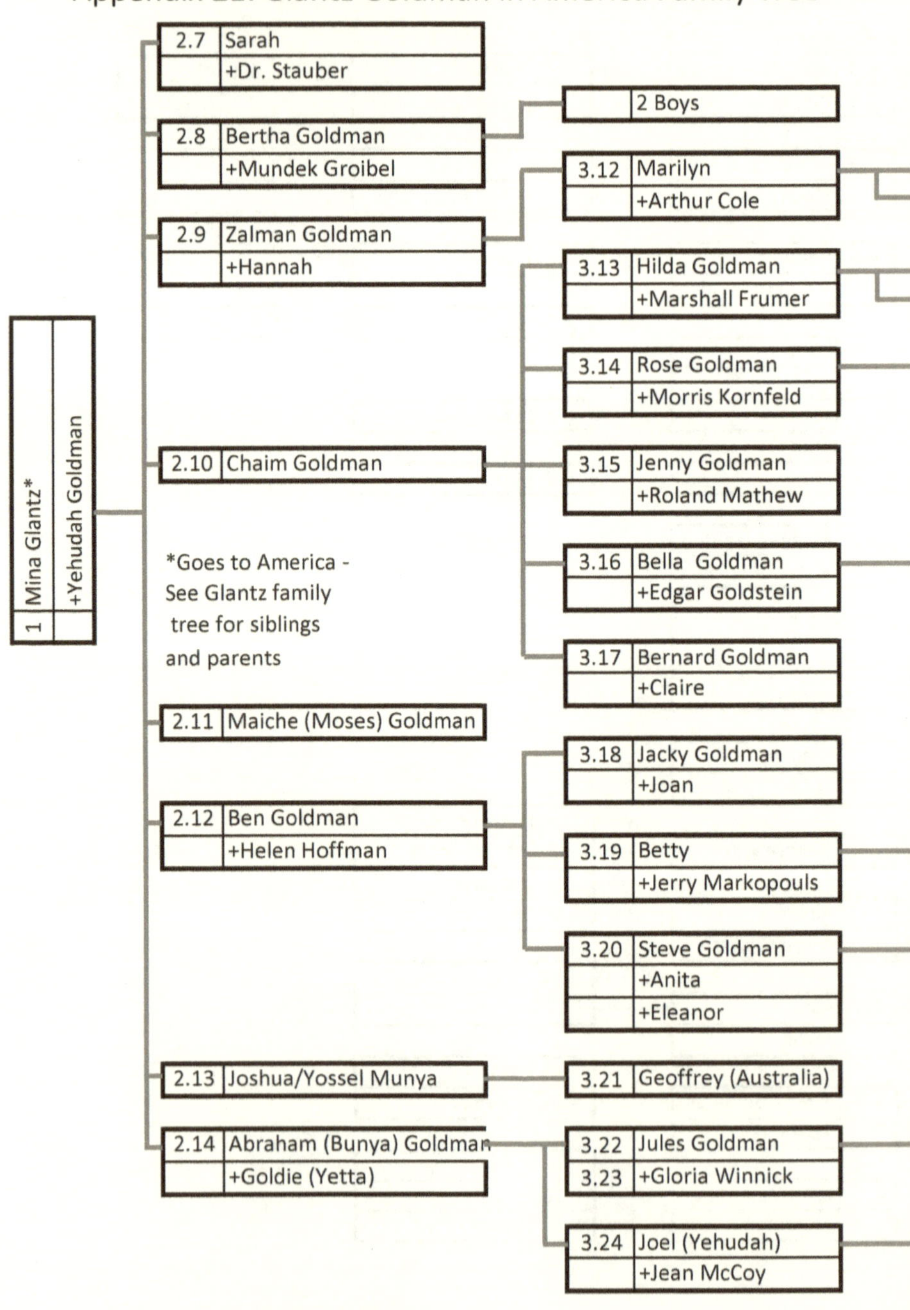

| 4.28 | Melissa Cole |
| 4.29 | Stewart Cole |

| 4.30 | Mark Frumer |
| 4.31 | Richard Frumer |

| 5.18 | Alexa |
| 5.19 | Lindsey |

| 4.32 | Julie |

4.33	Alan Goldstein
4.34	Therry Goldstein
4.35	Danielle Goldstein

Appendix 2F: Szylberstajn Family Tree

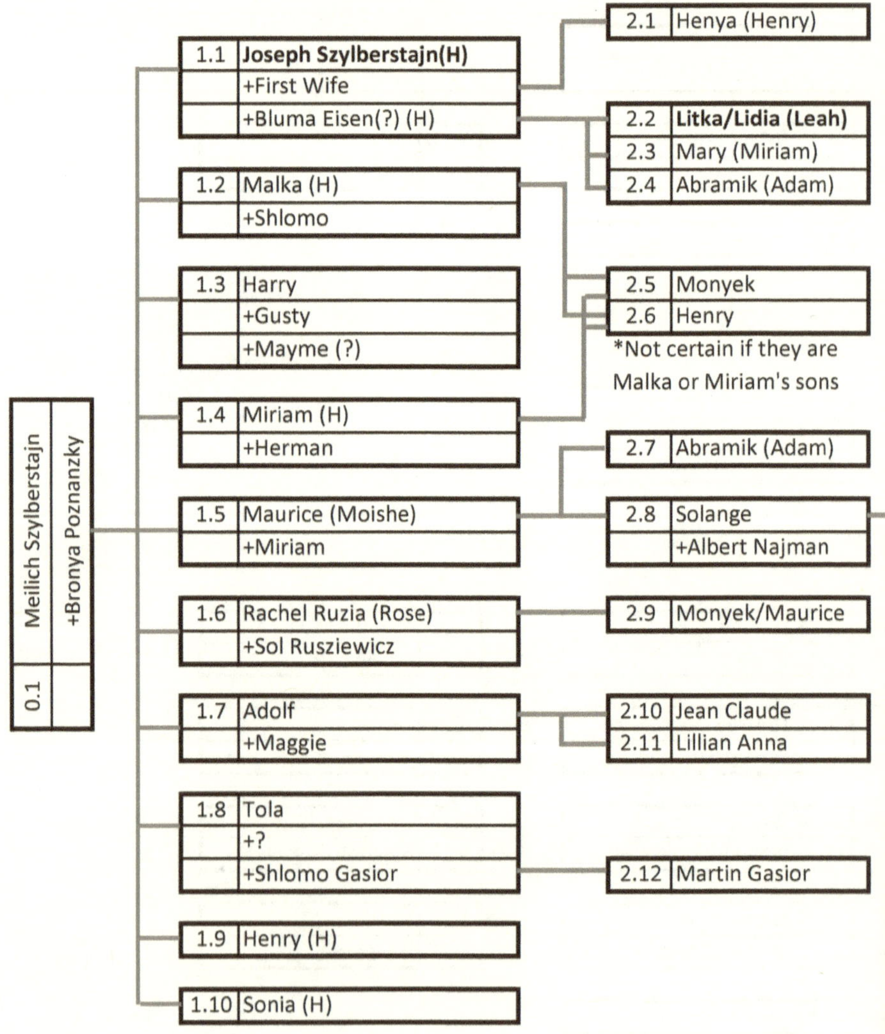

3.1 Maurice
4.1 Esther
5.1 Simon
3.2 Charles
+Emmanuelle Honorin
4.2 Areski Honorin

Endnotes

7.   https://en.wikipedia.org/wiki/Harte_Hanks

17.   https://en.wikipedia.org/wiki/Melamed
        https://en.wikipedia.org/wiki/Cheder

30.   https://en.wikipedia.org/wiki/Władysław_Anders
        https://en.wikipedia.org/wiki/Władysław_Sikorski

59.   https://en.wikipedia.org/wiki/Mandate_for_Palestine

103.   https://en.wikipedia.org/wiki/Oblast.

105.   https://en.wikipedia.org/wiki/SS_Bremen_(1928)
        https://warfarehistorynetwork.com/the-s-s-bremen-last-voyage-of-a
        -luxury-liner

108.   https://en.wikipedia.org/wiki/Bielski_partisans,

111.   https://en.wikipedia.org/wiki/Jerry_Blavat
        https://en.wikipedia.org/wiki/Hy_Lit
        https://en.wikipedia.org/wiki/Bruce_Morrow
        https://en.wikipedia.org/wiki/Wolfman_Jack

137.   https://jps.org/about/the-jps-story/
        https://en.wikipedia.org/wiki/Dropsie_College_for_Hebrew_a
        nd_Cognate_Learning
        https://congressforjewishculture.org/lexicon/t/5833

138.   https://www.library.upenn.edu/collections/notable/dropsie-coll
        ege-hebrew-and

139.   https://thehaddonfortnightly.org

142.   https://www.bancroft.org/about-us/history/

145. https://czestochowa.us

152. https://www.kadimahtorasmoshe.org/rabbi-halbfinger-eme
      ritus.html
      https://casetext.com/case/congregation-kadimah-toras-mos
      he-v-deleo

175. https://fr.wikipedia.org/wiki/Musique_légère

177. http://www.campdesmilles.org/home2.html

178. http://www.ajpn.org/juste-Monseigneur-Paul-Remond-234
      7.html

181. https://fr.wikipedia.org/wiki/Musique_légère

182. https://fr.wikipedia.org/wiki/Orchestre_lyrique_de_l%27O
      RTF

188. https://en.wikipedia.org/wiki/Édith_Piaf
      https://en.wikipedia.org/wiki/Jacques_Brel
      https://en.wikipedia.org/wiki/Montmartre
      https://en.wikipedia.org/wiki/Saint-Germain-des-Prés_(ab
      bey)
      https://lesdeuxmagots.fr/en/

192. https://en.wikipedia.org/wiki/Oskar_Kokoschka

197. https://www.frick.org/exhibitions/faience/technique_origin

198. https://en.wikipedia.org/wiki/Aix-en-Provence_Festival
      https://en.wikipedia.org/wiki/Archbishop%27s_Palace_of_
      Paris
      https://en.wikipedia.org/wiki/Aix_Cathedral

210. https://researchguides.library.syr.edu/vha

212. https://simple.wikipedia.org/wiki/Kapo

229. https://stilllifeinlodz.org

237. https://en.wikipedia.org/wiki/Dabrowski_Battalion

254. https://en.wikipedia.org/wiki/Man_Ray
      https://en.wikipedia.org/wiki/Dada
      https://en.wikipedia.org/wiki/Surrealism

256. https://m.wikidata.org/wiki/Q54869263

263. https://en.wikipedia.org/wiki/Rosa_Luxemburg
      http://www.leftfutures.org/2013/04/france's-l'humanite-the-
      secret-of-the-radical-daily's-success/

264. https://en.wikipedia.org/wiki/Protests_of_1968
https://en.wikipedia.org/wiki/May_68
https://leftinparis.org/people/michel-pablo-raptis/
https://fr.wikipedia.org/wiki/Michel_Recanati

265. https://en.wikipedia.org/wiki/Daniel_Cohn-Bendit
https://en.wikipedia.org/wiki/Jacques_Sauvageot
https://en.wikipedia.org/wiki/Alain_Geismar
https://en.wikipedia.org/wiki/Alain_Krivine
https://en.wikipedia.org/wiki/Dreyfus_affair

267. https://en.wikipedia.org/wiki/Coluche
https://en.wikipedia.org/wiki/François_Mitterrand

268. https://fr.wikipedia.org/wiki/Alliance_marxiste_révolutio
nnairep

269. https://en.wikipedia.org/wiki/Salvador_Allende
https://en.wikipedia.org/wiki/Farabundo_Martí_National
_Liberation_Front
https://en.wikipedia.org/wiki/Subcomandante_Marcos
https://en.wikipedia.org/wiki/Workers%27_Defence_
Committee
https://en.wikipedia.org/wiki/Lech_Wałęsa
https://en.wikipedia.org/wiki/Solidarity_(Polish_trade_
union)

270. https://en.wikipedia.org/wiki/Samizdat

280. https://www.festival-cannes.com/en/
https://www.premiersplans.org/festival/en/ressources-a_
propos.php
https://www.telluridefilmfestival.org

281. https://ifcinema-institutfrancais-com.translate.goog/fr/mov
ie?id=ba503e32-3ce7-6bd4-2c69-d35de43d0e5b&_x_tr_sl=
fr&_x_tr_tl=en&_x_tr_hl=en&_x_tr_pto=op%2Csc&_x_tr
_hist=true
https://en.wikipedia.org/wiki/Jean_Rouch

282. https://en.wikipedia.org/wiki/Surrealism
https://en.wikipedia.org/wiki/Ethnofiction

284. https://www.google.com/search?client=safari&rls=en&q=
Malem+Boussou&ie=UTF-8&oe=UTF-8#fp state=ive&vhi
d=tPrxtBtMYng9eM&vld=cid:56bea7e1,vid:Tyq47YfY2ZM
,st:0&vssid=1
https://www.youtube.com/watch?v=Mg9cpJDmH3U
https://www.piasgroup.net/blog/remembering-remy-kolp
a-kopoul-1949-2015/

285. https://en.wikipedia.org/wiki/Haitian_Vodou

286. https://en.wikipedia.org/wiki/Prix_Jean_Vigo

287. https://en.wikipedia.org/wiki/Jean-Bertrand_Aristide

289. https://en.wikipedia.org/wiki/A_Flag_Is_Born

290. https://en.wikipedia.org/wiki/USS_Cythera_(PY-31)

294. https://en.wikipedia.org/wiki/Simone_Schwarz-Bart
https://en.wikipedia.org/wiki/André_Schwarz-Bart

301. https://en.wikipedia.org/wiki/Hermann_Göring

301. https://en.wikipedia.org/wiki/Action_Reconciliation_Service_
for_Peace#Notable_former_ARSP_volunteers]

ACKNOWLEDGMENTS

Thanks to Robert Strauss, or just "Strauss", as he is known. He has been my friend since we were young boys. He traveled with me to my parents' home towns in the Ukraine and Poland.

Thanks to Solange Najman, Abe Fischer, Clara Glantz and my mother and father, whose conversations with me provided the substance of this work.

Thanks to Corinne Welger Barboza, for kindness she has shown me, help she has given, and friendship that has blossomed.

Thanks to Yves Flank, whom I met in Solange's kitchen the morning of her funeral. He befriended me from the beginning. Yves connected me to his cousin Zipi Newman, the Israeli Najman who straightened me out about a few things. Yves, who was on the barricades with Maurice in 1968 and knew Maurice and Charles their whole lives also made possible the connection with Cyrius Martinez.

Thanks to Cyrius Martinez without whom I would not have been able to tell as much of Charlie's story as I did, whose most poignant words about his dear friend were "I miss you Charlie, we miss you terribly."

Thanks to Zipi Naiman. Meeting her was one of the rewards of writing this book. We both now look forward to seeing each other whenever I travel to Israel.

Thanks to my dear friends, Phil Cohen and Dick Ravin, each more distinguished writers than I. It was Dick who found me my editor, Lynne Weiss,

Thanks to Lynne Weiss, my editor. She was more than just an editor, providing support as a coach and cheerleader.

Thanks to David Schreiber for listening to me work out various parts of the stories while we rode our bikes together.

Thanks to Glen Edelstein, my design editor, who got me through all that had to be done after I finished the writing.

Thanks to my son, Teddy, for designing and laying out the family trees so that they fit onto the page.

Most of all, thanks to my dear wife, Linda Jason, who put up with me, listened to me grapple with problems, read my draft manuscripts, bit by bit and piece by piece, editing the bits and pieces of this work, and helping me address all sorts of problems along the way.

About the Author

Andrew Fischer began this book as a legacy to his parents and to document their odyssey of survival through the holocaust. He recalls that when his father would tell his stories, he would be told to write the stories down. His father would answer "No one will believe them." Afraid that the stories would be lost, Fischer first set out to record his father's stories. The project soon grew to include the stories of other family members, those who survived and those who did not, up to the last of his family in Europe.

Although this is his first book, Fischer has been a writer for over fifty years, first and still occasionally as a journalist and newspaper reporter, music critic and feature writer. He has written opinion columns for various journals, including Jewish publications. Fischer has written innumerable briefs, memoranda and other legal writings in his forty years as a practicing attorney and attributes his success as an attorney to his writing experience.

Fischer is married to Linda Jason. He has three children and nine grandchildren. He looks forward to his next work, also related to stories of Jewish survival.